BEE COUNTY COLLEGE LIBRARY
3800 CHARCO ROAD
BEEVILLE, TEXAS 78102
(512) 354 - 2740

45991

ML
3507
.G5
1985

Giddins
Rhythm-a-ning

BEE COUNTY COLLEGE

You have accepted the responsibility of either
returning this book when due or paying the $1 a week
penalty. NO overdue notice will be mailed to you.
The college business office will notify you if money
is owed the college. This book can be renewed for
one week either in person or by phone (358-7032). A
book returned by 10 a. m. on the third overdue day will
not be charged a fine.

Rhythm-a-ning

ML 3507. G5 1985

Rhythm-a-ning

Jazz Tradition
and Innovation in the '80s

GARY GIDDINS

New York
Oxford University Press
1985

45991

Grady C. Hogue LRC

Oxford University Press
Oxford London New York Toronto
Delhi Bombay Calcutta Madras Karachi
Kuala Lumpur Singapore Hong Kong Tokyo
Nairobi Dar es Salaam Cape Town
Melbourne Auckland
and associated companies in
Beirut Berlin Ibadan Mexico City Nicosia

Copyright © 1985 by Gary Giddins
Published by Oxford University Press, 200 Madison Avenue
New York, New York 10016
All rights reserved. No part of this publication may be reproduced,
stored in a retrieval system, or transmitted, in any form or by any
means, electronic, mechanical, photocopying, recording, or otherwise,
without the prior permission of Oxford University Press.

Library of Congress Cataloging in Publication Data
Giddins, Gary.
Rhythm-a-ning : jazz tradition and innovation
in the '80s.
Includes index.
1. Jazz music——Addresses, essays, lectures.
I. Title
ML3507.G5 1985 785.42 84-20658
ISBN 0-19-503558-5

Printing (last digit): 9 8 7 6 5 4 3 2 1

Printed in the United States of America

For Alice and Leo Giddins,
who recognized the compatibility
of the Biblical and Constitutional
Decalogues, and raised their
children accordingly.

There is no music without order—if that music comes from a man's innards. But that order is not necessarily related to any single criterion of what order should be as imposed from the outside. This is not a question, then, of "freedom" as opposed to "nonfreedom," but rather it is a question of recognizing ideas and expressions of order.

—Cecil Taylor
Fly! Fly! Fly! Fly! Fly!

But, you know, no music is my music. It's everybody's who can feel it. You're here . . . well, if there's music, you feel it—then it's yours too. You got to be in the sun to feel the sun. It's that way with music too.

—Sidney Bechet
Treat it Gentle

Jazz is an art of the young, and it is a young art in itself. The progressive force of change will always fall chiefly into the hands of the young in mind and body . . . Will the jazz of today show greater durability and be just as enjoyable to the next generation? I think so!

—Count Basie
New York Jazz Museum pamphlet

Rhythm is life the space of time danced thru.

—Cecil Taylor
Unit Structures

It Don't Mean a Thing If It Ain't Got That Swing.

—Duke Ellington
song title

Contents

Introduction **xi**
Jaki Byard and the New Tolerance **3**
Pick a Card, Any Card **7**
How To Not Stuff a Jazz Classic **12**
Jack DeJohnette Beats the Band **17**
Moody's Moods Revisited **20**
Something Else Again **23**
Sarah Vaughan
   1. Soulful **26**
   2. Sassing Ellington **29**
Freedom Then and Now **34**
The Trombone's Connected to the . . . **38**
Fifty Years of "Body and Soul" **45**
Teddy Wilson's Golden Oldies **53**
Beyond Romance **56**
Composers Ascendent **59**
Big Noise from Missoula **63**
Tony Bennett Without Fear **65**
The Excitable Roy Eldridge **68**
Lester Young Grows Deeper **73**
Note: Andrew Cyrille Has a Band **75**
Miles's Wiles **78**
Blythemania **85**
Shining Trumpet **88**
Joe Turner, Unmoved Mover **92**
The Egg in the Meatloaf **95**
Songs Your Mother Never Sang **101**
Art Pepper, 1926–1982 **106**
Sonny Stitt, 1924–1982 **108**
Woody Herman
   1. Off the Road **111**
   2. A Fan's Fan **116**
Clarinets on Top **119**
Virtuoso Entertainment **122**

Motor City Classicist **125**
Stan Getz's Transfusion **128**
Hard Again **132**
The Jazz Singer **136**
Gypsy Soul **139**
Jolson's Greatest Heir **146**
Kind of Miles **152**
Wynton Marsalis and Other Neoclassical Lions **156**
The Latest Scat **161**
Return of the Organ Grinder **166**
Technicolor Repertory **168**
The Education of David Murray **171**
Illinois Jacquet
   1. Flying in Place **178**
   2. Jacquet Expands **181**
Life after Death **183**
School for Moderns **189**
Gunslinger, Phase Two **192**
Eclecticism: Ancient to the Future **194**
Chilled Classics and the Real Thing **201**
The Limits of Global Unity **207**
Carmen on Holiday **211**
Thelonious Monk
   1. In Walked Monk **214**
   2. Rhythm-a-ning **220**
Frank Sinatra
   1. An Appreciation **225**
   2. For Collectors **232**
Harmolodic Hoedown
   1. Ornette's Coloring Book **235**
   2. Speaking in Thumbs **242**
Not for Dancers Only **250**
The Definitive Bill Harris **259**
The Return of New Orleans **262**
Euphoria **267**
Orchestral Jazz **270**
Index **279**

Introduction:
Jazz Turns Neoclassical

We hear frequent talk of a renaissance in jazz. Musically, the signs are unmistakable; nevertheless, jazz remains nearly subterranean, a thing apart, a private cultural zone. Its state of alienation is frequently blamed on the Hydra that is variously known as the avant-garde, the new thing, the new wave, and free jazz—that is, the contemporary post-modernist jazz of the past twenty-five years. Avant-gardists are depicted, not always inappropriately, as musical Jackson Pollocks spewing sounds into the air without benefit of formal or narrative guidelines. Their music is considered esoteric when it isn't impenetrable, and erstwhile jazz fans, now repulsed by the gladiatorial anarchy that used to attract them, ask accusatory questions: where's the beat, the melody, the beauty? Musicians and critics continue to wonder when free jazz (allowing the supposition that free jazz *is* jazz—the debate here is unceasing) will be assimilated into the mainstream. In other words, when will Joyce become Dickens, and Bartók Mozart?

As I see it, the avant-garde has been studiously aligning itself with mainstream jazz for some time. The resurgence of jazz means in large measure the resurgence of swing, melody, and beauty, as well as other vintage jazz qualities such as virtuosity, wit, and structure—not that they've ever been entirely absent. If jazz, like other fine arts, had to be relearned in a period of avant-garde extremism, it has long since—and with a vengeance—turned neoclassical. Musicians weaned on the free jazz of the '60s now sift '20s' classicism, '30s' swing, '40s' bop, and '50s' soul for repertoire and expressive wisdom. They are, in effect, going home again.

From 1960 to 1975, adventurous jazz often meant indulgences on the order of 20-minute solos, or freely improvised polyphony, or endlessly repeated ostinatos layered over a single scale. Though the great figures of that period—John Coltrane, Cecil Taylor, Ornette Coleman, Albert Ayler, and a few others—could bring off the most demanding improvisational conceits, at least as far as the knowing, sympathetic, and determined listener was concerned, they spawned imitators who mistook freedom for license and justified excess with apocalyptic rhetoric. A backlash was inevitable. Not only were many listeners yearning for restraint but a younger generation of jazz musicians, many of them trained in conservatories, expressed horror that formalism appeared to be vanishing. Jazz has always been a dialectic between improviser and composer: when the improviser gets out of hand, the composer emerges with new guidelines, sometimes borrowed from the distant past.

A couple of years ago, while teaching at a university, I found—for the first time—a way to kindle students' interest in the new jazz players (they need only exposure to appreciate classic players). The course began with a survey of such jazz precursors as spirituals, marches, blues, and ragtime; I simply provided symmetry by concluding the course with treatments of those precursors by avant-garde musicians, including Arthur Blythe's version of "Just a Closer Walk with Thee," Anthony Braxton's march from *Creative Orchestra Music 1976,* "Blues," by Leroy Jenkins and Muhal Richard Abrams, and Air's arrangement of Scott Joplin's "Weeping Willow Rag." Nor was it necessary to stop there. Having traced the evolution of jazz from the beginnings to the present, I might have retraced it with modernistic but idiomatically satisfying interpretations—all recorded since 1975—of nearly every school and style. Indeed, I might have brought the course full circle by playing the Art Ensemble of Chicago's avant-garde parodies of the avant-garde. Jazz is so eclectic these days that you can find in it almost anything you please.

Jazz modernists rarely investigated the music's past before the avant-garde blew the old jazz truths out of the water. The composers and players of the era immediately following World War II ignored the traditonal repertory, and when they did pay homage to the ancients (ragtimers and New Orleans-style players), whatever regard they may have felt was often soured by condescension. Modernism, after all, was a rallying point, and a political movement—a transformation of mere entertainment into art. The genius-leaders of the movement—Charlie Parker, Dizzy Gillespie, and Thelonious Monk—knew better, of course; the traditions live in even their most volatile experiments, whereas their disciples, more obsessed with the propaganda of the new, were inclined to dismiss as passé the sweetness of Johnny Hodges or the showboating of Louis Armstrong. Still, what both the geniuses and their disciples propagated *was* new. By comparison, the neoclassicists of the '80s may seem to be offering, at worst, nothing more than half-baked historicism or, at best, an inventive reappraisal of the jazz repertory. In this regard, it's useful to remember that one saving grace of neoclassicism is its impatience with nostalgia. Whereas a modernist of 30 years ago might have used a plunger mute to demonstrate bemused affection for an outmoded style, a neoclassicist of today uses the mute because he knows that it can convey singular and immediate passions.

When all the post-modernist styles—expressionist and neoclassicist alike—are considered "avant-garde" (as, rightly or wrongly, they often are), they constitute an enduring sub-genre in jazz, one that dates back over 25 years. It has its own thesis ("the new wave") and antithesis ("the jazz tradition"). The distinction was made frustratingly clear to me by my students, who were enchanted by the contemporary restatements of classic styles, but resisted the unsettling innovations (works by Taylor, Coleman, etc.) of the '60s. I'm almost resigned to this response. Maybe only in a period of national tumult are people willing to listen to music for the pleasure of being battered and tested. The avant-garde, by definition, has no right to an audience larger than its true believers. Besides, the violent expressionism of the '60s made the current wave of neoclassicism possible; it freed the present generation to look on the jazz tradition with agnostic curiosity. And this generation—virtuosic, ambitious, and disarmingly unpretentious—has no axes to grind about the claims of art over entertainment or of freedom over form, except for the conviction, apparently widespread, that the future of jazz lies in a rapprochement between those putative opposites.

Still, when we talk about a renaissance in jazz, we are talking about a wealth of interesting music, not a broad-scaled awakening of interest in that music. Most of the neoclassical ventures discussed in this book are unknown outside the small enclave of New York clubs and European festivals. For, as all but the most provincial fans know, American jazz musicians are largely invisible in their own country. Few educated Americans can name even five jazz musicians under the age of forty. Jazz is virtually banished from television and commerical radio, and is usually conflated with pop in the press, when acknowledged at all—*Time* runs a Christmas music wrap-up that lists the best in classical and rock, as though jazz didn't exist. In four decades of prize-giving, the Pulitzer Committee has never recognized a jazz composer (the jurors who voted unanimously to award Ellington, in 1965, were overruled by the Advisory Committee). Booking agencies and record companies no longer scout for serious young jazz musicians. Even colleges, which once provided a network of concert halls for the Modern Jazz Quartet or Gerry Mulligan, now house lab bands that perform standard orchestrations but fail to book active innovators. Most significant jazz recordings of recent years were made abroad for labels like Black Saint in Italy, Hat Hut in Switzerland, Trio in Japan, Enja in Germany, SteepleChase in Denmark, and BVHAAST in Holland, or by tiny American labels, some of them little more than vanities; they are distributed in only a few American cities.

Yet, despite what amounts to a media blackout, jazz somehow

manages to replenish its audience and its musicians with every generation. Jazz festivals proliferate, at least in Europe, and so do independant labels and reissue series. Mail-order companies, from the Smithsonian Collection to Time/Life, have found a bonanza in jazz. The music may be in exile, but it isn't fading away. I intend to help spread the news of the increasing accessibility of swing and melody and beauty in the jazz of the '80s, but I'm fully aware that the bounding line between jazz and the mainstream of American life is a tradition unto itself. In 1965, Dwight Macdonald wrote an account of an arts fesival at Lyndon Johnson's White House that unwittingly embodied the problem. Macdonald, who was rarely unwitting about anything, complained that "no composers of any note were present." Several paragraphs later, he observed parenthetically that the "best thing at the festival" and "the only really happy-looking people, in fact, were Duke Ellington and his bandsmen." That's the way it is now, only more so. Nobody here but us happy-looking jazzmen, boss.

Acknowledgments

I've borrowed my title, *Rhythm-a-ning*, from Thelonious Monk, though I can't be sure he used it as I do—as a gerund or verbal adjective. As such, it seems a succinct way of getting at what jazz musicians do when they make music: they rhythm-a-ning. Steve Futterman came up with the subtitle. The chronicle that follows—written, with three exceptions, between January 1980, and June 1984—is made up of essays that first appeared in the *Village Voice* and other periodicals. They have all been revised. The pieces that precede 1980 are discussions of Jaki Byard (1978) and Cecil Taylor (1979), neither of whom should be overlooked in a survey of the present state of jazz, and a review of a Sarah Vaughan record. Although most of the pieces address the idea of an eclectic neoclassicism in jazz, several of them are only tangentially concerned with '80s' jazz, or with jazz itself. I don't apologize for my obsessions; I simply embrace the eclectic spirit.

I am much indebted to good editors—to William Whitworth of *The Atlantic*, which published the introductory remarks on neoclassicism, the first part of the Wynton Marsalis essay, and "Orchestral Jazz"; to Lisa Bain of *Esquire*, which published "The Egg in the Meatloaf" and "Off the Road"; and to Elizabeth Pochoda, who fought the good fight for jazz coverage at the lamentable *Vanity Fair*, which published "Gypsy Soul," "The Education of

David Murray," and the second part of the section on Wynton Marsalis. My thanks to William Livingstone, the editor of *Stereo Review*, which commissioned the Sinatra appreciation. I continue to marvel at the scrutiny of Robert Christgau, music editor of *The Village Voice*, which published everything else. I'm greatful to David Schneiderman for upholding the *Voice*'s commitment to jazz criticism, and to my colleague Stanley Crouch, with whom I've shared a non-stop decade-long dialogue that spurred many enthusiasms. I owe debts of many kinds to Mr. and Mrs. William Questel and the Four Rothchilds (a family that patterns itself after the Ritz Brothers). This book would not have achieved its present form without the care and enthusiasm of Sheldon Meyer and Leona Capeless of Oxford University Press. It would have been a lot longer in the making without the encouragement, acumen, and paste-and-scissors virtuosity of Deborah Eve Halper.

New York
September 1984

G.G.

Rhythm-a-ning

Jaki Byard
and the New Tolerance

For more than a decade, jazz has been unencumbered by the sort
of lodestar genius who so effectively points new paths that his
contemporaries lose sight of the old ones. The next stylistic
superman may be flexing his muscles in the wings, but the intervening calm allows us to look backward and sideways with renewed clarity. Jazz musicians of the '70s have sifted through the
ferment of the preceding decade, much as their antecedents in
the '50s and '30s refined the radicalism of the '40s and '20s. The
key difference is that present-day eclectics have so much more to
choose from: the old-line avant garde of Om mani padme chan-
ters has given way to a generation of vivisectional neoclassicists
(not for nothing does Lester Bowie perform in a surgical coat),
while archivists stake claims on every surviving shard from the
distant past, and hungry camp followers fuse with anything that
glitters.

All well and good, or most of it. A period such as this serves
as a corrective to periods dominated by the True Way. For a spell,
we come out of the tunnel, take a deep breath, and look over the
scenery. This changeover is illustrated by the career of Jaki Byard,
a full-time educator (primarily at the New England Conservatory
and the Julius Hartt School of Music), who frequently plays piano
in various New York cafes. Byard, the most ebullient jazz pianist

since Fats Waller, might even be considered the father of the new tolerance. In the mid-1960s, when he first attracted attention with a keyboard style that encompassed ragtime, stride, boogie woogie, bop, Garner (for want of a more meaningless term), and modernism, not to mention classical techniques ranging from Bach (counterpoint) to Henry Cowell (clusters), Byard was considered a pleasant anomaly. People were surprised when he expressed resentment at a *Down Beat* reviewer who described his stride playing at Charles Mingus's Monterey concert as "tongue-in-cheek." In those days, modernism was so much the norm that recourse to earlier styles was presumed to be intentionally comic.

Of course, Byard does play tongue-in-cheek quite often; his humor is broad, more on the order of Charlie Chaplin than of Noël Coward, though it's linked to the nostalgic piety common to both. Still, humorous content is not style itself. There have been schools of pianists devoted to the elaboration of a single style— whether that of Art Tatum or Bud Powell or Bill Evans—but Byard was one of the first to realize that all durable styles could be interwoven by a single pianist, and that modernism is just another option. His real achievement is not that he simply mastered diverse styles—on the order of, say Dick Hyman, who is an exceptional mimic—but that he personalized and integrated them with a highly developed sense of proportion and individuality. He is not an imitator; you always know when you're hearing Jaki Byard. For that matter, he isn't even dependent on stylistic allusions.

Two recent Sundays at the Blue Hawaii were illustrative. On the first, playing solo piano, he ranged freely through the panoply of jazz piano styles. He played medleys of pieces associated with Fats Waller ("Jitterbug Waltz," "Ain't Misbehavin'"), modern trumpeters (Gillespie's "Con Alma," Brown's "Joy Spring") and, quite stunningly, Ellington and Strayhorn ("Day Dream," "Johnny Come Lately," "Mood Indigo," and more). Another medley traveled from Italy to Spain to New Orleans via a "Hello Young Lovers" replete with broad arpeggios and tremolos, a "Besume Mucho" with Latin ostinato, and an original that combined tango and early jazz rhythms. Byard is a canny composer, and his originals invariably have purpose: "Hollis Stomp" is a stomp of the old school; "Hazy Eve" begins hazily but attains firm ground in bop territory (his fingers leap across the keyboard in asymmetrical patterns, every note punched square, the left hand alternating between staccato chords and a rolling bass); "Major Holley" employs block chords and reverse stride, where the left hand plays treble chords and the right improvises freely in the bass.

On the following Sunday, he offered another winning montage of jazz standards, evergreens, and originals, but this time he was accompanied by a young bassist (Ed Schuller), and the interplay tended to avoid familiar allusions. Other aspects of his music came more clearly into view. His tone, for example, is unfailingly bright. His middle-register improvisations are evenly articulated with a strong touch and pulsing time, and, though the general approach is indebted to Bud Powell with an assist from Lennie Tristano, the result is so individualized that no one could fail to distinguish Byard from his predecessors. He likes ringing tremolos and clanging fifths, and his accompaniment often consists of storming riff patterns that suggest a whole brass section. He breaks up his solos with skittering keyboard washes that float beyond the harmonic bounds but are ultimately anchored by the blues. Indeed, it is the heavy blues flavoring in this work that makes his approach to stride and ragtime particularly interesting. One of his earliest professional associates was Earl Bostic, and he has maintained through all the turns of his playing a fondness for Bostic-style rhythm and blues figures. Though Fats Waller is his model for stride, Byard prefers more expressive notes; like Waller, he doesn't hesitate to draw on his classical training, yet his use of blues tonality has a purifying effect whenever the etudes get out of hand.

Byard has recorded more than 15 albums as a leader and many more as a sideman. He has won a few prizes and has a loyal coterie. Yet he is persistently underesteemed. He hasn't recorded in America since 1972, most of his European albums (including duets with Earl Hines) have not been released here, and he has never enjoyed promotion by a major label. His finest albums on Prestige remain conspicuously out of print while the company regularly reissues lesser lights. Critics, however, feel protective of Byard; he is as much a critic's pianist as a pianist's pianist, since his approach to the instrument and the repertoire reflects an historical comprehension rare among musicians. Byard helped prepare the way for the multitude of young neoclassicists who presently roam the various realms of the jazz idiom. He was the ideal pianist for Mingus and Eric Dolphy, with whom he created two remarkably cliché-free homages to Charlie Parker. Supported by bassist Richard Davis and drummer Alan Dawson, he piloted the most commanding rhythm section of the '60s, excepting the Hancock-Carter-Williams trio in Miles Davis's band, though, like Louis Armstrong's Hot Five, it existed only for recording purposes.

The albums Byard made between 1960 and 1972 are dazzling in scope, and for his ability to make the most of limited situations. *Freedom Together* employs so many instruments that you might not guess from listening that it was a trio date. The title selection is a blues that develops thematically and instrumentally as Byard switches from electric piano to celeste to tenor. Throughout his albums, Byard displays various approaches to the blues, among them "Blues for Smoke," "Searchlight" (with Booker Ervin), and "To Bob Vatel of Paris/Blues for Jennie." One especially impressive example is "Twelve" from the inspired quartet performances recorded live at Lennie's: this piece has free episodes resolved by blues choruses, and Byard's comping is so rigorous that he makes the quartet sound like a larger band—the last five choruses of his solo consist almost exclusively of band riffs. Another triumph was *Jaki Byard with Strings!*, where the string section consists of violinist Ray Nance (whose solo on "How High the Moon" ranks with the one he recorded on Dizzy Gillespie's "Lover Come Back to Me" as the best work of his later years), guitarist George Benson, and two premiere bassists, Ron Carter and Richard Davis, making their only appearance together. On a piece called "Cat's Cradle Conference Rag," Byard achieved the ultimate exercise in congruent chord changes by having this quintet play five standards based on similar harmonies simultaneously. Byard, a fair saxophonist in his own right, works especially well with saxophonists, notably Booker Ervin, Eric Dolphy, Rahsaan Roland Kirk, Joe Farrell, Eric Kloss, and the dual tenors of Al Cohn and Zoot Sims, all of whom played at peak levels in his company. His recordings ought to be reissued chiefly for their intrinsic merit, but also to acknowledge a major precursor of the present mood in jazz.*

(March 1978)

Pick a Card, Any Card

The few magicians I've met charmed me with their enthusiasm, but I'd almost rather jog than attend their shows, so dampening is the frustration of not being let in on their secrets. Tricks without explanations are like detective novels without last pages—it's not fair playing show without tell, especially when magicians are the only mystifiers who *can* explain what they do. Artists, by contrast, get muddled in theories of inspiration and tend to dispel the whole question by deferring to a muse or a bitch goddess or something equally horrible.

---

*Byard, who still teaches and plays solo piano and also leads a big band called the Apollo Stompers, remains underrepresented in the record bins. Of the Prestige albums, only two early and relatively minor trio sessions *(Giant Steps)* and the highly stimulating *Jaki Byard Experience* have been reissued, the latter under Kirk's name *(Pre-Rahsaan)*. Two albums with Booker Ervin are available *(The Freedom and Space Sessions)*, as are the key works with Dolphy, *Far Cry* and *Outward Bound*. In addition to two volumes of *Jaki Byard Live!*, recorded at the 1965 Lennie's sessions and long since out of print, a third volume was readied but never released.

Music is the most mystifying of the arts, not least because few people have a clue as to how it's made. Nor are critics, whose collective batting average for missing every major development in music history is close to 1.000, of much help. The value of great invective of the sort James Huneker wrote—aside from its literary pleasure—is that it helps us remember what the educated ear was accustomed to when the Turks invaded. Critics who would rather strut naked at Carnegie Hall than miss placing a bet on the latest champ aren't very helpful either, often stumping for genius and excess alike in the name of tradition, thereby performing a kind of sleight of hand themselves; the newness is obscured by a system of mirrors that reflect only the past and other vaguely relevant tangents.

Cecil Taylor, whose extraordinary new record I'm slouching toward, has been "explained" ad nauseam in terms of the musicians and traditions he's absorbed. The theory is that if enough smokescreens are dropped—Bartók! Stravinsky! Cowell! Messiaen! Ellington! Monk! Powell!—the newness will disappear. This approach merits sympathy: If you don't know how the trick is done the temptation to lean on comparisons (particularly with the defenseless dead) is great. In fact, I'm so sympathetic to this approach that I've used it myself, but this time I've decided to get in line with the ignorant. I don't know how he makes his magic— that is, the more specific the explications I'm given, the more magical seem the results. But I do know that one can love all the foregoing names and still disdain Taylor—even the opposite, in theory, must be possible—and that rooting around in tradition doesn't help anyone understand what Taylor's music actually sounds like. He's an original. I doubt if you can even perceive the traditions that live in his music until you hear it with a sympathetic and familiar ear.

From my place in the dark, means are hazy, but the result is blindingly vivid. On every level, from sonorous image to the actual delineation in performance, Taylor is making a new music— his own music. One can argue that jazz and the academy provided him with a thesis and antithesis, but the baby must be loved for itself. There are always difficulties when an autodidact comes along to break all the rules, and never more so than in Taylor's case, Schoenberg could brandish his method, 12-tone techniques, in the most literal of terms; Parker's sorcery could be observed from the firm footing of song form, governing chords, and an evenly distributed beat. If Taylor's music were simply free expression, one might feel guiltless discussing it with buckets of impressionistic guesswork; but he is a composer. He orders his musicians and the elements of music with formal design, and the frustration of not knowing how it's done isn't allayed by the fact that his musicians aren't too sure either. They know that there are prepared themes with spaces for embellishment and improvisation, that concentration on interaction is essential to the development of a piece, and that its very shape is mutable—the same composition may be played in five minutes or an hour. Only part of the magic is explained by the arduous preparation entailed.

   The Cecil Taylor Unit (NW 201), the first of two albums recorded by New World Records last summer, is Taylor at his best. In the thrill of first discovery I thought it his finest ensemble recording, but on reconsideration the achievements of *Unit Structures* and *Conquistador!* are not to be denied. In some respects I find the new work more pleasing: melodies, while still terse, are less angular and taut, imbued with considerably more warmth; the role of each of the six musicians is more clearly defined; the overall effect is more relaxed, freer. With all those mores, one can presume maturity, but Taylor's method—that impossibly fine line he's sanded between composition and improvisation—has not changed. He is refreshingly conservative in instrumental precision and tonal gravity, and the instrumentation is Dixieland in its simplicity—three horns, three rhythm. In a music this personal, every change in personnel is precipitous, and we're lucky to have this sextet so well represented on disc. Its elements are diverse.

   If Taylor is the nervous center of his music, alto saxophonist Jimmy Lyons might well be considered its heart. His contribution is relatively spare, but his elegance of phrasing and warmth of sound resonate with modest wisdom; it is remarkable how he can body forth the ghost of Charlie Parker with a single, brief phrase, and how comforting is the effect. The presence of Ramsey Ameen's violin brings a new texture to the Unit, but it also recalls the role Alan Silva's arco bass played in the '60s; where Silva's high bowing contrasted with Henry Grimes's deep pizzicato, however, Ameen is often heard in tandem with Sirone's arco bass, producing a thicket of strings. The strength of Raphe Malik's trumpet is somewhat reminiscent of Eddie Gale; he plays written lines with stark urgency, and his economical embellishments put steel in the structures. The rhythm section is dynamic, steamy, earthy, unlike anything in previous Taylor ensembles. Sirone can walk as deferentially as Paul Chambers, but when he bears down his rhythm becomes the band's rhythm. Ronald Shannon Jackson is a revelation, and I recommend that you listen to the music at least once focusing on the drums. He is not afraid of dance rhythms and provides a stirring complement to Taylor's more diffuse rhythms, reminding me in spirit (not style) of Eddie Blackwell. Taylor feeds them, echoes them, connects the parts; he is the head and the motor nerve.

"Idut" is unusual among Taylor recordings for revealing him in a subordinate capacity. The striking theme is introduced by violin and bass, augmented by trumpet and alto sax. Taylor supports and encourages, responding to what they play and filling out the body of sound; he's in and out, pacing the entire work with unaccompanied transitional passages, and occasionally offering those big blue chords that you can recline on. Listen to how closely he tails Lyons's solo, and the ringing sound he gets from the extremes of the Bosendorfer piano, especially the bass notes. As soon as a beat seems to assert itself, Jackson jumps on it and drives it home; during the drums-piano episode, Taylor gives him the lead. There is a moment when the texture is dense and bruising, but this is anything but an unwieldy performance. On the contrary, I'm impressed with the variety of expression crammed into 14 minutes of faultless intra-ensemble mind-reading.

Taylor is the meditative center of "Serdab," and the horns repeat his melodies, including a figure in the bass that reminds me of one of the motifs Chaplin used in his score for *Modern Times.* The first tune intoned by the horns is rapturous, if that isn't too high-falutin a term for so bare a structure. The voicing is as much the point as the notes. After about a minute, he arpeggiates a simple minor chord—tonic, minor third, fifth—which is picked up by Lyons and then the others. It has the effect of an embrace by an old friend. The performance stirs itself into a whirlwind before it concludes symmetrically, being something of a looser second cousin to the 1966 "Enter, Evening." It's a beguiling example of Taylor's arranging technique in that the textures, however thick, comprise relatively few notes from each of the horns. The fullness of sound is more often a consequence of deft layering than of collective hollering.

The 30-minute "Holiday en Masque" begins with the blues, encroached upon quickly by the ensemble light brigade. There are piano-drums passages, and billowing crescendos, and after about eight minutes a moving, exotic melody introduced on violin. A bizarre merriment ensues: Ameen sings this gypsy song, and Taylor tickles it from below, Sirone groans, Malik whelps—eventually Ameen wins them over and everyone elaborates his mood. The work is studded with Taylor tunes that rear and fade, motifs flickering at odd moments. Jackson is a thunderstorm, both in concert with Taylor and in a stomp episode with Malik. There are so many changes that after a few hearings the performance seems very much like a journey, a "Holiday En Masque"; there are moments when you want to cheer, moments to be physical, moments to grope. There are also dead spots, but these are transitions and within a few seconds something new and substantive turns up.

Sam Parkins, who supervised the recording, has described Taylor's individual pieces as organisms that live and die in every performance. There's much truth here: however specific the prepared structures, the development of a piece depends on the interaction of individuals. At least two of the works on this album were painstakingly rehearsed, consolidated, and elaborated, but the takes are separate entities—far more so, because each take is defined by the entire ensemble, than in the alternate takes of bebop, where only the solos and tempo are changed. "Holiday en Masque" is a particularly vivid expression of that organic quality. There are grooves but there is no groove; there is a framework but it's elastic. It's music, with all the attendant glory and defiance and untranslatable emotion music ought to have, and that's magic of the highest sort.

(March 1979)

How To Not Stuff
a Jazz Classic

The movement to recreate or recapture classic jazz was launched six years ago by the New York Jazz Repertory Company and the National Jazz Ensemble, but the jazz past continues to frustrate its most reverent interpreters. Sincerity is not authenticity, and the laborious exercises that so often pass for rendition are usually a kind of taxidermy. It requires a valorous internalization of the old styles, or at least the realization that interpretation is an act of the imagination, to knock the stuffing out those varnished monuments. Jazz repertory is in its infancy, and its occasional successes notwithstanding, is not yet the respectable part of jazz discipline it will eventually become. Happily, there are veterans among us willing to provide cues and directions.

Panama Francis introduced his Savoy Sultans at one of the habitually underattended NYJRC concerts in 1974; he invited members of the audience to dance on stage, and spurred them with a rhythmic swagger that reasserted his stature as a swing drummer with few living rivals—perhaps only Gus Johnson, Buddy Rich, and, when the stars are in proper conjunction, Jo Jones. The Sultans never took off here, but in Europe the response was immediate and enthusiastic. The band was the hit of the Nice festival, and its first album (on Black and Blue) won France's Grand Prix du Disque and came in third in England's *Jazz Journal* poll. Inner City, which owns American distribution rights to the Black and Blue label, has yet to make it available, but that may change as a result of Francis's performance at Highlights in Jazz a few weeks ago and his forthcoming engagement at the Rainbow Room.*

The Savoy Sultans may seem an odd resource for a contemporary repertory group. Under the leadership of Al Cooper, the original nine-piece unit was the house band at the Savoy Ballroom from 1937 until 1946. Several of its 28 recorded sides for Decca are excellent, but they are overwhelmed by the band's mythology: Dizzy Gillespie called it "the swingingest band that ever was," and some top orchestra leaders reportedly declined to follow the Sultans on the bandstand. It was chiefly a jump band (the Sultans coined the term), specializing in riff-laden tunes that impressed dancers and listeners alike. The Swing Era—when congregations of reeds and brass cajoled each other in impassioned hallelujahs to rock the jitterbugs—encouraged rhythmic competition, and the "home of happy feet" obviously demanded a house band that could traverse swing's cutting edge. Yet the Sultans also had some fine if little-known soloists—especially Rudy Williams, the swing altoist who completely adopted the bop idiom after hearing Charlie Parker, and Sam Massenberg, a trumpeter who isn't listed in any jazz reference work and apparently never recorded again. Younger musicians looked up to them—Dexter

---

*Inner City's Classic Jazz label subsequently released *Panama Francis and the Savoy Sultans* (CJ 149) and *Panama Francis and the Savoy Sultans, Volume II* (CJ 150). Muse released a third album, *Jimmy Witherspoon Sings the Blues with Panama Francis and the Savoy Sultans* (MR 5288).

Gordon's "Long Tall Dexter," for example, is practically a be-
bopped version of the Sultans' "Little Sally Water."

The soloists were subordinated to the collective power of the
small ensemble, with the paradoxical result that the terse improvisations, craftily springing from the arrangements, showed
the players off to the best possible advantage. The same is true
of Panama Francis's edition, where the solos alternately relieve
and intensify the tension generated by the ensemble. The outstanding soloist is George Kelly, a driving, warm-blooded tenor
saxophonist in the Coleman Hawkins tradition, who gave Francis
his first job in 1934 (they were 19 and 16 respectively), joined
the Sultans in the '40s, and recently returned to active playing at
the West End Cafe after serving 10 years as the pianist and music director for the Canadian Ink Spots. Another find is Irvin
Stokes, a fluent trumpeter with a penchant for bop licks that
contrasts nicely with Franc Williams's mainstream vocalizations.
A somewhat analogous contrast exists between the two altoists,
Norris Turney and Howard Johnson, with the older and less
consistent Johnson essaying the riskier licks. Yet their solos
wouldn't be tuned nearly so taut if the rhythm section—pianist
Red Richards, guitarist John Smith, bassist Bill Pemberton, and
Francis—wasn't a precision machine.

For Francis, the project is obviously an act of love, a chance to
play the music of his heart—he apprenticed at the Savoy—after
a lifetime in the studios. He's never sounded better, and never—
insofar as records tell the story—swung with more dashing certitude. Although the Sultans provide him with a conceptual basis
for his potent concert-dance band, Francis's repertoire is more
diverse. "Gettin' in the Groove" and "Norfolk Ferry" bear the
Sultans' imprimatur though the latter came from Erskine Hawkins, while "Shipyard Social Function" originated as a Tab Smith
arrangement for Lucky Millinder; "Clap Hands Here Comes
Charlie" (with a storming solo by Kelly, paced and jolted by
Francis) comes from Chick Webb, "Moten's Swing" from Bennie
Moten, and "Girl Talk," a relatively recent Neal Hefti piece, from
Count Basie. Francis started the set on a doubly old-fashioned

note: the tune was "Song of the Islands," and the procedure allowed one soloist at a time to attain the stage and play a chorus
before the ensemble whacked the theme home. When a swing
band is on course, there is no mistaking its momentum.

The Highlights in Jazz concert was a salute to Roy Eldridge,
who, gave Francis his moniker and first recording date. When
Eldridge finally got to the stage, the Sultans had additional opportunity to display spontaneity in fashioning head arrangements for the trumpeter. The reunion was ripe with the kind of
emotion that makes everyone play as though each note could reverse time and settle the participants back into the halcyon days
when they ruled the world. Few musicians always give 100 percent; Eldridge always gives 150 percent. "I Can't Get Started" was
superb jazz repertory—a great jazzman accompanied through
familiar territory by his erstwhile drummer, and riffing section
men who know how to breathe as one. On Eldridge's subsequent
numbers, Dick Katz replaced Richards at the piano, but the
hornmen stayed on stage to provide organ chords and obbligato.
They all soloed on "Kidney Stew," Franc Williams playing in the
Eldridge style, after which Eldridge and Katz, reluctant to go
home, played a 90-second duet of whimpered blasts and scatter-
shot chords that sounded like Lester Bowie and Muhal Richard
Abrams. At sixty-eight, Eldridge is still a terror.

If Francis, Eldridge, and company proved that veterans can be
their own best custodians, the Smithsonian Jazz Repertory Ensemble's concert at Carnegie Hall illustrated all the pitfalls of the
discipline. Chief among the pitfalls is swing, the most elusive
fundamental of jazz. There are as many variations on swing—
which I would define, in the most general terms, as a rhythmic
consistency that elicits a physical response—as there are harmonies; if a repertory company fails to capture a music's distinguishing rhythm, the notes and sonorities won't count for much.
Also, a repertory soloist who is interpreting a classic performance can't make a mistake. Bix Beiderbecke can flub a note in
the heat of improvisation, and the ear registers forgiveness; let
an interpreter flub a note of Beiderbecke's solo and he has de-

filed art. Despite the able leadership of Bob Wilber, the Smith-sonian ensemble—eight strong—failed to bring the music of Bei-derbecke, Jelly Roll Morton, James P. Johnson, Fats Waller, Duke Ellington, and Thelonious Monk alive. The rhythms were limp and the errors plentiful. What is Beiderbecke without the purity of tone? What is Waller without the jollity and wit? The best so-los were by Bucky Pizzarelli, who alone remembered that Mor-ton should be fun, and Wilber, who handsomely recounted Johnny Hodges on "Day Dream" and Frank Trumbauer on "Singin' the Blues."

Even the academic aspect was unfocused. Wilber introduced the pieces on stage, with Martin Williams contributing appro-priate citations off, and while the sentimental banalities were harmless (Bix was "a doomed falling star,") the omissions (Trumbauer's name was never uttered) were puzzling. Before he got the Smithsonian to sit up and take notice of jazz, Williams—presumably a major force behind the program—established him-self as one of the most distinguished critics (of anything) this country has ever produced, and all the musicians are at least ca-pable, so there was no question about intentions or competency. The music simply eluded its supplicants, and you had to wonder how it is that Waller's lilt continues to stump pianists in a world of Liszt and Scriabin interpreters, and why violinists can race through Bach's D-minor chaconne but jazzmen turn to putty be-fore a few allegedly primitive blues choruses by Jelly Roll Mor-ton.

One reason is that formal interpretation is new to jazz. An-other is that recorded rhythms are a lot harder to render con-vincingly than written scores. But bands like the Sultans renew my conviction that repertory will be one of jazz's biggest chal-lenges in the years to come. It will produce a new kind of musi-cian, a new kind of listener, and a new kind of critic; it will force us to reconsider the elements of jazz, and how they can be made to live again in the contemporary concert hall and ballroom with the greatest effect and dignity. The abiding enemy of jazz rep-ertory is nostalgia. But if Mozart can be rescued from rococo preciosity, why not Ellington, Morton, and the other American titans?

(January 1980)

Jack DeJohnette
Beats the Band

Between 1966 and 1971, Jack DeJohnette seemed the most providential of drummers. He was present at Charles Lloyd's anointment *(Forest Flower)*, participated in the revitalization of Bill Evans *(Montreux)*, and presided over Miles Davis's ascension *(Bitches Brew)*. A lean, stark drummer, he requires only the basic components of the trap set, and makes his taut fillips, responses, and turnbacks sting. He can effect the snare's hollowest resonance, almost a flat smack; get the cymbals to shiver like nervous ghosts; and pedal the bass drum with such agility he approximates a roll. His playing is always intense, whether he's firing abrupt, dynamic fusillades against the time or fanning the drums in a relentless effusion of energy, and often charged with humor.

If his early work established him as a catalyst, his own quietly methodical, impressively diverse records show him to be an unusually capable leader. His albums on Milestone and ECM are uneven, but there is a fascinating continuity to them. They act as a kind of commentary on recent jazz directions, and are organized to inspire his collaborators' best work. Excepting his disastrous fusion band, Compost, DeJohnette's groups have intelligently explored the mystic suspense of late Davis, the let's-paint-a-landscape posturing widely associated with ECM, the ec-

lectic lunacy of the Art Ensemble, and—with his latest recording—the elegant homages of the World Saxophone Quartet. Along
the way, such cohorts as Alex Foster developed into an expressionistic altoist and John Abercrombie an impressionistic guitarist, and Lester Bowie was outfitted with some of the most gra-
cious rural funk imaginable.

The new record, *Special Edition* (ECM 1152), is his most satisfying yet, and one of the most entertaining of the new year. The
qualities that define meaningful leadership are present throughout—the compositions and arrangements make scrupulous demands on the increasingly familiar styles of Arthur Blythe and
David Murray. Jazz is at bottom a conflict between the will to
freedom and the desire for discipline, and DeJohnette's music,
in restricting his sidemen, illuminates their abilities. Moreover,
this is his first record where there are no windy stretches, no
stillwater pastels; something is always happening. The tautness is
perked by heady wit, the passions closely monitored. It's an additional tribute to his writing that so many textures are generated by a quartet (Peter Warren is exemplary on bass and cello).

The three originals have in common multiple themes, metrical
changes, and emotional directness. "Zoot Suite" will be the most
pleasant discovery for some, with its affectionate band riff (tenor,
alto, melodica, and arco bass) superimposing three against four,
and ebullient near-Dixieland dialogues between Blythe and Murray over Warren's staunch vamp and DeJohnette's roller-coaster
drums. "Journey to the Twin Planet" combines adroit rubato ensembles with an energy episode that manages to achieve lucid
polyphony. More challenging still is "One for Eric," an en-
lightening portrait of Mr. Dolphy with thematic and rhythmic
surprises, highlighted by Murray's quirky bass clarinet solo and
the sharply executed ensemble work. The piece has two themes,
one in 4/4 and a second in 9/2; during the improvisation, the
players have to work through both sequentially.

"One for Eric" is 10 minutes long on the record, but when
DeJohnette's quartet played Fat Tuesday's recently, its complex
structure was extended into an obsessive 50 minutes. With Chico

Freeman, John Hicks, and Eddie Gomez on board, DeJohnette opened each performance with some melodica-flute sketching, before establishing the primary theme's rigorous tempo. Inevitably, a pyramidal structure asserted itself as Freeman (soloing first on bass clarinet, then on tenor) and DeJohnette battled with a violence recalling the Coltrane-Ali duets. Freeman's warm sound and occasional Lestorian triplets provided some respite, and DeJohnette's crisp volleys and bass drum pulse suggested points of focus during his extended solo, but the performance was finally unwieldly, lacking the determined structuring of the record.

That structuring is particularly impressive on the album's arrangements of two Coltrane themes, because DeJohnette so thoroughly remodels them to his own needs. The devious ballad, "Central Park West," is voiced with four lines (two saxes, cello, melodica) that float in and out of synch for one deft chorus. "India" is a splendid surprise: DeJohnette substitutes the blues for Coltrane's Eastern borrowings, beginning with a churchy piano solo. The vamp is played with aggressive tension, until the horns diverge for a delicately balanced duet, followed by stirring solos. Murray, on bass clarinet, employs triplets, vocalizations, and cross-octave leaps; Blythe shoots into the high register and bites every note square and full. DeJohnette's slashing support is exhilarating.

My only quibble with *Special Edition* is the sound mix, which undercuts the cohesiveness of the ensemble by separating completely the two saxophonists. Nonetheless, the session has all the earmarks of a classic: It astutely assimilates two of the most individual contemporary saxophonists, registers the current revival of swing rhythms and sonorities, and holds two icons of the '60s (Dolphy and Coltrane) up to the light of the '80s. Taken in tandem with *Cosmic Chicken, New Rags,* and *New Directions, Special Edition* makes DeJohnette look like one of the most providential of bandleaders.

(February 1980)

Moody's Moods Revisited

There are few living musicians I enjoy hearing more than James
Moody, and because it's been six years since he lit out for the
security of a Las Vegas stage band, his appearance last week at
Sweet Basil was pure reverie. Everything was everything: the closer
and closer gyres of his double timing, the Casper-Milquetoast-gets-
zonked wit, the unqualified directness of expression, the beautiful tonal shadings, and those beguiling juxtapositions that make
his best solos mini-epics in which impassioned oracles, comic relief, suspense, and song vie for chorus time. Moody is a story-
teller, a manipulator.

   He's also enough of a showman to keep the itchiest dilettante
wondering what he'll do next. In addition to tenor, alto, and flute
(his soprano was absent), he made good use of his voice, which
sounds like fog and rain, and his repertoire is encyclopedic. The
first set was slightly nervous, as the rhythm players (a Mike Longo
trio with Paul West and David Lee) accustomed themselves to each
other and to Moody, and the house groped for the proper sound
balance. Still, the electricity was immediate when he stomped off
"Good Bait" at a medium-up clip, doubling the tempo for most
of his solo, and trading fervent fours with Lee. He played two
flute solos, the second over subdued rhythm, on "Wave" and two
more on his own blues, "Darben the Redd Foxx," interpolating
marital phrases and fleeting references to Horace Silver's "Dood-
lin'." He sang "Bennie's from Heaven" with outlandish vibrato, a
parody of Ray Charles melisma, and a falsetto close.

   The second set was immeasurably more relaxed, partly because the rhythmic gears had been tightened. On tenor, he played "Shadow of Your Smile" in straight four, making it a blues on the turnbacks, balancing jagged upper-register cries with rumbling tremolos, and ending in the hidden register. He sang his own apparently spontaneous lyric to the verse of "Stardust" (which explained with occasional rhyme that he didn't know the words and you don't care anyway and besides he just feels like singing) before playing one imperial chorus with smooth dancing lyricism, and then heading into the steamy climate of "St. Thomas," first over calypso rhythms and then in four, storming luminously into the darkest jungles at breakneck speed. It was the evening's pinnacle.

He switched to alto for "Moody's Mood," a straight reading embellished with gorgeous pitch shadings; Moody's 1949 improvisation on "I'm in the Mood for Love" is one of the best known of all jazz solos, and Moody makes it sound not only fresh with every reading, but rediscovered—much as Cootie Williams always seemed to be discovering his unchanging "Take the A Train" solo. But he brought those sinuous legato phrases up short by singing the release (originally the piano solo) in a screeching falsetto. He also sang a blues chorus as prelude and epilogue to "Oop-Pop-A-Da," hitting a three-note chord on the word "cry"; he used the song's frequent breaks to yodel, imitate Robert Goulet, scat, and play a half-time blues. His most efficient accompanist was David Lee, who mixes the time with oddball patterns on his tuned toms, and plays lucidly thematic solos.

Moody first attracted attention with a 16-bar solo on Gillespie's 1946 "Emanon," but it wasn't until he moved to Europe in 1949 that he won international acclaim for a series of recordings with Swedish musicians. Although Charlie Parker was the decisive influence on his playing, Moody had his own sound and his own fund of melodic resources. The former was evident on his first session, for example the demonic, freakish stuff on "Moody's All Frantic," a solo that prophesied the saxophone calisthenics of the '60s. His melodic gifts were sorely tested when he went over ground that Parker had made indelibly his own, "Embraceable

You" and "Out of Nowhere," and emerged whole and distinct. He was more triumphant still on the songs he discovered for himself, especially "I'm in the Mood for Love," where several pet phrases that flitted through his recordings settled down in one imperishable improvisation. He displayed a courageous mettle in those sessions, restlessly evading the hooks of very melodious songs, weaving silken legato phrases and then circling back on them with double time ferocity, like a fox burrowing after the beat, chomping it with his teeth for a few seconds, and then scooting off again. On "These Foolish Things," he audaciously invokes Lester Young for the first two measures, leaps away in the third—as the tenor begins to sound like an alto—and is doubling obliviously by measures seven and eight. When he returns for the last 16 bars, he suggests the dark wailing of Coleman Hawkins, and concludes with a flurry of a coda that, like Charlie Parker's "In a Country Garden" sign-offs, has the effect of announcing that it's all artifice.

Those qualities—passion, lyricism, control, distance, unpredictability, wit, tonal variation—are the essence of Moody's work, but above them all is the forthrightness that allows him to communicate with people who find other boppers monotonous or dizzyingly complex. It enabled him to lead an ensemble in the '50s that could please dancers as well as listeners, almost a modernist edition of the jump band Johnny Hodges led a few years earlier. And it enables him to communicate a variety of moods so intimately you think you know him personally just from listening. In the late '50s, Moody underwent his darkest time—a bout with alcoholism, compounded by a fire that destroyed his band's instruments and arrangements. He committed himself to a mental institution called Overbrook for five months, and when he got out he recorded the triumphant "Last Train from Overbrook," revealing an unmistakable revitalization in his music that has increased over the years. He spent most of the '60s in the finest small group Dizzy Gillespie led since the '40s (I still reard the quintet's recording of "Round Midnight" from this period as definitive), but jazz fell on hard times and we lost him for most of the '70s. Only the fact that the Osmonds have their own backup musicians made it possible for him to take the present sabbatical.

You don't know Moody's music? Here's where to start: *Workshop, Greatest Hits,* Kenny Clarke's *The Paris Bebop Sessions,* Eddie Jefferson's *Body and Soul* (all Prestige), *The Moody Story* (Trip), *Moody's Mood* (All-Platinum), *Everything You've Always Wanted To Know About Sax* (Cadet), Dizzy Gillespie's *Something Old, Something New* (Phillips,) *Feelin' It Together* (Muse) and *Sun Journey* (Vanguard). Even better is the chance to see him live: if the work was forthcoming in New York he might not be in Vegas.*

(March 1980)

Something Else Again

It's a terrible cliché to say of a jazz musician that he explored a familiar song to new advantage. It's worse still to get metaphoric about it, turning the song's changes into veils or rose petals or artichoke leaves, which the improvisor presumably peels in search of some ineffable core. The cliché nags because it's rarely true. Most players are content to personalize a theme (no mean feat), before discarding it for variations that have little to do with the concerns of the songwriter. Yet there *are* methods of illuminating a song: Art Tatum used amplified harmonies and juxtaposed rhythms, Miles Davis tried seemingly inapposite tempos and note substitutions; Thelonious Monk framed songs with stone and mortar, then chiseled away with minuscule deviations, while Sonny Rollins fixes on motifs and takes them as far as he can.

*Within a year, Moody returned to the East Coast for good.

Muhal Richard Abrams did a litttle of each in a breathtaking performance of Ellington's "Prelude to a Kiss" at Fat Tuesday's last week. He opened and closed with loving expositions of the theme, adding bass and drums (Brian Smith and Warren Smith) for a long middle section in which the melody underwent ceaseless alterations without ever getting submerged. His large hands rippled across the keyboard at a medium-up gait with scrupulous attention to the composition's details. Almost every measure suggested other ways the song might have gone, and as the penultimate chorus spun increasingly closer to the bare theme, Abrams appeared to be implying: These are some of the choices Ellington faced in crafting his song, but as you can see the choices he made were the best.

Every time I've gone to hear Abrams play during the past four or five years, I've left with increased admiration and not a little amazement at the scope of his music. Which is not to say that I've liked everything he's done. Abrams, like Jaki Byard, is a consummate jazz eclectic, but unlike Byard, he doesn't attempt to display the variety of his skills in every setting. So you never know what to expect. Some of my most vivid musical memories of the '70s center upon him—the ingenious trio with Leroy Jenkins and Jerome Cooper, the stomping blues he fashioned with Chico Freeman and George Lewis, the architectonic piano recital at Newport last summer; his playing last week was something else again.

The sets were unbroken montages of standards and originals, linked so seamlessly that the audience was afraid to intrude with applause. There were characteristic block chords and static rhythms (accompanied by Warren Smith's collection of gongs) and some burrowing into the innards of the piano, but the meat of every set was classic tunes. Abrams played in bop and post-bop contexts in Chicago for 15 years (with the MJT + 3 among others) before organizing the Experimental Band, yet he appeared to have put that part of his music behind him, drawing on it in fragments or for an occasional dedication (the excellent "J.G." on

Sightsong, for example). Happily, working a club put him in mind of the material he used to play in clubs.

Abrams played tough, dulcet variations on Gillespie's "Con Alma," then initiated fours with the Smiths and invented a strongly rhythmic vamp finish, with teeming left-hand chords. This led straight into a diaphanous statement of Thad Jones's "A Child Is Born," first rubato and then in waltz time, building with the rhythm section into a storming vamp episode that receded into another beautiful cadenza; this time, Warren Smith added a vibraharp counterpoint. Abrams demonstrated his openness to the contemporary jazz repertory with a version of Ray Brown's stride blues, "A Very Hip Rock and Roll Tune," that alternated elegant stride choruses with bluesy addenda. He outlined Johnny Green's "Body and Soul" with fat block chords, then lightened his attack with brisk single notes tumbling around the melody. He outfitted Ellington's "Warm Valley" in the glamorous chords Ellington favored in the '40s, with an emotional resolve that reminded me of Ellington's memorial performances of Billy Strayhorn's "Lotus Blossom." And he made Davis's "Milestones" roar (the drum solo was built on "Salt Peanuts").

Abrams's new Black Saint album, with Roscoe Mitchell, George Lewis, Jay Clayton, Amina Myers, and Yousef Yancey, will be out in a couple of months. Then he'll be back in the studio with a nine-piece orchestra. All the music is new, which is what you'd expect from so ambitious a composer. But it would be a shame if Abrams doesn't also document how distinctive an interpreter he is. A number of critics have responded to recent efforts by Arthur Blythe, Chico Freeman, and Air by wondering if their dabblings in the classic repertory were attempts at commercialism. This is "purism" at its most idiotic. Anyone who can play "Prelude to a Kiss" with as much feeling and originality as Muhal Richard Abrams can should.

(March 1980)

Sarah Vaughan

1. Soulful

I don't know if Sarah Vaughan is the finest living interpreter of American popular song—her playful irreverence and musicality make it clear that she regards Tin Pan Alley as a starting gate and not a shrine. I do know she is the most creative singer working within the standard pop-song repertory, that her control of timbre, pitch, articulation, and dynamics, and her ability to improvise harmonically, melodically, and rhythmically are without peer. Lyrics are additional tools with which she injects further irony and emotion into her performances. The current release of *How Long Has This Been Going On?* (Pablo 2310-821) is cause for breaking out the champagne for two reasons—it's one of the best albums she's ever made, and it documents another, if not a new, side of Sarah Vaughan.

During the five years since her last satisfying record, *Live in Japan*, there has been evidence in her concert appearances that she was moving away from her regimen of breathtaking ballad extravaganzas interspersed with fast, two-chorus throwaways, to more consistent, less showy, jazz-oriented programs. After so long a silence, the Pablo album, where she sings ten familiar standards aided by Oscar Peterson, Joe Pass, Ray Brown, and Louie Bellson, may seem an anticlimax, or a relief. Those who've come to admire La Vaughan as an opera singer without an opera may be disappointed, but those lonely for the kind of singer she was when Charlie Parker, Freddy Webster, and Miles Davis were

numbered among her accompanists will be elated—she swings just
as hard, her tones are richer, and her conception free of little-
girl coyness. This collection represents more than a return to a
casual jazz ambience. I can't think of another Vaughan album with
such an abundance of blues locutions, variations, and riffs.

Sarah Vaughan started singing in a church in Newark, but soul
orthodoxies have been repressed in much of her recent work.
Here they peek through. They are apparent in the three-note
melisma she attaches to the word "life" at the end of the first
chorus of "I've Got the World on a String," and to the word "see"
in the second chorus, and in the way she growls "anytime" in the
third. They are unmistakable in the way she has rewritten "Teach
Me Tonight," in the way she handles the second half of the bridge
on "How Long," in numerous blues phrases, and several riffing
out-choruses. The high note right before the tag ending on "Teach
Me Tonight" reminds me of Jackie Wilson—it is not standard
Vaughan procedure, although the range itself is nothing out of
the ordinary for her (usually she works her way up with an arpeggio, as in the final release on the 1973 "My Funny Valentine").

How Long Has This Been Going On? was recorded in one day,
and that kind of thing has been going on too long. A not especially inspired "Easy Living" deserved a retake if for no other
reason than that she botched the lyric; her pacing and pronun-
ciation on the first eight bars of "Midnight Sun" are faultless, but
the song finally gets away from her and she compensates with
overindulged vibrato. Still, there are at least six stirring performances, more than on most people's records. Start with the first
cut, "I've Got the World on a String," and then proceed directly
to side two, where she does only one number with the quartet,
and one number with each member. It's hardly necessary to note
how difficult it is to sing a ballad creatively with just piano or guitar
or bass, or to effectively trade two-measure breaks with drums.
Vaughan makes it seem effortless and natural. Peterson introduces "More Than You Know" with a few notes from the Ada-
gio from Rodrigo's *Concerto De Aranjuez,* and Vaughan sings the

verse (note the way she puts the affected emphasis on "true" in perspective with the soulfully phrased "remain") before setting up the chorus in her mightiest trombone intonation. This is a masterly, emotive Vaughan performance: she picks up the first release with the same breath as the preceding phrase; the second release is patterned with descending parallel arpeggios; and the protracted ending has her repeating the title line four times, returning to the tonic only on the very last note. "My Old Flame," accompanied by Pass, is just as good. It's true that Vaughan sometimes seems oblivious of lyrics, but her strongest performances emphasize the meaning of words, and when she sings of thoughts that "go flashing back again," she sounds as though she has a particular old flame in mind. She makes the crawling tempo swing (especially on the release), and she resolves a treacherous ending so cleanly it seems planned, though I'm sure it wasn't.

The new version of "Body and Soul" is her third, and it relegates the recordings of 1946 and 1954 (as good as those were) to apprentice work. Accompanied only by Ray Brown's bass, she begins with the release at a medium-up tempo. The practice of starting a song in the middle is pretty unusual, although it's an obvious way of creating immediate tension and surprise. In his 1961 recording of "Let's Fall in Love," Frank Sinatra began with the release, moved backwards to the verse, and then, after a dramatic pause, forward into the chorus. "Body and Soul," with its strenuous key change, lends itself better to such tinkering, and Vaughan heightens the drama by halving the tempo as she begins the chorus fresh. She keeps you alert to every measure's nuance, and a couple of gambits are outstanding—the paraphrase melody she introduces on the line, "I spend my days in longing," and the single, bulleting arpeggio she makes of two sentence fragments, ". . . you're making. You know I'm yours . . ."

Excepting his splendid work on "More Than You Know," Peterson's solos are superficially bluesy, but he's a good accompanist and there are moments when Vaughan works closely with him, as when she scats his segue chords coming out of the release on "I've Got the World." Pass's best work is his counterpoint on "Teach Me Tonight"; Brown and Bellson play well together, as usual. Vaughan doesn't require much more from a rhythm section than reliable, attentive backing, and when she's singing as well as she does here she inspires it to keep pace. It will be interesting to see if she continues to work with producer Norman Granz, because if he parades the entire Pablo stock company through her sessions (including, one hopes, a set of Benny Carter arrangements), he will be mining the most valuable lode since Ella Fitzgerald discovered songbooks.

2. Sassing Ellington

My ambivalence about *Sarah Vaughan: Duke Ellington Song Book One* (Pablo Today 2312-111) was exacerbated partly by the extraordinary expectations I brought to the record and partly by the simultaneous reissue of Ella Fitzgerald and Duke Ellington's 1957 *The Duke Ellington Songbook* (Verve VE2-2535). The Ellington orchestra practically swooned its accompaniment to Ella, and the maestro was so pleased with her philanthropic interpretations (the phrase is basically his) that he appropriated the fourth side for an instrumental suite in her honor. Three of the Vaughan performances are equipped with faceless orchestrations by Billy Byers; for the other seven, she has only a four-piece rhythm section plus one or two soloists. Moreover, Sarah isn't nearly so philanthropic. Whereas Fitzgerald sings the songs straight, keeping her embellishments to a minimum, Vaughan occasionally threatens their integrity with her mannerisms.

I'd fantasized a Vaughan sings Ellington (more precisely, Vaughan sings Ellington and Strayhorn) album for years—and not simply for the obvious pleasure of hearing some of my favorite songs sung by one of my favorite singers. Ellington's songs are difficult to sing, with their oblique harmonic contours, strangely plotted blues notes, and, most characteristically, octave or larger intervals. These often occur at the beginning of a song (i.e., "I've Got It Bad," "Day Dream" "I Let a Song") and are more often finessed than sung. Ellington was the master of the luxurious arpeggio (i.e., "Sophisticated Lady," "Come Sunday," "In a Sentimental Mood"), and these require not only accurate pitch but tonal richness and dramatic sensitivity to do them justice. Considering the challenges they impose, it's surprising that so many have become popular standards. Billy Strayhorn's songs, which, excepting the problematic "Lush Life," have never been given their due by singers, are even more challenging.

The singers Ellington hired were, generally speaking, a motley bunch. The best of them was the cheerfully emotive contralto, Ivie Anderson, who handled the whole gamut of his songs with obvious pleasure and minimal fuss. After Ivie, when Ellington wasn't recording vocalists for specific orchestral effects or presenting superficially soulful entertainers to his concert audiences, he preferred baritones and sopranos. But they weren't definitive interpreters as, for example, Johnny Hodges and Ben Webster were, a failure that is only partly explained by the fact that many of Ellington's best tunes originated as instrumental pieces. Usually, the singers weren't up to the material; in some cases, they misinterpreted Ellington's intent, applying jazzy melisma where none was needed. In Ella Fitzgerald, he found a marvelous interpreter: She could spark the swingers and court the ballads, and her tone was never more beautiful than in her Songbook period, the '50s. Yet even Fitzgerald couldn't realize the full potential in Ellington's songs.

Which brings us to an irony in Ellington's relationship to Tin Pan Alley. Many of the great tunesmiths—Berlin, Rodgers, Kern— disdained the license jazz musicians take, but their songs inspired and in many instances demanded embellishment. The chords of a tune like "All the Things You Are" facilitate improvisation to such a degree that the melody seems relatively unimportant. Ellington, on the other hand, wrote songs that inhibit improvisation—songs in which melody and harmony are fused so perfectly that they force the musician to think in terms of interpretation. Consider the intriguingly unsuccessful album Thelonious Monk made of Ellington tunes; he pecked at them timorously, never quite able to inhabit them. By contrast, the cheap sentiments of "These Foolish Things" and "Just a Gigolo" were more conducive to Monk's idiosyncratic explorations. (Of course, Ellington wrote many pieces specifically for jazz improvisors; several of the most played jam session tunes are from his book, including "Take the A Train," "In a Mellow Tone," "C Jam Blues," and "Perdido." It's no coincidence that Monk's most energetic Ellington performance was on such a vehicle, "It Don't Mean a Thing.") The intransigence and ambitious design of Ellington's (and Strayhorn's) best ballads make them art songs in a way that few Tin Pan Alley products are. Ellington did not, after all, write them for musicals or movies—the songs he *did* write under that kind of pressure (or merely in the hope of producing a bills-paying pop hit) were usually failures.

In fact, the Ellington-Strayhorn trove would provide a compelling body of work for classical singers (European school) no less than jazz and pop singers. That's the one treatment that hasn't been tried—opulent readings by an operatic voice with a complement of strings. Evidence that Ellington wanted to hear his tricky intervals hit squarely and with a tonal purity that eluded him in America is circumstantially available in his enthusiastic collaborations with Sweden's Alice Babs. But even at the time of his death, Ellington was not considered quite "serious" enough by the arts establishment, and it would have taken a singularly knowing and adventurous singer to broach the project.

There was, however, a jazz singer with operatic range, exquisite intonation, and harmonic savvy. Strangely, Sarah Vaughn had never shown much interest in Ellington's songs. In the '50s, she had a hit with Juan Tizol's "Perdido" and recorded stunning versions of "Prelude to a Kiss" and "Lush Life"; in the '60s, she tackled "Sophisticated Lady," "In a Sentimental Mood," and "Solitude." That was it. I had hoped someday to hear her essay not only the established Ellington-Strayhorn repertoire but—commissioning lyrics when necessary—several instrumental gems waiting to be turned into songs, such as "Black Beauty," "Serenade to Sweden," "Blue Serge," and "Blood Count." Dreams, all dreams.

The actual album (a second volume will be released in the fall) is disappointing first in its production standards. As noted, Norman Granz, who also produced Ella and Duke, gave Sarah skeletal support. But the real problem for me is the way Vaughan takes liberties with the material. Those liberties, in other contexts, are the key to her greatness. She makes Rodgers and Hart's "My Funny Valentine" a good deal more than it is on the printed page; she makes Ellington's "All Too Soon" something less. I don't mean to suggest that Ellington's songs are sacred texts—though I would have preferred a straight chorus before the change-ups— but Vaughan's playfulness trivializes the original phrases, at times suggesting a lack of conviction.

The outstanding ballad selection, "In a Sentimental Mood," is the exception—brilliant Vaughan that dwarfs everything else on the record. She works the arpeggios with scrupulous care, her luscious voice swelling and decaying with total control, her low notes booming sonorously. Byers's arrangement is, for once, rich and supportive; after the strings interlude, Vaughan returns not at the release but five bars early. Her "Solitude," however, sacrifices Ellington's poignancy and clarity with coy variations and a brassy second release in which she whoops it up with trombonist J. J. Johnson. "Day Dream" is a spare and elegant song in which every note is essential, and Vaughan's ornaments aren't improvements: The three notes she applies to the word "glow" (and "came" in "Sophisticated Lady," and the two notes she uses for "heart" and "part" on "All Too Soon") obscure the gracefulness of the original line. And while the half-note/dotted-quarter/eighth-note rhythms of the song's release can seem facile, I don't think her dotted-half/two-eighths substitution helps. She scats most of "I Didn't Know About You," with results that are no more than pleasantly glib.

Elsewhere, the Vaughan imprint is so beguiling that I can forgive her willfulness, for ultimately this is a personal testament. She never goes near the original melody of "I'm Just a Lucky So and So," turning it into a febrile blues with falsetto and stop-time episodes. I don't prefer it to the original, but it's pure Vaughan in a histrionic mood, and she seems to be having fun. She also toys with "I Let a Song," displacing rhythms in the first release, then swinging the out chorus, concluding with a trumpet-like high note and glissando. She makes the flame in an otherwise perfunctory "Sophisticated Lady" really flicker, and she's so authoritative on the release of "All Too Soon" that you wonder why the rest of the interpretation is so pale. The new "Lush Life" hasn't the rich certainty of the 1956 version (a comparison of the two is particularly damning to Byers's arrangement and the sound mix), but her huskier voice, subtle parlando, and diminished tempo are earmarks of the mature and tougher Vaughan. Although the band arrangement on "In a Mellow Tone" is nondescript, this is one piece that she's made her own through frequent performances. On the combo selections, Jimmy Rowles is the most helpful accompanist; obbligati are provided by Frank Foster, Frank Wess, Zoot Sims, J. J. Johnson, and Waymon Reed— never more than two men to a selection.

The only Ellington song Vaughan sang during her recent opening night at the Grand Finale was "In a Mellow Tone," which she invested with even more pizzazz than on the record. The room is large, uncomfortable, and overpriced, but I didn't hear many complaints: It *was* thrilling to see her in a nightclub. The intimacy seemed to loosen her up, possibly because she didn't have to worry about projection: We hung on her every word. The rhythm section (Butch Lacy, Andy Simpkins, and Grady Tate) was a little unfocused because of Lacy, who played cocktail-lounge chords and accompanied every tremolo with a grimace, so you'd know he was feeling them blues. Not even that mattered. Vaughan was magnificent, and she had a few surprises. She opened with a fast "Lullaby of Broadway," introduced "Easy Living" with wordless crooning (she sang the bridge without taking a breath), scatted Waymon Reed's "46th and 8th" (including his trumpet solo from the record of that name), and burned through "Cherokee." There were several show-stopping ballads, of course, including an alchemical rendition of the ever-unappealing "Over the Rainbow." She finished it by riffing the line "I wanna fly," with "I" dropping an interval and "fly" rising one each time. She also got off a funny bit and a funny line. The bit took place on "Misty," where her voice suddenly took on a masculine edge and the audience stared unbelievingly for the three seconds it took to realize that she was lip-synching Grady Tate. The line was in reference to her perspiration: "I come up here looking like Lena Horne and walk off looking like Sarah Vaughan."

She still introduces herself as June Carter (well, there are worse people she could introduce herself as), and still invites requests as a prelude to the only request she'll take: "Send in the Clowns." It's a remarkable performance, and though I always think "no, not again," I always get goose bumps when she homes in on the big a capella climax: "Losing my timing this late/in myyyyyyyyyyyyyyyyyyyyyyyyyyyyyyyyyy career." If she can do as much for Sondheim, why not Ellington?

(October 1978/March 1980)

Freedom Then and Now

For some time now, it has been insufficient to say of Max Roach that he is the most widely admired drummer since the advent of modern jazz. He's become something more—a tough-minded monitor of the music's best instincts. This status springs not merely from his role as spokesman and teacher, or his insistence that art cannot be divorced from the social pressures that produce it (and I don't mean to underestimate the courage with which he challenged the solipsism of the jazz establishment or the invective he withstood), but from his ability to detect signs of genuine musical progressivism and redefine them through his own authority and craftsmanship. Like Mao, or Coleman Hawkins, Roach seems to believe that you can either criticize the vanguard from the ranks, oppose it, or lead it. Roach leads, and in 35 years he has yet to make a compromised or meretricious recording. The diversity and constancy of his input are illuminated by two new recordings and the reissue of a classic that was more heard of than heard.

Roach's reputation as a musician was firmly established by 1956, when Clifford Brown's death brought the last great bop band to a tragic end. If his idol Jo Jones played like the wind, Roach was often a typhoon, though too conceptually oriented to court chaos. His quicksilver accompaniment was astonishing; his solos, models of thematic organization, taught the drums to breathe; his partnership with Brown brought a warmth and fire into the music at a time when it appeared most susceptible to a cool academicism. After Brown's death, he worked like a demon, recording over 15 albums as a leader during the next six years. He was composing in earnest, experimenting with voices and odd time signatures, and making reparations for having led a movement which had whittled down the trap set from a garage sale of percussive accoutrements to the austere essentials of snare, tom, cymbals, and bass drum. That period ended with a trilogy of records in which he brought it all to bear on the civil rights movement here and in Africa: *We Insist! The Freedom Now Suite,* Abbey Lincoln's *Straight Ahead,* and *Percussion Bitter Sweet.* Although the first of these is the most celebrated—it has been choreographed, expanded, and filmed—it is the least well known, having remained unissued since Candid Records went under in the early '60s. Columbia is now making it widely available for the first time (as JC 36390), and though, the *We Insist!* has been dropped, the music remains as effective as it was 20 years ago.

The subject matter was hardly new to jazz in 1960. Indeed, the first two movements—"Driva' Man" and "Freedom Day"—echoed Duke Ellington's "Work Song" and "Emancipation Celebration" in the 1943 *Black, Brown & Beige.* Louis Armstrong had spurred interest in Africa with his widely publicized visit to the Gold Coast, and Sonny Rollins served notice with a paragraph that accompanied the original release of his "The Freedom Suite" that jazz musicians were committed to the struggle. What was compellingly new was Roach's fervor (which helped make possible the rhetoric of Archie Shepp and others), his militant stance, and the ingenious marshaling of various musical elements—alternating or superimposed time signatures, modes, vamps, pointed lyrics (by Oscar Brown), wordless vocals, Third World percussion, discordant harmonies—for the harsh yet lucid expression of an intolerable situation. He chose his cohorts well: Olatunji leads the percussion quartet on "Tears for Johannesburg," which prefigures M'Boom by a decade; the extraordinary trumpeter Booker Little, whose solos are highlights of "Tears" and especially "Freedom Day," shares the front line with tenorist Walter Benton and trombonist Julian Priester; and Coleman Hawkins plays with dignity and drive over a slow 5/4 pulse on "Driva' Man," in which Roach's accents ring like the blows of an axe. (To really appreciate how inspired Hawkins was by Roach's music, you also have to hear his solos on "Blue Monk" and "Left Alone" on *Straight Ahead*.)

Abbey Lincoln has never sounded more effective than she does on *Freedom Now*. The tendencies toward sharpness and plaintiveness that mar other performances are firmly controlled here, particularly in the bitter chanting of "Driva' Man," where she's accompanied only by a tambourine, and the stirring "Tryptich," where her clamant moaning and hollering presage the instrument glossolalia that would dominate jazz for much of the '60s. Last weekend, Roach and Lincoln were reunited to perform "Tryptich" for Diane McIntyre's dance company at Symphony Space. Roach, Lincoln, and McIntyre were silhouetted for the first movement, moving into the light for the "Protest" episode, as McIntyre caught every contorted accent of the music with stabbing undulations of her body, her long, sculptured arms slicing through the air, her face an unrelenting mask of resolve. It was a riveting performance, and Roach, armed only with a snare, monitored the passions with imperturbable finesse. In some ways, *Percussion Bitter Sweet* represented an advance over *Freedom Now*, not least because Eric Dolphy was an essential voice of the age, and Roach's own solo on "Mendacity" set the standard for freely phrased drum solos; yet *Freedom Now* holds together better and has more immediate impact. It remains relevant politically and musically.

In 1970, Roach formed M'Boom Re: Percussion, an ensemble of eight drummers who played trap sets, percussion keyboards (vibes, marimba, xylophone), concert percussion (tympani, bells, chimes), and Latin, African, and Oriental percussion. Once again, a precedent could be found in Ellington, who assembled nine percussionists in 1959, for "Maletoba Spank" and "Tymperturbably Blue." M'Boom gave several memorable concerts, and has finally recorded a solid album for Columbia's new Mastersound series, *M'Boom* (IC 36247). The music thrives on subtle contrasts—deadened versus crystalline sounds, pitched versus unpitched instruments, little instruments (employed for detailed effects) versus big instruments (that carry melodies and propel the rhythms). The structures are familiar—ostinatos plus variations—but freshly conceived, with an accent on compositional restraint rather than the slambang forays that the group sometimes achieves in concert. All the pieces but Monk's "Epistrophy" were generated by the nine percussionists, and the variety is impressive: the delicate lyricism of "Twinkle Toes" (a simple theme meticulously developed), "Morning/Midday" (an evocation of the jungle), and "January V" (an ethereal dirge for Mingus); and the wonderful menace of "Kujichagalia," which evolves from cowbell and temple blocks to an echoic steel drum melody abetted by lockstep trap drumming, and the Middle Eastern-sounding "Caravanserai." Particularly outstanding are "Onomatopoeia," a concatenation of bells and chimes, "Rumble in the Jungle," in which the accents suggest five superimposed over eight and a lovely pentatonic melody serves as a running motif (both pieces are by Omar Clay), and Roach's "The Glorious Monster," in which variations on a vamp that changes signature from six to seven to an alternation of six and eight are intoned by the mallet instruments, a saw, tympani, traps, and tom-toms.

Finally, there is an album by Roach's current quartet *Pictures in a Frame* (Soul Note 1003). The band troubles me in concert:

trumpeter Cecil Bridgewater (whose tone often blares) and reed-
man Odean Pope are not sufficiently distinguished to justify the
very long solos they play on very long structures. But the record
is a triumph of creative producing. The average length of the
nine selections is four minutes, and only two pieces receive conventional quartet performances (the others are duets, trios, and
solos); the writing is substantial, and the brevity brings out un-
suspected discipline in the hornmen. Bridgewater is convincing
on "Magic," where he reminds me a little of Booker Little, and
on "A Place of Truth," in which his smoky phrases are subtly
shadowed by Roach at the piano; Pope is superb in a tenor-bass
recitation of Clifford Jordan's "Japanese Dream." Calvin Hill's
agility in the low register of the bass and the quality of his writing are impressive. And Roach, in addition to varying the rhythms
and darting through every opening (i.e., "Mwalimu") with his
customary elan, adds another dazzling piece for solo drums to
his canon: "Reflections," a seven-note theme with roiling responses and an intensity in execution that recalls Bud Powell. Since
he embarked on an academic career eight years ago, Roach has
only been intermittently on the scene, but his current recordings
prove that he's still thinking and listening. And still leading.

(June 1980)

The Trombone's
Connected to the . . .

Owing to the economy of its design, the trombone is a peculiarly
modern-looking contraption: cylindrical tubing elegantly arranged in unbroken parallel lines with a small input bell and a

large output bell. Actually, it is the oldest instrument in the orchestra after percussion, having achieved something very near its present form 500 years ago. Its reputation for versatility, range, and multiphonics was earned recently, however, largely through the efforts of jazz musicians. The trombone didn't become a familiar presence in the orchestra until Beethoven employed three of them to beef up the climax of his Fifth Symphony; when, a century later, Ellington added three to *his* orchestra, he was as much intrigued by their tonal diversity (a trombone in the hands of Lawrence Brown was a different animal than one in the hands of Tricky Sam Nanton) as their punch.

At the time Ellington began experimenting with brass voicings, the trombone was thought to have limited legato and mobility, and a range just short of three octaves. Within a few decades, Jack Teagarden showed how smoothly the trombone could phrase; Joe "Tricky Sam" Nanton, using muting devices, created alternate sequences of pitch; J.J. Johnson demonstrated mobility almost equal to that of a trumpet; Albert Manglesdorff developed the trombone's harmonics to such a degree that he could play two- to five-note chords; and Bill Watrous helped to enlarge its range to five and a half octaves, up from double pedal B flat.

Still, the trombone was relatively slow to develop as a jazz instrument. Its role in the ensembles of New Orleans was mimetic, chiefly because it was expected to perform the function of a tuba or bass, but also because it lent itself to barnyard buffoonery. Indeed, the shenanigans contributed to the popular image of the trombone as a comical instrument. (A few bandleaders of the '30s, notably Tommy Dorsey, mitigated that popular image with the slickest sort of romantic balladry.) Yet the trombone made up for lost time in the '20s, evolving so quickly that last year's trailblazer was this year's antique. Kid Ory was the model traditional trombonist, with his brusque, rhythmic counterpoint and swooning glissandos, but his younger compatriot, George Brunis, whose bandstand antics preserved the trombone's vaudeville antecedents, recorded the first solo on the New Orleans Rhythm Kings' 1923 "Tin Roof Blues." By 1926, Miff Mole's cool sound and technical aplomb, exemplified on the Edison recording of "Hurricane" and the Brunswick version of "Alabama Stomp" (both with Red Nichols) relegated Brunis and even Charlie Green, the lusty bluesman who accompanied Bessie Smith, to the primeval past. The arrival only two years later of Jimmy Harrison and Jack Teagarden made Mole sound like a Dixieland dinosaur.

Harrison was the more economical player; his unperturbed use of space on the Chocolate Dandies' "Dee Blues" and Fletcher Henderson's "King Porter Stomp" still sounds knowingly modern, and his dark, warm tone (well captured on Charlie Johnson's "Walk That Thing") and blues feeling are said to have influenced Teagarden. But the influence and admiration were mutual: Teagarden's impact on Harrison is unmistakable on Chick Webb's "Heebie Jeebies." Teagarden's virtuosity was already well in hand by the late '20s, in such wonderful choruses as "She's a Great, Great Girl" and "Ridin' but Walkin'." Within a few years, Teagarden jettisoned his vibrato, achieved unparalleled fluidity, and innovated a technique whereby he replaced his bell with a water glass and phrased so effortlessly that some who heard his records assumed he was playing a valve trombone. By contrast, J. C. Higginbotham, whose work with the Luis Russell orchestra often found him serving as a rapacious foil to Louis Armstrong (as on "Dallas Blues" and "Bessie Couldn't Help It"), made the trombone aggressive and violent with his thunderclap timbre and large intervallic leaps. The trombone was firmly established in the '30s. There were schools of hot players (Benny Morton, Dickie Wells, Sandy Williams, Trummy Young, Keg Johnson, and Claude Jones), and cool players (Tommy Dorsey, Floyd O'Brian, and Jack Jenny). There were those who, in the spirit of Harrison and Teagarden played hot *and* cool, like Lawrence Brown, Vic Dickenson, Bill Harris, and Fred Beckett. And there were the muted warblings of Tricky Sam Nanton, a school unto himself, whose later disciples included Quentin Jackson, Booty Wood, Tyree Glenn, and Al Grey.

The tonal variety was staggering, but there was some question as to whether the trombone could adapt to the challenges of bebop in the '40s. In a period that found such traditional jazz standbys as the clarinet and the rhythm guitar falling by the wayside, the trombone's survival would depend less on personal intonation than on a thoroughly noneccentric mobility—fast, light, attenuated. J. J. Johnson, in his 1946 "Jay Bird" session and his 1947 collaboration with Charlie Parker, "Drifting on a Reed," proved the trombone's adaptability, and in a matter of months jazz was swarming with his imitators. They dominated the instrument for nearly 20 years, but it would be a mistake to suggest that the new virtuosity suppressed individuality. Personal style existed on a subtler level, perhaps, but was certainly discernible in the work of Kai Winding, Eddie Bert, Earl Swope, Curtis Fuller, Slide Hampton, Frank Rosolino, Carl Fontana, Britt Woodman, Jimmy Cleveland, Jimmy Knepper, Willie Dennis, and Bob Brookmeyer (who, like Juan Tizol and Stu Williamson, played valve trombone). The reaction against bebop that fueled the avant-gardism of the '60s helped to restore the trombone's intonational eccentricities, but this time they were bolstered with a technical command that gave the instrument a conceptual range without peer among brass instruments. Yet despite the tremendous impact of Roswell Rudd and Albert Manglesdorff, the trombone remained on the periphery of the new music. Only in the past five years have the technical discoveries begun to reap a musical harvest.

That harvest is exemplified in a pandemic approach to the horn that acknowledges the punching violence of Higginbotham, the suave shadings of Dickenson or Harris, the unshakable authority of Johnson, and the amazing overtone discoveries of Manglesdorff. The key transitional figure of the '60s was Rudd, who came to the new music after a decade's apprenticeship in Dixieland bands. (Bill Watrous, whose technique rivals that of Manglesdorff but who has opted for a life in the studios, played with Rudd in the strange Dixie/swing bands piloted by Herbie Nichols.) Rudd's work with the New York Art Quartet, Archie Shepp,

Charlie Haden's Liberation Music Orchestra, the Jazz Composers Orchestra, and in his own masterful album *Everywhere* (a homage to Bill Harris, who, in his tenure with Woody Herman, played insinuating solos on such trombone tone poems as "Bijou" and "Everywhere") demonstrated a revitalization of expressive techniques and a concern with restoring the trombone's brassy, refulgent sound and dynamic sensitivity. His Dixieland background prepared him for the resumption of jerky glissandos and mooning sighs when the meticulous phrasing of bop was no longer sufficient. There is an idiomatic element in his work, reflected in his vocalizations, his patience with muffled aftertones, and a general willingness to substitute sound for notes—to rediscover melody as a consequence of tonal properties.

Rudd's recordings during the past 10 years have been jarringly inconsistent, occasionally so wry as to seem disingenuous. But a recent album, recorded in Italy in 1978, is as good as anything he's ever done, and documents real maturity in melodic and harmonic cogency. *Sharing* (Dischi Della Querica), a collection of duets with pianist Giorgio Gaslini, covers a lot of ground: "Simona" finds him employing diverse sonorities in a more straightforward, less vocalized manner than in the past, and exemplifies his ability to find and sustain fresh melodic ideas; "Four Lessons from the Third World" ranges from bebop articulation to pentatonic primitivism to compelling dissonance; "Tango-Barcarola" shows him to be Bill Harris's truest and sultriest heir; and "Ow-Wah Blues" demonstrates his authenticity as a bluesman. Rudd doesn't use multiphonics, but a new album by Manglesdorff, *A Jazz Tune I Hope* (MPS), recorded in Germany in 1978 with Elvin Jones, Eddie Gomez, and Wolfgang Dauner, shows that overtones can be eventfully assimilated in a rather orthodox jazz setting. He uses multiphonics to build up the themes, for rhythmic chording, and to simulate strumming. Most impressively, he uses them to color his solos, to amplify without distracting from the linearity of his ideas.

Many of the best jazz trombonists of the past 20 years—from Buster Cooper, Grachan Moncur, Garnett Brown, and Julian

Priester in the '60s to Raul De Souza, Dave Bargeron, Jim Pugh, Dennis Wilson, and Steve Turre in the '70s—have honed a fairly conservative line; for them the cutting edge borders on hard bop. The hardcore avant-gardists—of whom England's Paul Rutherford is the most implacably, flatulently hardcore—are found in greater abundance in the classical vanguard (Garrett List, Jim Fulkerson) or in Europe. But in recent years, a middle ground has been attained by a few trombonists who experiment with several kinds of improvisation and have emerged as grand instrumental entertainers. Some are associated with such European groups as Willem Breuker's Kollektiev and Loek Dikker's Waterland Big Band, in which the umbilical cord linking the New Orleans tailgaters and the modern expressionists is viewed with evenhanded irony. Yet the most satisfying, at least from a New Yorker's vantage point, are the young Americans, George Lewis and Ray Anderson.

Anderson, who arrived from California just as jazz loftdom was peaking, is a busy player, but his prolixity is made interesting by the tonal and temporal resources with which he varies his notes, and by his compelling energy—he has fun with the horn. Barry Altschul's *Somewhere Else* (Moers 6059) is trio music, and Anderson knows exactly when to promenade out front and when to hold back. The best moments are the three-part inventions, as on "Slickophonic Shuffle," when Anderson comes in on bassist Mark Helias's solo, followed by Altschul, and each sustains a merrily static give-and-take. On the ballad, "Onea," Anderson's playing is somewhat reminiscent of Rudd's New York Art Quartet performance of "Sweet," but he's too recondite and the result is oddly vacant. On "Martin's Stew," his rough-hewn playing recalls the vibrant attack of Higginbotham and Benny Morton. Anderson also performs on *Anthony Braxton's Seven Compositions 1978* (Moers 01066), and he positively transforms Side One/Cut One, a rhythmically plodding pseudo-bop head, by entering with high riffs stretched across the beat—suddenly Thurman Barker asserts himself, and the music swings—and an impressive density of melodic notions. He uses multiphonics to comical effect on Side

One/Cut Two, but fails to make the most of Braxton's fine contrapuntal writing on Side Two/Cut One. Perhaps the high point is the very brief Side Two/Cut Two, in which the band really achieves unity, spurred by the controls of the leader's ingratiating piece. Here, Anderson is a delightfully quick-witted foil for Braxton.

George Lewis, a young AACM member whose most important associations have included Abrams, Braxton, and Roscoe Mitchell, is every bit as flexible a sideman as Anderson, and has also proven himself as a conceptualizer—as a soloist in his tour de force *Solo Trombone Album,* where he accommodated each improvisational style with a different tone, and as a composer on *Homage to Charles Parker,* a thoughtful tribute to Parker which avoids specific references to Bird's music by combining a static, electronic opening that extends and abridges the concept introduced by Miles on "He Loved Him Madly," with solos by Douglas Ewart, Anthony Davis, and Lewis. His approach is a good deal less robust than that of Anderson, and his tone generally darker and more studied. On Fred Anderson's *Another Place* (Moers 01058), he makes notes and whole phrases sound as though they were played backwards, the result of breathing effects and a highly developed terminal vibrato. He recalls the Harris-Rudd connection in sections of "The Bull," caressing the melody without wasted gestures, encouraging—by the sheer conviction of his playing—the rest of the band to settle around him like filings around a magnetic field. On the title selection, his phrases unfold with yawning ease, and the rhythms spring naturally from his melodies. Lewis also plays a significant role in "Triverse," from Muhal Richard Abrams's *Spihumonesty* (Black Saint 0032). The piece is a quicksilver colloquy between Lewis and Roscoe Mitchell over a furious keyboard scrim with bass added at beginning and end.

In some ways, Lewis stands apart from the new trombone virtuosity, generally eschewing harmonics and plunger effects; he tends to be smooth and introverted—if Anderson explodes with the revelation of J. C. Higginbotham's power, Lewis often suggests the whimsical offhandedness of Vic Dickenson. What they share is a devotion to the trombone, in all its guises. If they make us think of trombones of the past, it is less the consequence of specific references than the fact that in representing the trombone as it exists in 1980, they encompass all that's gone into its making. They make us enjoy the instrument as much as they do.

(September 1980)

Fifty Years of "Body and Soul"

In the year of its 50th anniversary, let us now praise a song—the most recorded American popular song of all time (nearly 3000 versions). Few songs have survived as long or as well, and none have inspired as many durable interpretations by successive generations of musicians. "Body and Soul" first became famous as the showstopper in a 1930 Broadway revue called *Three's a Crowd*, starring Libby Holman, Clifton Webb, and Fred Allen. Ironically, Arthur Schwartz and Howard Dietz, the show's chief songwriters, tried to have it cut. According to Robert Sour, who collaborated with Edward Heyman on the lyric, the song was actually deleted from several performances at the tryout in Philadelphia, where they wrote several sets of lyrics in a plea to save it. Fortunately for everyone, Libby Holman sang it in New York, and thus was born the ballad that earned its 22-year-old composer, Johnny Green, a grateful footnote in the annals of jazz.

It's hard to imagine jazz without "Body and Soul." Excepting the blues and those songs (such as "I Got Rhythm," "Honeysuckle Rose," and "How High the Moon") that were transformed by jazz musicians into untethered chord progressions, no other piece has been interpreted as frequently or with such consistently rewarding results. Yet it's an unusually difficult example of the 32-bar AABA song, with three key changes in the chorus (and three more in the rarely performed verse), intricate major/minor circuitry, and a wide range; moreover, it has a cloyingly powerful melody. Jazz musicians favor "Body and Soul" not because the harmonies provoke vivid new variations, as is the case with Jerome Kern's "All the Things You Are," but because they like the tune.

Ironically, the improvisation that secured the song's place in jazz—Coleman Hawkins's 1939 masterpiece—suspended the melody almost entirely. Yet even his most demonic and irreverent descendants, including Charlie Parker and John Coltrane, found it difficult to shuffle off Green's imposing melodic coils. Basically, there have been three interpretive approaches: (a) personalized recitation; (b) whimsical variation employing fragments from other songs; and (c) genuine melodic variation. Perhaps only Hawkins, Teddy Wilson, and two or three others have achieved the last, which is a fairly commonplace goal in jazz improvisation. And yet performances of "Body and Soul" continue to proliferate, and several artists have recorded it repeatedly.

Johnny Green has spent most of his life writing movie music in Hollywood. His songs are few, but of high quality: "Out of Nowhere," written in 1931, became as much a part of the bop era (thanks to Charlie Parker, Tadd Dameron, and Fats Navarro) as "Body and Soul" was of swing, and "Coquette," "I Cover the Waterfront," and "I'm Yours" have also enjoyed the respect of jazz musicians. But "Body and Soul" is in a class by itself. Within a period of about eight weeks in the fall of 1930, at least eight versions were recorded, including those by the three torchiest ladies of the era—Libby Holman, Ruth Etting, and Helen Morgan. Louis Armstrong transformed it from a lament of unrequited love to a ballad with greater interpretive potential, and established it as a jazz standard. In trying to trace its progress during the past

50 years, and the progress of jazz as reflected in approaches to
that one song, I listened to over 90 versions.

I encountered not only dozens of first-rate performances, but
several milestones indicative of the development of jazz itself: the
first fruits of what would be the most influential keyboard style
of the '30s (Wilson), the long-meter approach to ballads (Eldridge), the culmination of the vertical style of improvisation
(Hawkins), the rise of virtuosity in jazz bass (Blanton), the initial
explorations of Charlie Parker, and the fullest realization of talented stylists (Chaloff, Cohn, Betty Carter, and others). The
magical qualities of "Body and Soul" lay in its ability to inspire
musicians to plumb the depths of their own creativity. I've nar-
rowed the list to my favorites, plus a few interesting curios. Two
sets of lyrics from the song's Philadelphia tryout are in circulation; Billie Holliday recorded the second set, but almost everyone else sings the first. Also, three writers are officially credited
with the occasionally ungainly words ("my life a wreck you're
making"). The ringer is Frank Eyton, a staff arranger at Chap-
pell & Co., which offered to publish the song on condition that
he work on the lyric. Eyton was cut in, but according to Sour,
"He didn't even change a comma." Incidentally, the best "straight"
recording is the 1947 rendition by Frank Sinatra (Columbia), who
except for dotting one quarter note at the expense of another,
sings it just as Green wrote it, thereby demonstrating that the song
is pretty wonderful to begin with. I've dated the entries that follow not by the artist's first recording but by the one that seems
to me most indicative.

1930: Louis Armstrong (Columbia). No one translated more
pop into jazz than Armstrong, and though this effort with the
Les Hite orchestra isn't as prepossessing as some of his other gems
from the period, its feeling and drama make the torch singers
sound like holdovers from a previous century. His trumpet swings
the turnbacks and heats up the last eight bars, but his vocal,
seemingly tenuous in its determination to rethink every phrase,
is what you remember.

1935: Benny Goodman Trio (Bluebird). The trio's first record, and one of Teddy Wilson's most celebrated solos—a 16-bar variation that sounds almost like an inversion of the melody. But it's a mistake to isolate Wilson's contribution. The record is gripping because of the constant colloquy between Wilson's melancholy provocations (in accompaniment as well as solo) and Goodman's straightforward recitation. Wilson offers a somewhat different paraphrase in the trio's 1938 version (Columbia), and reworks some of the same ideas in his 1941 solo performance (Smithsonian/Columbia).

1937: Django Reinhardt (Capitol). The guitarist's superb solo includes a rubbery stop-and-go phrase at the first turnback, a folkishly plucked release, and lightning strumming, as well as a doubletime passage in the third chorus. His 1938 version (EMI) with Larry Adler is charming, but less adventurous.

1938: Chu Berry and Roy Eldridge (Commodore). After Hawkins, Eldridge has the most claims to B&S, and it's his technical brilliance rather than Berry's rather decorative statement that makes this a classic, the epitome of swing. Eldridge was the first to play the song in long meter (each measure is doubled), a practice that is still widely imitated. He merely embellishes the melody—but what embellishment, and what velocity. Note Catlett's drumming during the release and when Roy returns to the original tempo. Among other Eldridge versions are a 1939 fragment (Jazz Archive), an amazing, extended blitz from a 1941 jam (Xanadu), a 1944 studio version in which a stunning reading is foreshortened by a piano solo (Decca), and a moving 1967 concert without long meter (Pumpkin).

1939: Coleman Hawkins (Quintessence/RCA). One of the most celebrated improvisations in music, and a gauntlet tossed at every other saxophonist in jazz. There is nothing to compare with it. For two choruses and a brief coda, Hawkins rhapsodizes over the chords, never even hinting at Green's melody after the first seven notes, and the profusion of ideas, the sustained tension, the incomparable rhythmic authority build dynamically, phrase after phrase. Incredibly, it was a huge hit—Hawkins's variations became as much a part of jazz as the original melody; Benny Carter orchestrated part of it, Eddie Jefferson wrote lyrics to it, Hawkins used his improvisation as the basis for subsequent improvisations. In 1948, Hawkins recorded "Picasso" (Verve) after eight hours of preparation; it was the first unaccompanied tenor solo in jazz, and based on the changes of B&S. Of his many other versions, a 1959 concert reading (Verve) was outstanding.

1940: Jimmy Blanton and Duke Ellington (Smithsonian/RCA). A milestone in virtuoso bass playing. Blanton's arco is notable for its warmth, rudely attacked low notes, and glissandos, but his pizzicato half-chorus shows how remarkable an improvisor he was.

1940: Billie Holliday (Columbia). She made all kinds of subtle alterations in the melody, and Eldridge took eight memorable measures. I slightly prefer her 1946 version (Verve), in which the phrasing is more legato and the alterations braver. She always sang, "My life a hell you're making."

1940: Charlie Parker (Onyx). Bird's first recording, from a Wichita broadcast transcription, is a curio—but note how confidently he toys with Hawkins's phrases in bars 9-14. A 1950 concert (Sonet) found him flying high, yet not beyond the tune's gravity.

1942: Lester Young (Phoenix). Naturally, he had to try his hand at it, and he's wistful and sure; Nat Cole's famous solo routine is here in embryonic form. Young's deeply considered 1950 version (Savoy) is an often overlooked gem.

1944: Jazz at the Philharmonic (Verve). Les Paul plays a comical Django solo and J. J. Johnson pays homage with a couple of Hawkins's phrases, but Nat Cole's whimsy just about wins out. His solo consists almost entirely of cleverly juxtaposed quotations, which he'd refined in his trio version (Capitol) earlier that year.

1944: Cozy Cole (Savoy). Ben Webster's turn. He's sensuous and breathy for the first chorus, and ardent to the point of violence when he tips his hat to Roy Eldridge for the long-meter chorus.

1944: Art Tatum (Comet). He left more than a dozen versions, including broadcast and army recordings, but his first try—with his 1937 Swingsters—was inconsequential. A 1940 after-hours gem (Onyx) shows hat he viewed the tune with irony similar to Nat Cole's—he alternates Monkian asceticism with flighty asides and makes the release a potpourri of off-the-wall quotes. This propensity came to fruition in the 1944 trio gambol with Tiny Grimes and Slam Stewart, which is to all previous versions what *Animal Crackers* was to drawing-room comedy. Here, and in his 1953 solo (Pablo), he showed greater ingenuity in long meter than at ballad tempo.

1946: Don Byas (Prestige). Yet another ravishing tenor seduction of the melody, virtuosic and ardent. A more relaxed but no less impassioned reading was captured after-hours in 1941 (Onyx).

1946: Boyd Raeburn (Savoy). George Handy's sumptuous arrangement is outerspace schmaltz with swirling harp, punctuating French horns, and a Ginny Powell vocal.

1947: Teddy Edwards (Onyx). I think this is the first bop version. B&S didn't appeal to the boppers right away, probably because its melody demanded attention, while the soloists were looking for new melodies. Edwards broadened his vibrato to suggest Hawk, but his nifty triplets and the injection of Latin rhythm are signs of the times.

1949: James Moody (Prestige). He ejects from the melody by the second bar, doubletimes his pet licks (while avoiding long meter), and swings with relentless creativity. Not quite up to "I'm in the Mood for Love," but Eddie Jefferson wrote lyrics to this solo too. Moody's 1956 version (Chess) is notable for a splendid Johnny Coles long-meter trumpet solo that coolly navigates the major/minor changes.

1955: Serge Chaloff (Capitol). Perhaps no other recording demonstrates the full dynamic range of the baritone sax for such emotional effect. Chaloff, suffering from spinal paralysis, cut this from a wheelchair, and though "Thanks for the Memories" and "Stairway to the Stars" are contenders, this may well be his masterpiece, and is certainly one of the most compelling ballad performances in jazz. It's been out of print for nearly 25 years.

1956: Hank Jones (Savoy). Among the bebop piano versions are those by Erroll Garner, Bud Powell, and Barry Harris, but this is the most beautiful—lush chord modulations and a fanciful second chorus (until the release). How did we allow this man to disappear into the studios for so long?

1957: Gerry Mulligan and Paul Desmond (Verve). A four-part ricercar, though the saxophonists encircle the melody and each other so limpidly (the heat rises subtly but steadily) that you might forget that bass and drums also play "parts."

1958: Sonny Rollins (Verve). For his second attempt at an unaccompanied tenor solo, Rollins turned to tradition, and played two choruses plus an intro and coda (built on a single motif). Its chief interest is rhythmic, and though the playing is often magnificent, a comparison with the abstractions of Hawkins's "Picasso" makes the Old Man look godlike.

1960: John Coltrane (Atlantic). He plays long meter throughout, and gives B&S a new character with minor-key alterations. But he never gets beyond the surface, and the most interesting solo is McCoy Tyner's burrowing chorus. Interestingly, Coltrane played a better solo on a rejected alternate take, where Tyner's solo was relatively dull.

1961: Buck Clayton (Inner City). A personalized, melancholy statement with authentic drama, and a vividly Armstrongian open-horn finish.

1962: Thelonious Monk (Columbia). Studious stride in the left hand, and slapdash minor seconds in the right, and all the alterations in the world can't keep the ancient lament from shining through.

1966: Henry Red Allen (Impulse). The superbly eccentric New Orleans-born trumpeter-vocalist first recorded the song in 1935 (Columbia), but this version, his solo feature from a concert with the compatibly eccentric Pee Wee Russell, is looser and more inventive. He plays two trumpet choruses, over slow and fast rhythms, and sings with bellicose conviction.

1969: Betty Carter (Bush). From her famous medley with "Heart and Soul" (in which she "lost control . . . yes I lost it");

there is no more sultry or heart-rending ballad performance than her chorus and a half of B&S. She reprises Billie's "hell" and does the last eight bars a cappella. **1970: Buddy Tate (MPS).** There is a jaunty after-hours version from 1941 (Xanadu), but this is close to definitive, although I've heard him do it even more effectively in concert. It's a beautifully controlled, piercingly vocalized recitation. **1970: Dexter Gordon (Prestige).** The performance is shaped in part by Tommy Flanagan's minor-key vamp and the subtle long-meter manipulations of Alan Dawson, while Gordon moseys into fantasyland, combining methods B and C (see intro above). His 1978 version (Columbia) overdoes the vamp, and after a good beginning, he gets bogged down. **1973: Al Cohn (Muse).** In which all the distinctive aspects of Cohn's style came together in two masterful, immensely communicative choruses—the second, especially, is a straight-from-the-heart marvel, in which hollow moans footnote the compelling sureness. **1977: Benny Carter (Pablo Live).** He plays the first chorus fairly straight on trumpet, but his prolix alto chorus skirts through the chords with admirable independence, the melody peeking through and amplifying his own tale. **1978: Archie Shepp (Horo).** The most recent extravaganza by an uneven tenorist, accompanied only by guitar. There's no escaping the melody for Shepp, who rummages through it songfully, ultimately taming it with his penetrating tone (his cries recall Buddy Tate) and acerbic asides. **1978: Sarah Vaughan (Pablo).** Her 1946 performance (Everest) was merely flawless, the one from 1954 (Emarcy) expertly poised, as she imbued every syllable with nuance and worked in a long-meter section. This version, a duet with Ray Brown, starts with a long-meter release and circles back through the ballad for a creative tour de force. **1978: The Heath Brothers (Columbia).** Percy Heath's "In New York" is a rarity—a bop line composed on B&S changes, inspired by Blanton's last half-chorus with Ellington. Jimmy Heath plays a chorus, but his real confrontation with the tune came in 1975 (Xanadu).

1978: Bill Evans (Warner Bros.). This bears comparison with the Goodman trio, since Toots Thielemans dominates with a locked-in harmonica solo, and the real breakthrough is a romantic and highly inventive half-chorus of piano; it's something of a disappointment when Thielemans returns.

1979: Helen Humes (Muse). What a surprise!—proof that a good singer can still invest the song with emotional fortitude and make it work anew. It's startling to hear her riff the second chorus, and take risks throughout. The allure of B&S continues.

(October 1980)

Teddy Wilson's Golden Oldies

Teddy Wilson is so conservative and orderly a musician that it was impossible to glean from an hour of his music at Fat Tuesday's last week the revolutionary impact he once exercised on jazz. More than most of his peers, he seems devoutly old-hat. And yet his talent has not dwindled, the radical aspects of his style have not hardened into mannerisms, and he's never compromised commercially. The problem is that his playing hasn't changed at all, and neither has his repertoire. A typical set is a medley of songs he's been doing for 45 years. Of course, that's true of many musicians in jazz and popular music. The subversion of revolu-

tionaries into grand old men and women, as innovation is flat-
tened through acculturation and the innovator placated by flattery, is no less evident in jazz than in the other arts.

Flattery, and the obligations it imposes, may be the key issue.
If Louis Armstrong exists in the popular mind as a safe harbor
for indiscriminate reverence, like Robert Frost, it's because the
popular mind is no more aware of Armstrong's breast-beating irreverence than it is of Frost's neurotic bitterness. Radicals who
have been hugged to death either die or pledge allegiance. Wilson, who will be sixty-eight in a couple of weeks, was twice a radical in his twenties—socially and musically. By touring with the
Benny Goodman trio in 1935, he played a role in entertainment
analogous to Jackie Robinson's in baseball 12 years later. As a pianist, he refined the woolly cross-rhythms and improvisations of
Earl Hines, the imperious stride of Fats Waller, and the harmonically advanced filigree embellishments of Art Tatum into a cool,
unshakably lucid style. His playing embodied the optimism and
tenderness of the swing era with a grace, modesty, elegance, and
confidence all his own. Moreover, he devised a modern improvisational approach which stressed melodic variation, influenced
every young pianist of the period, and provided a direct link between his predecessors and Bud Powell. The small-band recordings he piloted, including such timelessly evocative masterpieces
as "Blues in C-Sharp Minor" and the many collaborations with
Billie Holliday, are among the most celebrated in jazz.

Yet all of these accomplishments were notched by the time he
turned thirty. Perhaps the most telling moment in the career of
an American musician comes with the inevitable shift in taste.
Wilson played it safe. After the end of his own big band (where
he revealed unexpected and, soon thereafter, neglected talents
for composing and arranging), he led a sextet at Cafe Society for
four years. He started teaching, did studio work, and participated in the first of countless reunions with Goodman and company. His 1956 appearance in *The Benny Goodman Story* enabled
him to tour with a trio, and at this point he became a regular in
high-class nightclubs, playing requests for well-heeled barflies. At

fifty, he embodied nostalgia; he was a classic—someone you didn't have to listen to very hard.

At Fat Tuesday's, it was fitting if irritating to find him imposed upon by a table of drunken tourists, who sang the beginnings of every tune. That kind of audience contributed to the notion that Wilson, his innovations thoroughly absorbed into the mainstream, had somehow become a cocktail pianist. And the fact remains that excepting history-minded jazz buffs, the under-thirties are less familiar with Wilson than they are with Waller and Tatum. The amount of awe musicians generate seems proportionately related to their availability. If Tatum wre alive, and playing annually at Carnegie Hall, his ability to sustain a clamorous following would undoubtedly be greater than if he were moving from one piano bar to another. If Waller had lived, he might have remained an invaluable pomposity-deflator by going after every new wrinkle in popular song (imagine what he would have done with "Raindrops" or "I Am the Walrus," or a thousand others) but it's more likely he would have been forced to recline on his royalties. In any case, Tatum and Waller did not survive, and didn't have to suffer the accusations of sameness and conservatism that have followed Wilson for 30 years.

The problems Wilson raises for the audience are partly his fault and partly the audience's. His failings are obvious: by playing the same tunes, even the same Goodman-trio intros and riffs, he flirts with superficiality in a style that seems emotionally detached to begin with; his unchanging approach encourages sentimental responses even when the music avoids sentimentality. He doesn't want to surprise himself or the listener. The failings of the younger audience are perhaps not so obvious: 20 years ago, it complained of long solos ("self-indulgent" and "aimless" were the critical clichés), but now it gets bored *without* a lengthy, vamping groove. Wilson rarely plays more than two or three choruses, and he's a subtle melodist. That means you have to listen for the gems as they fall. The paradox is that the familiarity of his music lulls you into a false security, and you miss the sensitive melodic inversions that illuminate the feeling lurking just below the immaculate surface. Wilson remains a distinguished pianist. His impeccable time, his inimitably delicate yet foursquare touch, and his exacting embellishments are far beyond the ken of any cocktail pianist, and with a good trio (Major Holley and Ronnie Cole were fine), he crafts a consistently swinging set. Still, you have to sluice through a lot of silt to get to the gold, and there may never again be a sizable audience willing to do that.

(November 1980)

Beyond Romance

Until I saw the Pat Metheny–Charlie Haden–Dewey Redman–Paul Motian quartet at the Village Vanguard last week, and heard Metheny's new record, *80/81* (with Jack DeJohnette replacing Motian and Michael Brecker added), I assumed that any ties between Ornette Coleman and Keith Jarrett were purely circumstantial. Haden and Redman had worked with both leaders, and Haden enticed them to share a disc if not a piece of music when he recorded *Closeness*. Metheny's music, on the other hand, attempts a syncretism between the two. He doesn't quite succeed in forging a new compound, but the correlations are intriguing, and the stark, jaunty influence of Coleman offsets the mawkish theatrics of Jarrett long enough to allow Metheny to emerge as an incisive improvisor.

Incisiveness is not a quality I previously associated with Metheny. For all his instrumental bravura, his music is often swamped in a Brahmsian gloss, as dollops of superficial Weltschmerz vie with folkish tunes—a tendency exacerbated by the presence in his quartet of a rather precious pianist named Lyle Mays. I invoke Jarrett as a source of Metheny's sugary modal lyricism, but it was probably ingrained in him during the time he worked with Gary Burton and Steve Swallow. At times, they all intone plush melodies with excessive sobriety, as though the notes were transmitted directly from God, and the gospel chords they lean on originated not in the sweaty hallelujahs of a slave culture but in the pristine structures of Burt Bacharach. Metheny's new music has more spine in it, especially as sampled at the Vanguard, and for that I credit the Coleman influence.

The first of five selections in an exhausting 100-minute set was Coleman's "Broadway Blues." After a unison theme statement and a lithe Redman solo, Metheny romped through several choruses with enthralling if nearly manic command. With a silvery sound, he executed long, lean, fast phrases, obsessively at first and then with meaningful pauses to accent the cadences; the theme was voiced in various registers as a working motif, and flawless legato passages bounded and swayed across the fretboard. Redman and Haden played in the rhythm; Metheny pushed against it with acerbic confidence. Haden's warm, melodic solo provided ideal contrast—the band, which sounded like a band, might have short-circuited if everyone had been plugged into the same socket. For the first of his two originals, Metheny switched to a guitar synthesizer, and after an attractive Bach-like theme for which he simulated organ chords, the Jarrett element appeared in soupy glissandos and grace notes. The other Metheny line, "Off Ramp," had a tough Colemanesque quality, and Metheny proffered a vigorous vamp for Redman's cool, strutting solo; his own solo ignited quickly, but eventually suffocated in that yearning romanticism that is Jarrett's curse, as chromatic puttering led to predictable intervallic leaps. He saved himself with jagged Ornette-like riffs—great equalizers, too short and rhythmic to be sentimental. On Haden's "Silence," the ballad of the set, Metheny used his synthesizer to fashion a chordal backdrop to the shivering bass solo. On Redman's "Rush Hour," with its discordant, martial figures, Metheny's intricate improvisation was suffused with bleeding overtones over splashing drums and swooping arco bass.

The chemistry is similar on the record, particularly the title theme, which cleverly suggests a Coleman-Jarrett collaboration; the peppery rhythms and riffs of Metheny's solo are concise, intelligent, and free of bathos. Another exceptional theme is "Pretty Scattered," a blues with a Colemanesque bridge as well as unexpected accents and a stop-time passage. Metheny's at his best when the theme provides a firm underpinning to improvise on. He plays even better on another blues, Coleman's "Turnaround," beginning behind the beat, making maximum use of the minor changes at the turnbacks, and pushing into increasingly complex and funky terrain with each lucidly prepared chorus. On "Two Folk Songs," he contributes energetic acoustic strumming and a pretty solo that meshes chords and single-noted lines in a Spanish vein. The two songs, by Metheny and Haden, work well together (they have in common the pentatonic scale and a seventh), and Michael Brecker executes a compelling tour de force in a long statement that searches sonically for Albert Ayler without quite finding him. DeJohnette's crystalline drive is especially welcome here, though he plays a heroic role throughout—his accompanying cymbals anticipate Metheny's every move on "The Bat." A couple of pieces don't work: the plodding "Every Day" and "Open," which sounds like something devised to fill out the album. "Open" is free jazz without energy—Redman is too smooth for his own good, Brecker recites Wayne Shorter licks from 15 years ago, Metheny turns to romantic striving, and DeJohnette's fast and busy work sounds just fast and busy.

My responses to Metheny's music are contrary, I'm sure, to those of his longtime fans. Easy romanticism is always popular, and just as songwriters have known at least as far back as Chopin that audiences find a well-placed sixth or ninth irresistible, Metheny (like Jarrett, Burton, et al.) knows that similar modulations over a churning modal surface will excite similar enthusiasms. Cheap thrills. But whatever Metheny decides to do with his talent—and

he has a lot of it and is very young—*80/81* (ECM 2-1180) and
the Vanguard gig serve notice that his potential is great.

(November 1980)

Composers Ascendent

In the essay accompanying his current record, Anthony Davis
describes a "shift from the pre-eminence of the performer, the
player, to what I believe is the natural ascendance of the composer," and complains of widespread resistance. Jazz is forever
marked by quests for and away from compositional form, but
never as urgently as in the 20 years since the avant-garde violated the sanctity of blues and song structures. Davis's generation
needs to "feel free to draw from any influence." The resistance
will be allayed only by music of such unqualified success that
questions of pedigree disappear. *Lady of the Mirrors* (India Navigation 1047), Davis's most impressive album to date is that kind
of achievement. In five pieces for solo piano, he sustains interest
through purely pianistic means, demonstrates a technical aplomb
that doesn't shout its virtuosity all over the place, and marries
composition and improvisation in new and persuasive ways. This
last point is perhaps the most significant. Many jazz players have
written themes that sounded like their improvisations, but a primary objective of musicians like Davis is to make the two inseparable, so that the listener isn't always sure where notation ends
and extrapolation begins.

James Newton, a sometime associate of Davis, faces the same
problem in *The Mystery School* (India Navigation 1946), and though
the album is uneven, he offers a nearly irresistible solution in the

best of his works for wind quintet, "The Wake." Newton's nine-part memoriam to the composer Howard Swanson is built on an attractive theme introduced by bassoon, to which clarinet, flute, and oboe offer consecutive and eventually simultaneous counter-point, while tuba lines out the bottom. The theme is reharmon-ized into a suprisingly lovely dirge, and feeds a succession of inventive solos and duets. If the piece is notable for its delicate melodic material, lucid structuring, and seamless incorporation of elements from jazz and Europe, the execution is winning not least because the participants never sacrifice their individual styles. The tonal mischief of Newton and John Carter is unmistakable, and Charles Owens's performance on oboe and alto oboe may create interest in an instrument that hasn't been much heard in jazz.

The success of "The Wake" is linked to its episodic design. By contrast, the album's two other pieces, though shorter, seem interminable—"Central Avenue" opens with the lower pitched instruments creating an ostinato for an excitedly boppish theme, but the effect is vitiated by a slow movement and a long passage of heated chattering, and "Past Spirits" attempts to avoid tedium with little more than shifting colors. On the Davis record, there simply aren't any tedious moments. Not a second passes when you don't feel the performer in conscious control. The shadows of Cecil Taylor and Duke Ellington are apparent, but they never obscure Davis's originality. For example, "Lady of the Mirrors" begins with a Taylorish cluster and recalls Taylor's famous state-ment about imitating a dancer's leaps in space, yet the discursive design underscores a very different set of concerns, most signif-icantly hand independence. Davis's music is overridingly poly-phonic: his left hand constantly works away at ostinatos, pedal points, broken rhythms, and contrapuntal phrases to set off the right. In "Under the Double Moon," he even attempts contrast-ing meters—6/8 in the left, 7/4 in the right—and in "Five Moods from an English Garden," technically the most impressive per-formance, he switches the lead from treble to bass and back.

The relationship between Davis and Taylor is not unlike that between Thelonious Monk and Art Tatum. In both instances, the younger men edited the relative extravagances of the older men, and by economizing, forged new avenues from what had previously seemed dead ends. One thing Davis has in common with those giants is an unmistakable touch, an even-handed meticulousness more percussive than Tatum but considerably lighter than Monk or Taylor. He succumbs to a few mannerisms, especially single-note hammering in the left hand, but his approach is generally sober. "Beyond Reason," the first selection, and "Man on a Turquoise Cloud," the last, exemplify Davis's ability to sustain and multiply levels of tension with artful restraint; and though the former is indigenous and the latter a dedication to Ellington that captures, as perhaps no other pianist has, the imperious savoir-faire with which Ellington tossed arpeggios into the bass clef, they are cleverly related. Davis uses a three-note motif, actually something of a blues cliché (i.e., G-G flat-E) in both pieces, albeit in very different ways, to unify the record and suggest his own place in the tradition.

Lady in the Mirrors solidifies Davis's position in the vanguard of pianists who've embraced jazz in the past decade; its conscious meld of formal and improvised invention ought to serve as an antidote to the indulgent esoterica that has characterized so many piano recitals of the '70s. Along with Newton's "The Wake," as well as recent performances and records by Abrams, Threadgill, Blythe, David Murray, and a few others who presently embody the ascendancy of the composer-player, it justifies Davis's belief that "today is a pivotal time for our music."

•

James Newton is a romantic; his favorite composers are romantics. He plays the flute with a measured yet burnished tone, and favors dramatically chromatic phrases, soaring cadences, and juxtapositions of major and minor chords, dissonance and consonance. As an instrumentalist, he has perfected a glossary of microtones and multiphonics that, as a composer, he uses for maximum impact. Much of his writing is concerned with minimizing the distinctions between composition and improvisation, an obsession of many jazz composers going back to Jelly Roll

Morton. Along with a handful of his contemporaries, Newton has
assimilated the influences of jazz, Europe, and exotic folk musics
with greater equanimity than any academic composer has done
or is likely to do in the near future. That's partly because he
doesn't patronize any of these traditions.

In many ways, Newton's most impressive recording to date is
the 1982 *Axum* (ECM-1-1214), a series of short mood pieces inspired by the Ethiopian Auxumite Scrolls, and performed solely
by Newton, sometimes with overdubbing on flutes of various sizes.
Considering the tour de force nature of the project, this is a surprisingly varied and listenable record, ranging broadly in style
and content. The overdubbed flutes often achieve a haunting
quality, from the Ligeti-like harshness of "Axum" to the Ravel-
meets-Grieg lyricism of "The Neser" to the riff- and blues-based
"Addis Ababa" and "The Dabtara." The spiraling "Malak 'Uqabe"
and the furious "Susenyos and Werzelya" are among his most
impressive improvisations.

Although Newton's selection (a dedication to Mingus) from the
1982 Kool Festival's Young Lions concert is omitted from *The
Young Lions* (Musician 60196IR), his performances on the pieces
by Anthony Davis and Craig Harris, whose ambitious big band
arrangement includes an alert duet between Newton and Davis,
prove how relaxed and skillful a jazz player he can be. The best
evidence on that score, however, is *James Newton* (Gramavision
8205), a handsomely orchestrated and reflective work that illuminates Newton's affection for and debt to Billy Strayhorn. The
opener is Strayhorn's "Day Dream," with solos by violinist John
Blake and Newton, who plays one chorus at a tempo that is unusually brisk for this piece. The two successive Newton originals,
"Budapest," featuring Jay Hoggard on vibes, and "Ismene," with
Slide Hampton on trombone, show how well he's listened to
Strayhorn's chromatic mood-setting—especially the latter, with its
close ensemble chords behind Anthony Davis, and a duet by Davis
and Hampton. After an odd blues (16½ bars) by Davis, the al-
bum concludes with the most inventive of Newton's pieces, "The
Crips," in which written episodes employing canons and fugues

tie together two freely improvised quartet passages (one for vibes, piano, and rhythm, the other for flute, violin, and rhythm) that suggest some of the lyric magic of Ornette Coleman's *Free Jazz*.

(April 1981/May 1983)

Big Noise from Missoula

The Big Sky Mudflaps, a honky tonk band from Montana that rocked, rolled, and swung for two nights at Cody's last week, lacks one quality found in most of the young white bands that have revived post-depression pazz and jop during the past decade: pretentiousness. That is, they don't affect "authentic" clothes, they don't imitate the mannerisms of aged blacks, and they don't attempt fussbudget transcriptions of arrangements that have already been done to a faretheewell. Instead, they appropriate a panoply of musical styles with the naive conviction that all this stuff, black or white in origin, is America's public domain and anyone who performs it honestly will do it honor. The musicianship isn't top-drawer, but the infectiousness and spirit make up. After listening to five sets, I was ready to hear more.

My interest in the group stemmed from the discovery that Judy Roderick was featured. In the mid-'60s, during my 15 minutes as a confirmed folkie, I went to see Phil Ochs at the Gaslight, and was enchanted by the opening act, a singer-guitarist whose repertoire included things like "Miss Brown to You," "Baltimore Oriole," and "Wild Women Don't Sing the Blues." It was Roderick, and I thought she was probably the most convincing white woman blues singer since Lee Wiley; no one in the intervening years has changed my mind. In 1964, at twenty-one, she cut a

record for Columbia called *Ain't Nothin' but the Blues*, and though
the production values were misguided, it preserved her unself-
consciously vital and emotional vocal style, and unusual breadth
of repertoire. But she disappeared, and no one I queried over
the years (such is the loyalty of unrequited fandom) knew why
or where, until a publicist-manager (her sister, it turned out) called
to tell me about the Mudflaps and mentioned Roderick's name.

So it was chiefly to hear her that I went to see the Mudflaps at
the Bottom Line two weeks ago, when they were scheduled to
open for J. J. Cale. Shortly before the gig, however, manage-
ment informed them that they wouldn't be allowed to play because of an overlooked rider in Cale's contract prohibiting an
opening band. "If they set up," Cale reportedly said, "we'll walk
out." It seemed incredible to me that a prominent performer,
himself an extension of the folk movement, would sabotage seven
relative unknowns who'd driven in a van from Montana for what
they assumed would be a big break; when I finally caught them
at Cody's, I figured he was right. They are a tough act for anyone, let alone a somnambulist, to follow. The Mudflaps are the
only band I've ever seen keep lindy hoppers on the dance floor
through the likes of "Billie's Bounce," "Scrapple from the Apple," "Yardbird Suite," and "Groovin' High," to mention only their
bop repertoire.

Roderick, unfortunately, just travels with the group as a friend,
and sang only two songs per set, though a couple of the musicians said they were hoping she'd do more. Her best numbers
included Patsy Cline's "Walkin' After Midnight" and an original
called "Austin-tageous," and though her singing (she doesn't play
guitar in the group) had a more countryish flavor than her earlier work, it retained the same haunting urgency in the middle
register and the strangely compelling pinched sonorities of her
high notes. In any case, my disappointment at not hearing more
of her, as well as the songs she used to sing, was mitigated by the
vivacity of the band. Coincidentally—Roderick became associated with the Mudflaps after moving to Montana from Denver,
where she led a group called 60 Million Buffalo—the band is al-

most an extension of the kind of performer Roderick was in the '60s. In addition to bop, the material includes songs from the Boswell Sisters, Bob Wills, Louis Jordan, Helen Humes, Count Basie, Hank Williams, Duke Ellington, Ruth Brown, Big Joe Turner, and Charles Mingus.

All of it is interpreted with a streamlined backbeat (the able drummer is Michael Lea), and given a spare but rollickingly rural punch by the open chords of pianist Steve Powell, the economic riffing of altoist and clarinetist Dexter Payne, and the rippling, fluid solos of the group's most engaging soloist, guitarist David Horgan. Horgan's tone recalls the deft brightness of Hank Garland, and his ideas the vivid harmonic thinking and rolling triplets of Arv Garrison. Completing the personnel are two women who alternate on bass and vocals: Beth Lo (who outfitted Mingus's "Jelly Roll" and Parker's "Yardbird Suite" with lyrics and painted the group's funny-surreal backdrop and album cover) and Maureen Powell play trim, incisive solos reminiscent of Tommy Potter, and sing in pale lilting voices that get the job done. They took up bass less than four years ago, because "you can't amplify washboard." The group's first record, *Armchair Cabaret* is characteristic of the band's scope and is worth hearing, but it doesn't do justice to their present accomplishment.

(May 1981)

Tony Bennett Without Fear

The two (out of four) performances I saw Tony Bennett give last week in support of the Police Athletic League underscored the jarring discrepancies between Bennett assured and Bennett un-

nerved. Had I caught only his Bottom Line debut, these comments would be hallelujahs over how high and radiant an arc he
can trace when all is well, plus a self-examining atonement for
past doubts; but his wind-up at Carnegie Hall rekindled those
doubts—though now more respectfully noted—and reminded me
that when Bennett isn't very good, he's close to silly. The decisive
factor would appear to be his own doubts, as evinced by his de-
pendence on Pope Frank I's decree that he's "the best singer in
the business." A decade ago, he actually opened a Playboy Club
concert with a film of Sinatra uttering his famed encomium. In
the present series, it was merely repeated by an emcee and re-
printed in program notes.

Bennett, at his best, *is* one of the best. The first time I saw him,
in 1961, I thought he was spellbinding; too many disappoint-
ments in the intervening years made me dismiss the vivid memory of that evening as adolescent enthusiasm. The Bottom Line
gig reversed my reversal. He was everything we've come to expect—charming, friendly, energetic, excitable, emotional; yet he
also had a steel grip on his pitch problem, and he was swinging
not in the manner of a well-meaning but alienated jazz lover who
has to settle for a businessman's bounce, but as a knowing rider
with both feet firmly planted in the metric stirrups. Not counting
a dire soliloquy written expressly for him by Stevie Wonder, which
Bennett seems to love despite its unwonderful melody and words
("yesterland" indeed), he sang 20 first-rate songs. The rhythm
section—pianist and music director Ralph Sharon, bassist John
Burr, drummer Joe LaBarbara—played hard, thanks chiefly to
the relentless LaBarbara, and Bennett pushed them without fal-
tering. His appealingly bald and husky voice seemed a little dry
in the middle register, but he had no problem shooting for fire-
cracker endings and rather obvious but effective embellishments, and even when he reached for something slightly out of
grasp (which happened very rarely), he saved himself so quickly
that I was willing to applaud the risk.

Bennett knows how to read a lyric; on some ballads, he's even
better at it than Sinatra. Sinatra calls himself a saloon singer

though he wouldn't be caught dead singing anyplace smaller than a Vegas ballroom, but Bennett—who'll sing anywhere—really is a saloon singer, in the best way. He's an audience-lover who presents himself as real, unpretentious, part of the crowd. He's too straightforward to impart irony to a lyric, so he conveys meaning with a sense of wonder, using his hands and face for nuance and emphasis; at "It's hard to conceive it" in "Body and Soul," he tapped his noggin and looked like he was having a hard time conceiving it. He can also underline meaning without visual help; there's a marvelous moment at the outset of his recording of "The Touch of Your Lips," with Bill Evans, when he utters the word "sweet" as though he were first realizing what sweetness is. On ballads, the big-hearted bellowing voice is honed for dramatic effect, as vowels and phrase endings linger in fuzzy exhalations of breath made especially piquant by contrasting rapier shouts.

By contrast, the Carnegie concert was mostly mannerisms. Strangely enough, he was greeted with an ambience of real intimacy at the Bottom Line, while the older audience at Carnegie was nearly rowdy with whistlers, foot-stompers, and singalong buffoons. Bennett's trio was amplified by four discreetly arranged string players in the first set, and he sang eighteen of the Bottom Line songs. Yet something was off from the start. Amiable gestures were now stratified routines—not only the rehearsed stuff, like putting his hand in his pocket for the last half-chorus of "I Guess I'll Have To Change My Plans," or throwing the mike from one hand to the other during the bridge of "My Favorite Things," but in the swinging motions he made with his body to compensate for the fact that he wasn't swinging, and in the big high-note finishes that were now gaudy tails wagging recalcitrant dogs. He missed notes; he introduced almost every tune with the phrase, "Here's a song I'd love to sing" or "Here's a song I'd really love to sing"; he tried to milk the audience with what looked like reverse curtseys, jerkily throwing up his arms and chest; and he gave the feeling of a marathon résumé, speedily moving from one song to the next without quite doing justice to any. A failing that was acceptable at the Bottom Line became troublesome at Carnegie: he has no microphone technique. He holds it in the same place whether whispering or shouting, so that opening consonants are often gusting winds. Things didn't improve in the second set, when he was supported by a full orchestra and many more strings.

There may be a moral here: perhaps Tony Bennett should spend more time in saloons like the Bottom Line and the Village Vanguard, where he can just . . . relax.

(May 1981)

The Excitable Roy Eldridge

Through much of its history, jazz made avid converts with the simple promise of undying excitement, whether maximized by throbbing rhythms, blood-curdling high notes, violent polyphony, layered riffs, hyperbolic virtuosity, fevered exchanges, or carnal funk. Yet excitement often gets a bum rap from those converts who, having mined the music's deeper recesses, suspect all crowd-pleasing gestures of vulgarity. At bottom, the distinction between the two is subtle but clear: if you like it, it's exciting; if not, it's vulgar. As Sidney Bechet noted, "You got to be in the sun to feel the sun. It's that way with music too." If you're cold to a musician's impassioned yowling, that passion will seem awfully dim if not aimless, and since crowds more than individuals thrive on excitement, your response to musical rabble-rousing may depend on your willingness to get lost in a crowd.

The showiest expressions of passion frequently border on outright pandering, but immoderation of that sort is a healthy symptom—it tends to proliferate in a milieu where authentic excitement also flourishes. Over the past decade, excitement has been scarce to a degree that not even the spaciest '50s cool-jazz hipster could have anticipated, while vulgarity continues unabated in its new garb, substituting pretentious meditation for caterwauling. Still, that part of the audience that hasn't been rendered insensible by ECM-styled stabiles of sound, in which slowness indicates profundity, hungers for le jazz hot, as witness the gratitude with which it greets the appended swing theme that, in so many contemporary performances, caps an hour's worth of esoteric clamor.

The most exciting new record I've heard recently was recorded 30 years ago in Paris, but never issued here. My high opinion of "Oh Shut Up," one of several gems—the others a good deal less tempestuous—on Roy Eldridge's *I Remember Harlem* (Inner City 7012), is not universally shared, presumably because it's vulgar, an objection which is raised from time to time in the more somber discussions of Eldridge's music. I suspect even the musicians might have thought it a boozy jest, the kind of incendiary outburst that happens when two highly charged and sophisticated swing fiends (Eldridge and Don Byas) decide to mock their Dixieland forebears. The not inappropriate reproof of the title would seem to support this, except that it is obviously a reference to "Please Don't Talk About Me When I'm Gone," which provides the performance with chords and structure. "Oh Shut Up" drives furiously along the dividing line between excitement and vulgarity. The noisy French rhythm section is intractably overenthusiastic, and the poor engineering recalls the crackling static on the first Gary U.S. Bonds records. Yet Eldridge and Byas are a storm above the storm. I can't think of another piece quite like it, or a better example of what makes Eldridge the most electrifying of jazz trumpeters.

Eldridge first came to prominence in the '30's with a flashy, passionate, many-noted style that rampaged freely through three octaves, rich with harmonic ideas and impervious to the fastest tempos. In part, his secret was to transfer ideas patented on the more facile tenor saxophone to the trumpet; his ability to play Coleman Hawkins's solo on Fletcher Henderson's 1926 "Stampede" got him his first job, and more than a decade later, when

Hawkins, lording it in Europe, heard the first Eldridge recordings, he vowed to work with the younger man when he returned
to the States, not realizing that one of the things he admired in
Eldridge was the transposition of some of his own phrases—as
well as those of Chu Berry, Lester Young, Ben Webster, Ike
Quebec, and other tenors that Eldridge loved and worked with.

The decade preceding the emergence of bop was rife with
frantic, exhilarating trumpeters. After the war, the tenor sax
would assume that role of crowd pleaser, honking and moaning
like a Baptist who'd just heard the word. But in the '30s and early
'40s Louis Armstrong's instrument was still king, and while many
of its best practitioners pursued the course of lyrical composure
(among them Buck Clayton, Bobby Hackett, Bill Coleman, Harry
Edison, and Doc Cheatham), others—Eldridge, Red Allen, Bobby
Stark, Hot Lips Page, Charlie Shavers, Shad Collins, Rex Stewart—strove for an agitated, coruscating approach as thrilling as
anything heard in American music. If they were more likely to
overstep the bounds of good taste, there was a payback—they took
the most expressive risks. Eldridge was the most emotionally
compelling, versatile, rugged, and far-reaching. His ballads were
complicated but stirringly lucid, and his bravura numbers were
played with such bracing authority that they dwarfed the competition. To a young Dizzy Gillespie, "He was the Messiah of our
generation."

In one way or another, Armstrong fathered all the trumpeters
mentioned above. Eldridge started listening to him in 1931, at
twenty, taking cues from his dramatic storytelling intensity, his
logic, his gleaming high-note flourishes. When he started leading
his own bands in Chicago, after years of touring with Teddy Hill,
Henderson, and others, Eldridge challenged Armstrong with
flamboyant performances of "King of the Zulus" and "St. Louis
Blues." It was a genuine if respectful competitiveness that kept
his motor wound, as it does today, and in one area at least—excitement—he may have surpassed Armstrong. The signal,
matchless aspect of Armstrong's music was his fatted, New Orleans sound; even when he busted his lip punching skeins of high

C's, his every note was shaped and effulgent. Eldridge never had a pure or golden tone; his sound was always underscored by a vocal rasp, an urgent, human roughness that gave his music an immediacy of its own. You felt you could hear the sound start in the viscera and work its way through his small body, carving a path in his throat, and bursting forth in breathtaking release. Nor were Eldridge's high notes rounded like Armstrong's. Instead, shaded by a rapid shake, they seemed a spontaneous, uncontainable explosion of feeling. And this was only the beginning, because by the mid-'30's, Eldridge was able to fashion whole phrases and, eventually, whole solos ("Wabash Stomp," "Rockin' Chair," "The Gasser," "The Man I Love," "After You've Gone," and dozens of others) that sustained the internal excitement, as though built on a constant series of infinitesimal tremors. His high notes were never merely high; and rather than concluding performances, they tended to prefigure fiery parabolas of melody. Orson Welles once explained that the screaming white cockatoo in *Citizen Kane* was inserted to keep the audience alert. Eldridge's expressive cries and banshee whistles serve the same purpose, telegraphing his own excitement.

In 1950, after touring Europe with Benny Goodman, Eldridge settled in Paris, where he recorded for Vogue and wrote a newspaper column for a couple of years. "Oh Shut Up" is the highpoint of his Vogue session with Don Byas. After a four-bar piano introduction, trumpet and tenor play the raucous theme in antiphonal style. Each man is alive with so much enthusiasm that it's surprising to realize how fresh and coherent their solos are; neither ever quotes the "Please Don't Talk About Me" melody. Byas follows with two rocking choruses, playing on the beat with short, heated phrases, and growing increasingly strident and brawny as he rises to a climax. Eldridge is extraordinary: his embouchure never fails him, and his lengthy phrases attest to the uncommon thoughtfulness he brings to every performance. He starts high, building to a six-measure phrase that traverses the first turnback, and barking the release while crafting yet another extended and wily phrase, as if to say, "I'm in heat but still in control." He finishes the chorus with a siren blast—a note sustained in excess of four measures that lands him in the last chorus, at which point Byas returns to egg him on. Here the record gets so inflamed that you can sympathize with the rhythm section, which, lacking the panache to stay relaxed, simulates a herd of maddened buffalo in its attempt to keep up. Eldridge, sparking ever upward and out, signals the close by appending an eight-bar Dixieish coda that would be pure corn if it weren't a perfectly appropriate resolution to inspired hysteria.

The best of the remaining pieces with Byas is "The Heat Is On," Eldridge's variation on "I Never Knew"; Jimmy Dorsey's "Hollywood Pastime" is notable for its languid tempo; and Benny Carter's "I'd Love Him So" for Eldridge's long-meter episode. But there are several great moments in this collection from other Vogue sessions: "I Remember Harlem" is a beautiful, cantorial masterpiece—Eldridge's "Blue Lester," if you will—in which the trumpeter seems to fade up from the ether of a vamp; "L'Isle Adam," constructed from "Swing Is Here" riffs, concludes with Eldridge playing a protracted coda over drums in the grandest Armstrongian style; the first take of "Une Petite Laitue" has one of his best vocals, complete with stop-time suspensions; and "Tu Disais Que Tu M'Aimais," on which he sings the blues in French, has a stark and powerful solo. One of the most interesting aspects of the collection is its three daring homages to Armstrong: Fats Waller's "Black and Blue" has 16 bars of riveting trumpet that is very much up to the master's standards, plus an effective vocal (he changes the phrase "what is in my face" to "what is on my mind"); "Wild Man Blues" and "Fireworks," duets with Claude Bolling in the role of Earl Hines, are noteworthy for screaming poignancy and rhythmic momentum in the former and two- and four-bar exchanges in the latter. The album is rounded out by three Eldridge piano solos, in which he tries boogie, rubato improvisation, and stride.

(May 1981)

Lester Young Grows Deeper

Lester Young started recording relatively late in life, at twenty-seven, and finished early, at forty-nine. But with a musician as poetic as Young, obsessed with finding precisely the right note and timbre to convey the specifics of every bright or sullen inspiration, 22 years documents too lengthy a chunk of life to fit the facile categories—early Young (1936–44) and late Young (1945–59)—with which jazz history has often been content. Admittedly, the year he spent in an Army Debilitation Barracks makes for a convenient demarcation. That frightful experience altered Young and his music, encouraging an already shy and aloof man to further isolate himself with various antisocial affectations, not to mention a very real problem with alcohol. Yet he never stopped searching and evolving; the simplistic conceit that blames the Army for an irreversible decline in Young's art is sentimental.

Young's music changed over the years, as did John Coltrane's and Miles Davis's. To compare his early and late work with an eye on proving that the light-footed ebullience of his Basie tenure is the true Young, and the later work a pale attempt to recapture his youth, you have to be not only sentimental and naive, but deaf to the distinctive beauty and instrumental mastery of his last 14 years. Moreover, you have to ignore the stylistic changes *within* the pre- and postwar periods. The bigger, drier tone, eccentric tonal devices, and straightforward swing that characterize his recordings of the late '40s are apparent on the prewar Keynotes and Savoys; the postwar "Crazy Over J-Z" sounds

more like "early Prez" than the prewar "Jump, Lester, Jump";
the recordings immediately following his discharge ("D.B. Blues,"
"These Foolish Things") contain some of the most impressive
performances of his career. And just as the 1944 "Lester Leaps
Again" shows a marked change in attitude from the 1939 "Lester Leaps In," the long era of "late Prez" reveals countless sub-
tleties and turnarounds in his thinking, as between the 1945 "Mean
to Me" and the 1955 "Mean to Me," which is superior in expressiveness and inventiveness.

"Sweetness can be funky, filthy—anything. But which part do
you want?" Young asked an interviewer shortly before he died,
and the same question can be asked of Young's music, which also
could be anything. You don't listen to 1956 Young when you want
to hear the way he played 10 or 20 years earlier, but in disre-
garding the later work, you neglect an exquisite body of saxophone music quite unlike anything else in jazz. Certainly, there's
nothing in early Prez that can take the place of such late recordings as "Up 'n Adam," "This Year's Kisses," "Star Dust," "Come
Rain or Come Shine," "Gigantic Blues," "Polka Dots and Moon-
beams" (hear his perfect single chorus on *Prez in Europe*), or the
music made on that most savory of Washington nights—December 7, 1956—when Young was recorded privately by his accompanists at Olivia's Patio Lounge. Pablo Live has just issued the
third volume of *Lester Young in Washington D.C.* (2308/228) and
it's fully in a class with its remarkable predecessors. It's one of
the best Lester Young albums ever.

A performance of "Just You, Just Me," taken slower than the
original Keynote version, exemplifies Young's ability to conjure
lovely, wistful paraphrases that pay homage to the song while
suggesting the integrity of fresh composition. Where does he find
so many ideas? He boots and then retards the tempo, riffs one
series of chords only to invest the next with expansive melody,
and imparts feeling and urgency into every measure; he says more
in an eight-bar exchange with the drums than most musicians do
in a lifetime. For the last chorus, he plays the riff that Coleman
Hawkins called "Spotlite" and J.J. Johnson "Mad Be-Bop." His
tone on "Sometimes I'm Happy" is at once austere and rosy, es-

pecially during those seductive triplets when the air escaping his embouchure provides ghostly resonance. Young's cool imitators in the '50s frequently suffocated swing with an airless preciosity, but Young never sacrifices vitality for lyricism. The exceptional version of "Up 'n Adam" is a lesson in controlled blues playing and modulated power. He begins by shrugging off four notes in twice as many measures, and then builds each chorus with increasing energy, the dynamics complementing the diverse intentions—melodic or rhythmic, convoluted or spare—of each of a dozen stirring choruses. Another blues, "G's If You Please," is replete with singing, bending sighs, and a bright, cantering "Indiana," which concludes with an ironic reference to "Manhattan," is a textbook in temporal equilibrium, as long phrases are unexpectedly extended, and contrastingly simple riffs ride ahead of, on, and after the impervious beat.

This is the music of a man who can't play without evoking deep feelings. Like many great musicians, Young used art to scumble the frustrations of his life, making from them bemused and sanguine dreams of undeniable power. Those who besmirch such work by invoking the standards of youth are probably unwilling to face the trials of maturity. Like Yeats, Lester Young found the strength to "wither into the truth."

(June 1981)

Note: Andrew Cyrille
Has a Band

It's often difficult for a musician who's been associated almost exclusively with a classic ensemble to break away and assert himself as a leader, especially if he plays drums. Yet Andrew Cyrille, the bedrock of Cecil Taylor's Unit from 1965 to 1974, has piloted so pleasing and distinctive a quartet since his departure from Taylor that I'm surprised Maono, as he calls the band (the name is Swahili for "feelings") hasn't caused more of a stir. The group's third album, *Special People* (Soulnote 1012), though not up to its inspired predecessor, *Metamusicians' Stomp*, underscores Cyrille's virtues as a leader: his concern with form and diversity, his ear for interesting material, and his editorial knack for getting the most from his players.

A résumé is probably in order. Cyrille's first record, *What About?* in 1969, was a tour de force for solo percussion that continued along the lines pioneered by Milford Graves and Sunny Murray; his subsequent association with Graves produced their 1974 duets, *Dialogue of the Drums*. The name Maono was applied a year later to the ensembles, employing from two to nine participants, assembled for *Celebration*. Though the side-long "Haitian Heritage" was diminished by the intrusion of a pretentious poem pretentiously read, it demonstrated Cyrille's ability to construct a long, mutable canvas with minimal voicing; and in "Non-Expectation Celebration," he created what in retrospect seems like a free-form rap record, an obnoxiously amusing montage of male voices, drums, and synthesizer. Maono's present members were introduced in 1976, except that Lisle Atkinson was the original bassist, but only one of the four selections on *Junction* featured the full band. It was apparent that as a leader Cyrille was something of a rhythmic minimalist, preferring a light and fanciful attack to the thundering barrage he produced with Taylor, and that in saxophonist David Ware and trumpeter Ted Daniel he'd found an effective textural blend.

The payoff came in 1978, when he made two excellent records in Italy. *The Loop*, recorded in July, represented, for all its spontaneity, a measured, articulate sequel to *What About?*. *Metamusicians' Stomp*, recorded two months later, was a splendidly authoritative quartet session. The way the disciplined solos referred to the themes suggested that Cyrille's long apprenticeship in mainstream bands had instilled in him a genuine regard for conscientious variations. Perhaps to counterbalance *The Loop*, the leader played no solos, but he was clearly in control. The new bassist, Nick DiGeronimo, provided a firm undercurrent; the contrast between Daniel's complacent tone and Ware's acidic edginess guaranteed tension and excitement; and the compositions, including an exceptionally moving arrangement of Kurt Weill's "My Ship," displayed a wit and refinement only hinted at in the early work. *Nuba*, the following year, was an atmospheric poetry-and-jazz reunion with Jimmy Lyons, from the Taylor band, and Jeanne Lee, who appeared on *Celebration.*

So *Special People* is the first album by Maono in two years, and if it lacks something of the excitement of the last installment, it benefits from the increased intimacy of its members. Most notable of the three Cyrille originals are "Fortified Nucleolus," a blues with tricky variations made cohesive by a 4/4 walking bass line, modest use of counterpoint, and fastidious allegiance to the theme in the improvisations; and "High Priest," a lengthy, involuted theme, also in 4/4 but rooted to a two-measure ostinato that animates the variations. Daniel is rather reminiscent of King Oliver in his half-valved coyness, and DiGeronimo keeps the ostinato firmly in view no matter how far he seems to depart from it in his solo. The title selection is little more than an eight-bar fragment, but it's enough to bully the foursome into frenzied improvisation.

The remaining compositions are Ornette Coleman's "A Girl Named Rainbow," written for Leroy Jenkins but here given its recorded debut, and John Stubblefield's "Bay Man," which Cyrille arranged so that the solos precede the theme. Coleman's languorous piece is tied to a repeated interval, but Ware, winningly buoyed by bass and drums, stalks the intervening territory with warmth and purpose. I take the general clarity of his work with Cyrille as a tribute to the leader, since it's not nearly so evident in his own recordings. Daniel, an entertaining chameleon who elsewhere suggests Don Cherry and Miles Davis, steals a few burnished plums from Clifford Brown in his attractive prelude to "Baby Man."

Drummers are often thought to be particularly qualified to

compose jazz pieces, and Cyrille's work supports that contention. His music breathes with the confidence of a leader who knows all the twists and turns in his music, and doesn't have to beat the rhythms to death to make them reverberate; that knowingness gives the whole session an unwound, loping quality. This is the kind of group that should be working the local clubs, but to my knowledge it's never played more than isolated concerts in the United States. Maono is modern and accessible and adventurous, and at a time when working bands are at a premium, it merits a lot more encouragement.

(August 1981)

Miles's Wiles

Five years in the life of Miles Davis can seem like a generation in the life of jazz. It's the distance, for example, between "Israel" and "Walkin' " and *Kind of Blue* and *My Funny Valentine* and *Bitches Brew* and *Get Up with It.* The 1949 blues was heralded as the birth of the cool, and the 1954 blues as a return to the hot, but the distinction was to be found not so much in Davis's trumpet playing as in the settings he encouraged. This business of cool and hot is the jazz dialectic in a nutshell, and one reason Davis felt at home in both camps is that, more than any other instrumentalist of his generation, he knew that hot and cool could mesh without turning lukewarm; in fact, it is at that point where they are insoluble that we find the Prince of Darkness prancing on his eggshells. The bottom line of his ceaseless innovating is to be found in his obsession with form and texture. His trumpet playing changed plenty in the course of 35 years, but his phases—first a brief apprenticeship in the shadows of Freddie Webster and Dizzy Gillespie, then the emergence of a thoroughly original style built on the acknowledgment of technical limitations, then a renewed assault on those limitations—might almost be an incidental by-product of his restlessness. His evolution as a soloist is personal, a matter of the id; it's in the directions he sets for his cohorts, near and far, that his ego comes into full play. Which is why the four albums mentioned above seem less like signposts of one man's growth than measured attacks on the status quo.

The status quo in jazz is protected as much by obeisance to the pathfinders as by principled conservatism. Radicals are too much worshiped, their innovations shamelessly bled for new clichés to replace or supplement the old. Good musicians, justly proud of the individualism that is at the core of jazz, may invent new sounds and variations, but how many have addressed the fundamental issues of structure, instrumentation, and repertoire? Miles Davis does, constantly, and every time he comes up with a new answer, the whole music shifts in its seat. He didn't originate all the directions that became associated with his records, but he found ways to make them palatable, even popular. His popularity probably accounts for the frequent omission of Davis's name from discussions of jazz radicals. We associate the avant-garde with privation, which Davis has never known, and with a specific approach to improvisational freedom, which he rejects. Still, he is a terribly conscientious avant-gardist, continuously remaking jazz in his own image, and often remaking himself in the process. Harold Rosenberg defined avant-gardism as an "addiction that can be appeased only by revolution in permanence." Davis's addiction has proven as unkickable as that of Coltrane or Coleman and perhaps more so than that of Taylor, and he's been in its throes longer than any of them.

I began by invoking the five-year cycle because of the five-year silence from which Davis has just emerged. His return is freighted with unique expectations: should Thelonious Monk return, we'd be delighted with new choruses of "Evidence" and "Straight No Chaser," but we refuse to accept from Davis a mere continuation

of where he left off. To this extent, he's made good on his promise. But the comeback has also been taxed by his own silly arrogance. During his absence, young zealots apotheosized him in a
way that wasn't possible when he was actively performing, and
though I don't think he actually bought their bill of goods, they
may have convinced him he could get away with anything. His
only New York interview was with a dilettante at the *Times* who
was satisfied to reproduce his gibberish about money, women, and
fast cars. His bumping of Blood Ulmer from his Kool concerts
was widely attributed to competitive fear. Worst of all, he recorded a narcissistic sop to the airwaves with a title, "The Man
with the Horn," that is scarifyingly close to Dorothy Baker's day-
dreams about trumpet players. Davis once told an interviewer that
his hobby was "making fun of white folks on television." With
this wilting performance, he appears to have expanded his field
to black folks on radio.

The rest of Davis's new album is another story. *The Man with
the Horn* (Columbia FC 36790) is hardly top-drawer or second-
drawer Miles, but it's interesting in surprising ways, especially in
tandem with his current concerts. In several important respects,
Davis is surveying his past and expanding his options. Playing pure
trumpet without benefit of electronic gimmickry, he has diversi-
fied his repertoire and put together his first homogeneous, studio-
produced album since *Jack Johnson* in 1970. All the intervening
records were either edited from concert tapes or collated from
two or more widely divergent sessions. Though carefully edited
to promote his continuing addiction to change, they were quite
unlike the thematic statements that made Davis a major force in
recordings in the late '50s and the '60s, when he produced the
orchestral projects with Gil Evans, the pioneering essays in form
(Kind of Blue) and texture *(Bitches Brew),* and the incisive "in between" albums *(Milestones, Miles Smiles, Miles in the Sky)* that mapped
out the steps leading to the major breakthroughs.

The degree to which Davis and producer Teo Macero have
succeeded in making a varied album is all the more impressive
given its two major drawbacks: the sidemen, excepting Al Foster,

are faceless, and Davis is chopsless. He compensates for the failings of others by hiding them. Excepting guitarist Mike Stern,
who mercifully plays on only one selection, the sextet's only soloist other than Davis is saxophonist Bill Evans. He compensates
for his own deficiencies by facing them head-on, renouncing even
the wah-wah machine that made his *Agharta* wimperings sound
like deathly chortles. Indeed, *The Man with the Horn* is something
of a tour de force for him, and there are moments, especially his
two solos on "Aida," where he broaches the high register with
nervous punctuating notes and pressing arpeggios, that put me
in mind of the pride that animated some of Billie Holiday's last
performances. I don't mean to make much of the comparison:
Holiday was at the end of her rope, while Davis, judging from
his concert, has already toughened his embouchure in the few
months since this record was cut. The point is that he isn't cheat-
ing.

The album's big surprise is "Ursula," a swinging if monochro-
matic 4/4 jazz walk that could have been recorded in 1968. Because it consists exclusively of short, punching, middle-register
phrases, much emphasis is placed on the triologue between Davis,
Foster (who leans into some splashing Tony Williams stuff behind the sax solo), and a Fender bassist named Marcus Miller; it
even ends with that ancient Milesian tradition of the trumpeter
rasping, "Play that, Teo." Other ties to the past are explored in
"Back Beat Betty," which has a good, simple theme strongly
reminiscent of both "Shhhh/Peaceful" *(In a Silent Way)* and the
improvisation on, but not the theme of, "Petit Machins" *(Filles de
Kilimanjaro)*. The rhythm section is discreet except for some psy-
chedelic interludes, and Davis meanders nicely with a concatenation of mutters, tremolos, and shouts made cogent by his intensity and sound. Bill Evans enters with a squeaky, yearning cry
and continues his solo in Davis's vein.

The conservatism elsewhere isn't so rewarding. "Shout" is tepid
soul music by the threesome that crafted the noxious title selection, although it's no disgrace as a bid for the airwaves—at least
Davis makes a yeoman try at a solo, and the saxophonist once

again attempts to sustain the leader's mood. The uninvolving vamp
on "Fat Time" undercuts the poignancy of Davis's tone; the orderly rhythms and modulations of the guitar solo sound anti-
quated compared with John McLaughlin's febrile work of 10 years
earlier, and I find the heavy-metal sonority as inappropriate here
as it would be in a Beethoven quartet.

I don't think Davis sustains a single melodic idea on the entire
record, but I suspect that had his chops been more in order, he
might have displayed the ardent lyricism with which he once made
cool hot and hot cool. The evidence was in his Kool concert performance, when he resurrected "My Man's Gone Now." It was
the first time I'd heard him play something from the standard
repertory since 1970, and it reminded me of a rumor that was
circulating shortly before he took his sabbatical: a musician talking to Davis backstage at a European concert said that Davis expressed the desire to reinvestigate ballads, but added "they won't
let me." Oh, ominous apocryphal tales! For all the sludge that
pervaded his Kool recital, I find that two weeks later his two choruses of Gershwin's melody remain fresher than most of what I
heard at the festival. But I'd better explain my use of the word
"chorus," because it was in the restructuring of that piece that
Davis's impish radicalism returned. He didn't play choruses per
se; instead, the piece was poised over a scale or a pedal point that
allowed him to phrase with complete freedom, though this didn't
much affect his choice of notes. He followed the pattern of the
song with few deviations, but when he wanted to breathe he didn't
have to concern himself with chords and measures and the way
they relate to each other. Here, Davis was working through an
idea he'd been mulling over for more than 20 years.

What made Davis radical in the '50s and '60s wasn't that he
did away with song form but that he opened it up. Even Duke
Ellington, the cleverest of all jazz radicals, who worked every
variation imaginable on traditional song and blues forms, never
went beyond the basic parameters of those structures. The challenge for Davis was illustrated unintentionally in the second take
of his 1954 recording of "The Man I Love": Monk plays a piano

solo in which he repeatedly bedraggles the six-note motif over the bar lines, until finally he gets lost—Davis puts him back on the track by playing the appropriate chord at the release. Monk subsequently settled the issue for himself with subtly rubato, un-accompanied solos—an option not open, or at least as appealing, to a trumpet player. Davis had to think the problem through for his whole band. He had already worked to simplify the harmonic labyrinth of bop as a soloist: he made an art of choosing stimu-lating tempos, and drew on his considerable knowledge of har-mony to choose the odd but tellingly right notes. This ability, added to his painstaking development of a personal approach to timbre (abetted by a Harmon mute), gave him the charismatic sound that forced the music community to suspend its disbelief.

In the next few years, Davis adapted his regimen of simplifi-cation to a band context by exploring modes and scales. The turning point was the seminal *Kind of Blue,* that gorgeous, in-trospective collection of first takes so smoothly executed that hardly anyone recognized it for the insurrection it was. He revitalized the blues with "All Blues" and "Freddie Freeloader," introduced modulating tempos in "Blue and Green," replaced chords with modes while retaining the traditional song form in "So What," and improvised form itself in "Flamenco Sketches." "So What" has always seemed the most significant piece—a 32-bar song based on the Dorian mode with a second scale used for the release—because of its immense impact in popularizing modality. But now, "Flamenco Sketches" appears more relevant. Its challenge was to play a series of five scales, the duration of each to be improvised by the soloist. For the most part, Davis and his musicians played it safe, modulating every four or eight bars, and telegraphing those modulations by a mile. Within a few years, however, he was play-ing remarkable improvisations on standard tunes—"Autumn Leaves," "My Funny Valentine"—which, though almost always cleaving to the metrical rules, often gave the illusion of im-promptu modulations, and of a structural freedom denied his sidemen.

At the same time, narcissism began to creep into this work.

Fluffs became marks of honor, even aesthetic signposts. It started subtly: there's that magical moment during the "Strawberry" episode of *Porgy and Bess,* when the trumpeter's technical failure seems preordained, as though he were deliberately cracking his notes to convey the dolorousness of the lament. By the time of "My Funny Valentine," which has one of the most notorious fluffs ever released, one got the feeling that his every crackle and splutter was to be embraced as evidence of his spontaneous soul. On the other hand, his cavalier attitude toward mistakes was more than balanced by an astonishing ambitiousness in his overall performance: he began increasingly to forage into the upper register at breathtaking tempos, the ideas spilling from his horn like leaves in October. This spiraling aplomb, matched by a constant quest for new song forms (Wayne Shorter's impact here can hardly be overestimated), resulted in some of the most fiery playing of his career: "Country Son," "Petit Machins," "Right Off." And it is just at this point that he trades the bite and brilliance of his reclaimed virtuosity for the often mud-colored electronic ensembles, which, for all their rhythmic excitement, vitiated his sound before finally disguising it with gadgetry, limited his options, and substituted tribal chatter for the dagger-edged ego-play of his quintets. This time when he remade the music in his own image the accent was almost entirely on texture, sometimes with notable results—for example, "Mtume," an electrified Ellingtonian jungle in which Davis, gargling like a recently spayed cat, provides compelling poignancy around which the churning rhythms coalesce. But for the most part, his playing lost its charisma, and even the "Interlude" solo on *Agharta,* with its urgent blues licks and pungent glissandos, suggests more of the pain than the grandeur in his music.

The new record and the concert I saw do make for an anticlimactic return, but they are promising nevertheless. He doesn't fudge notes on the record—maybe you can only do that when you're full of confidence, and he has reason to be guarded. Yet he's letting his own sound resurface. In editing down the band, he's cleaned away some of the gratuitous colors. In looking backward, he's opened up his repertoire. Gil Evans has also looked back to the *Porgy and Bess* triumph, and his current band plays a revised arrangement of "Here Comes de Honey Man." A reunion between Evans and Davis may be the only hope of hearing the most lyrical soloist of our time collaborate with a peer. The last time they worked together, the evocative *Filles de Kilimanjaro* resulted, though Evans wasn't credited. The fact that one can even imagine a sequel is the best news about Davis's return. Five years ago, he appeared dead-ended; now, he seems cautious but open. After five years of silence, cautious but open is good news.

(August 1981)

Blythemania

Moderation won't do: Arthur Blythe's performance at the Village Vanguard last week was extraordinary, and so is his new record, *Blythe Spirit* (Columbia FC 37427). His "In the Tradition" band, floated by the rhythm section of John Hicks, Fred Hopkins, and Steve McCall, could be the one to lead jazz out of bondage and into the competitive arena where people can reject it *after* they've had a chance to hear it. Only they won't reject it. This is the band to sweep through campuses as Brubeck did in the '50s, and to be assaulting radio and, dare I say it, TV. Usually commercial ambitions fill me with dread; compromise sets in like cancer and what you originally wanted to sell is eaten down to a trembling husk. But Blythe's band needs no commercial fine tuning; it works the way it is.

Blythe hasn't only developed an original sound on alto, but an original-sounding band, notwithstanding its commonplace instrumentation. Other contemporary bands are melodic and swinging and tight, but Blythe's is illuminated by the colors of the day; it's as unmistakably a band of the '80s as its methods and convictions are of tradition. It's not Top-40 music, thank heavens, but it *is* the music to reach the untapped potential jazz audience that the record industry suicidally stopped trying to reach 15 years ago. Having the commercial viability of contemporary jazz placed on his velour-covered chest is not a responsibility Blythe needs, and he would be wise to laugh it off. But Columbia shouldn't laugh it off: if the company has any desire to take a marketing gamble and open up music in this country,* it's never held better cards. The company's own best interests will be served by creating a mid-line audience, nesting between the consuming masses and the low-rent aficionados—and jazz, real jazz, could nourish it.

The Vanguard set roared from the first notes: Blythe's "Miss Nancy," an AABCA confection in which the variations never stray too far from the triplet-flooded theme. Blythe's sound has ripened into gold, an image usually associated with trumpeters but one which he encourages with whistle-stop phrases that travel angularly from the keening uppermost register through the plump middle one into the bedrock lower one. When he plays, Blythe holds his fingers away from the keys; unlike the veteran saxophonists of earlier generations, whose fingers ripple over the keys with a minimum of movement, Blythe uses his like pistons, and the pumping action shapes his phrasing and rhythms. Some of his solos evolve into dialogues between banshee cries and low-note rumblings, resolved by supple, darting figures. Such was the case with his version of Monk's romantic masterpiece, "Ruby, My Dear." Blythe's improvisation had an integrity worthy of composition— worthy, in fact, of Monk's composition. He raced through "Jitterbug Waltz," but his control made every note an ember; when he lashed into some low-register Coltrane multiphonics on "As of Yet," the riffs forged in granite, he checked himself by easing

*Fat chance; in 1984 Blythe was importuned to make a funk record.

back into his own honeyed tone. "Jitterbug" was John Hicks's best chance to strut, and what an exhilarating pianist he's become. Playing around and against the theme at a whizzing tempo, he made each note ring true, mounted waves of excitement with every chorus, and never violated the structure of the song. What was finally most compelling about his solo was the confidence with which he resolved every blazing, razzle-dazzle gambit in eight bars, only occasionally pacing himself with some I've-gotta-rest chords in the left hand. Hopkins and McCall are not as showy as they used to be, and the undercurrent is smoother and surer. McCall gets a dashing sound from the ride cymbal, and all three of the rhythm players have gotten to the point where they can anticipate Blythe without thinking about it.

This quartet only plays one tune on the new record, but it's exemplary. Garner's "Misty" has been so overdone that, like "Satin Doll," it has to prove itself all over again; Blythe makes the case with a deeply personal recitation and variations that take it to a new realm. The album's other standard, "Strike Up the Band," is treated as a joke—a jerky march anthem that totters against increasingly violent assaults. The album's gem, the one most likely to get radio play, is a jaunty treatment of "Just a Closer Walk with Thee," that is both idiomatically correct and jazzily exalted. Bob Stewart, who wins Best Supporting Instrumentalist for his tuba work throughout the disc, begins by accenting on the one and three, but progresses to an offbeat counterpoint as Blythe lifts himself from the theme. Amina Claudine Myers somehow makes a Hammond sound like a pipe organ, providing a background of muffled, stately chords. The prettiest of Blythe's new compositions is a waltz called "Faceless Woman," but the most impressive is "Reverence," which mines a six-beat rhythm in a way that makes subtly explicit the relationship between Blythe's current music and his roots in the church and rhythm & blues. This music is too bright and singing and forthright to remain the province of an audience disenfranchised by the mass media. Maybe after Columbia makes its mint with Blythe, it or its brethren will sign up Air, the Okra Orchestra, Andrew Cyrille &

Maono, Hannibal, Gil Evans, the Decoding Society, and . . . others. Some of them aren't as accessible as Blythe, but each has legions of admirers who've not yet even heard of them out there in the great untapped.

(September 1981)

Shining Trumpet

Pee Wee Erwin was a short, stocky, diffident-looking man who might have been mistaken for a small-town pharmacist, except when he was holding a trumpet or cornet. From the way he handled his instrument, wedging it in the crook of his left arm or pressing it high on his chest with his right hand, you knew it was an old and intimate friend. When he raised it to play, which he tended to do only a second before his first note was required, he enacted no lip-smacking or lung-filling preliminaries in order to make an immediately beautiful and distinctive sound. Erwin died a few months' ago at sixty-eight, but he was much on my mind at Dick and Maddie Gibson's 19th annual Colorado Jazz Party, held during the Labor Day weekend. It was at their 1975 party that I first heard him, and found myself enchanted by a musician I had considered little more than a studio hack.

Erwin was one of those musicians who existed on the periphery of jazz, more than capable of playing it but never wholly committed to it. His commitment was to the trumpet, which he could play in any context, having been classically trained (originally by his father, who worked territory bands in Kansas City), and subsequently apprenticed with several despotic danceband leaders, including Isham Jones, Ray Noble, Benny Goodman, and

Tommy Dorsey. Erwin was a couple of months short of his 24th birthday when he joined with Dorsey in 1937, replacing Bunny Berigan. His first widely noted solo was on "Who?" a sequel to Berigan's feature, "Marie," and Erwin dutifully played in his style. But as Billy Butterfield, Erwin's good friend and one of the last of the Swing Era's golden trumpets, notes, there was a difference: "First there was 'Marie,' and everyone was talking about Bunny's solo. But then 'Who?' came out a few months later and even though the trumpet solo was in Bunny's style it seemed to take it to the next step. As soon as I heard it I knew I had to meet Pee Wee."

The years with Dorsey produced a number of memorable Erwin solos, among them "Canadian Capers," "Little White Lies," "Oh Promise Me," "Shine On Harvest Moon," "Yearning," and "Comin' Through the Rye," as well as performances with Dorsey's Clambake Seven. But after so auspicious a beginning, Erwin slid into the workaday routine of radio. There was a stint with Raymond Scott, and at least two attempts to start his own band, including a singular foray into bebop with a rehearsal orchestra in 1946; Red Rodney remembers it as one of the first bop orchestras in New York, but though its ranks included Rodney, Al Cohn, and Gerry Mulligan, it never recorded. In 1949, Erwin brought a sextet into Nick's, which became his home base for more than a decade and established him in the dubious world of Dixieland. The Dixie circuit has never been known to broaden a musician's scope or ambition—the repertory is narrow, the routines codified, and the demands of the audience stultifying. Yet in the '50s, it was a haven for scuffling mainstream musicians, and among those who treaded water with "Royal Garden Blues" and "Fidgety Feet" were Henry Allen, Buck Clayton, Pee Wee Russell, Bobby Hackett, Vic Dickenson, Jack Teagarden, and J. C. Higginbotham. Some had long been associated with Eddie Condon's brand of jazz ("the boppers flat their fifths, we drink ours"), but all eventually transcended the idiom, even adapting pieces by Monk and Coltrane.

By entering the television studios in 1960, Erwin moved from one relatively faceless enterprise to another. He was an ideal studio man—expert reader, flawless technician, dependable soloist. Kenny Davern, who received an early break in Erwin's band of the '50s, points out that the economic security of the studios was difficult to resist, but thinks that the real reason Erwin never became recognized as a stylist was his unwillingness to assert himself as a jazz player. He seemed to fall into jobs and the styles that went along with them. With Dorsey, he took on Berigan's mantle; at Nick's, it was Phil Napoleon's; with Jackie Gleason, it was Bobby Hackett's. Yet a personal voice was audible in each of his incarnations. One reason may be, as Bob Wilber suggests, that Erwin listened closely to King Oliver, an influence which may have mitigated Berigan's. Davern used to give him Jelly Roll Morton records, for the George Mitchell trumpet leads. In any case, by the '70s, Erwin was particularly well equipped to take part in the burgeoning interest in jazz repertory, as evinced by his participation in Dick Hyman's tributes to Morton and Armstrong and the Perfect Jazz Repertory Quintet. The best repertory players are knowing interpreters, not simply duplicators; Erwin had the chops to essay any assignment, and the poise to express his own temperament. This was what struck me when I first heard him at the Gibson jazz party in 1975. The band was jogging through the inevitable "Royal Garden Blues," but the trumpet solo, noticeable from the outset for its sure tone and game rhythm, had an inward, almost demure quality. The phrases were long, fluid, and graceful; the delicate but firm sound was colored with dabs of vibrato and glowing smears. Part of the annual pleasure of subsequent parties was the chance to confirm those individual qualities; an abiding frustration was the absence of recordings.

Last year, Erwin was enthused about sessions he'd made for a mail-order label started by a friend, Bill Muchnic, for the sole purpose of recording him. Three records have just been released, and the best of them, *Pee Wee in Hollywood* (Qualtro Music 101), does full justice to his lyrical inventiveness ("Farewell Blues" and "Bye Bye Blues"), his precise use of vibrato ("Rose Room") and honeyed glissandos ("Old Fashioned Love"), and the unerring yet plaintive quality of his lead work. On these selections, his cohorts include the unfailingly captivating Davern, who is often cheated on records, but plays consistently well here—notably a "Bye Bye Blues" solo in which 20 out of 32 bars are filled with tremolos; a chalumeau statement of "Blues My Naughty Sweetie Gave to Me"; and gently invigorating exchanges with Eddie Miller on "Rose Room" and "Hindustan." Miller, an introvert Bud Freeman who has never played an unlovely note, is particularly effective on "Old Fashioned Love," and Bob Havens, the Lawrence Welk trombonist with an affinity for Teagarden, shines brightest on "Bye Bye Blues." Pianist Dick Carey, whom I've admired since I first heard the 1947 Armstrong Town Hall recordings, duets with Erwin on "Monday Date," and is especially effective on "Old Fashioned Love," in his solo chorus and in a quasi-boogie backing for Davern.

The record's highlight, however, is one of two duets with Dick Hyman: Jelly Roll Morton's "Shreveport Stomps." Morton introduced it in a superb 1924 piano recording filled with racing, stiff-legged bass patterns and mad glissing in the treble; a few years later, he revised it as a trio with Omer Simeon and Tommy Benford. Over the past decade, Hyman refurbished it in a performance with Joe Venuti, reproduced the Morton trio with Bob Wilber, and played it solo. But his duet with Erwin is the best performance of "Shreveport Stomps" since the 1924 recording, and one of the finest examples of jazz repertory I've heard. The first two strains, 16 and 14 bars respectively, are played in the Morton tradition, but the trio is extended so that Hyman and Erwin can each wail for a few choruses, and they never miss a beat in building to the final resolution. Erwin's clean, remarkably long phrases strut over the original melody, every note singing. By contrast, their other duet, "When My Sugar Walks Down the Street," is a lovingly nostalgic gambol.

Pee Wee in New York (Qualtro Music 100) is almost all nostalgia. Bob Wilber wrote a series of handsome band arrangements that recall the '30s and allow Erwin to spread his tone a bit. The songs are good standards, and the ensemble as led by Erwin is rich and creamy, but there aren't enough solos to satisfy a jazz appetite, and the medium dance-band tempos are too much the same. Still, Erwin embraces Gershwin's neglected ballad, "He Loves, She Loves;" renders "What's New" in pure silk over Milt Hinton's leathery bass; and wistfully recalls "Buddy Bolden's Blues." The real gem, however, is "Creole Love Song," with a deliciously quizzical Erwin solo that suddenly becomes declarative in the stop-time episode; here, his indulgently golden tone and wry emotional understatement go hand in hand. The third album, *Pee Wee Playing at Home* (Qualtro Music 102), finds him deliberating over a dozen well-chosen melodies—among the best are Beiderbecke's "In the Dark," "The Touch of Your Lips," and "Moonlight on the Ganges"—with just the guitars of Bucky and John Pizzarelli; the jazz content is lowest on this album, though admirers of Hackett's mood records may want to test its powers of seduction. The quality that raises Pee Wee's best solos above the crowd and into the rarefied atmosphere of jazz was addressed by Joe Newman: "Pee Wee's timeless. What he played doesn't fit into any categories—it's not Dixieland or bop, just a great musician playing what he feels."

(September 1981)

Joe Turner: Unmoved Mover

The mental picture I have of Kansas City in the 1930s, the image that resurfaces when I listen to the barnstorming music financed by the city's notorious Pendergast regime, is a fleeting moment from Gordon Parks's otherwise unmemorable 1969 film, *The Learning Tree*. As I recall it, swinging doors frame a crowded, noisy, blueish saloon—arid with smoke, irrigated with liquor. Behind the bar, Jimmy Rushing is running a cloth over the shiny wood, and shouting the blues. There is no tension in the partying; it will go on all night, possibly interrupted—though not for long—by an unruly drunk. I can imagine all the Kansas City legends taking place in this setting: Count Basie improvising head arrangements until sunup, Lester Young doing battle with Coleman Hawkins, Charlie Parker bringing his patched-up alto around to sit in. The image is romantic, but not entirely false. Big Joe Turner really was a singing bartender. Still in his teens, he dispensed booze at the Sunset Cafe, where a PA system was installed behind the bar so that when he felt like emoting, his sonorous voice would spill onto the streets and serve as an advertisement for good times at the Sunset.

After five years at home in Los Angeles, when he was too ill to travel, Big Joe is back in New York, looking a lot thinner, a little older (the surface of his face hasn't changed much in 40 years), and walking with the aid of crutches. Yet when he unburdens himself into the microphone, it's still Kansas City in 1930, even if the audience is now white, polite, and humbled by history. The acoustic miracle that is Turner's voice is as cavernous and majestic as ever, almost a kind of human thunder. It makes all the points about fickle women and troubled nights quickly, dispassionately, and without fanfare, and it brooks no appeal. To my mind, Turner at seventy is the most commanding blues singer alive—the very embodiment of the blues as survival weapon, and the blues as triumph.

Actually, "blues singer" puts too fine a line around what he does. At Tramps, he tells the audience, "We do some rock and roll, some jazz, and some blues," and there's no way you can mistake when he's doing what, even though it's all based on the same 12-bar recipe. The distinction is in the rhythms and in the calibrations of pitch, which measures the shadings between a moan (a moan to turn back rivers) and a shout (a shout to start the world dancing). Percy France's quartet provides serviceable backing when it gets warmed up (drummer Wes Landers winks with an occasional Baby Dodds pressroll), and Turner, suggesting a nonchalance that borders on insolence, alternates between the sermon-on-the-mount admonishments of "I'm Going Away To Get You Off My Mind" and the rocking insouciance of "Flip, Flop and Fly." When Big Joe is out of spirits, he sounds lethargic (as on, for example, Pablo's *Everyday I Have the Blues,* which is to be avoided by even the most ravenous of his admirers). He doesn't sound lethargic these days.

He sounded positively godlike on a recent night at Greene Street, when he sat in with two other prophets from the Kansas City diaspora, Jay McShann and Claude Williams plus bassist Paul West. First he wandered upstairs to where WVNJ's Les Davis broadcasts nightly, and Davis showed him the new MCA reissue of Turner's great 1940s' Deccas—*Early Big Joe* (MCA-1325), a faultless compilation with several Turner classics, a glorious reworking of "Trouble in Mind" (retitled "Nobody in Mind"), and the aid of Hot Lips Page, Don Byas, and Art Tatum. Turner hadn't seen the album, and he expressed curiosity about "Blues on Central Avenue"—B. B. King's been asking him about it, but Turner couldn't even remember cutting it. He listened intently as Davis played it, and said it sounded pretty good. Downstairs, he walked haltingly to the bandstand chair, chitchatted in a deceptively small voice, and suddenly popped the first notes of "Hide and Seek" into the mike. McShann played piano, drums, and all the horn parts on keyboard, Williams—who has emerged from inexplicable obscurity to reestablish himself as a premier jazz violinist—fiddled rhythmically slippery responses, and Turner, the unmoved mover, conversed regally with deities that only he can hear.

(October 1981)

The Egg in the Meatloaf

It's always gratifying when innovation shatters the complacency of jazz. Until recently jazz iconoclasm was associated almost exclusively with youth; the innovators made their marks by their mid-twenties—Louis Armstrong and Charlie Parker at twenty-five, Coleman Hawkins at twenty-two, Miles Davis at nineteen. Now, however, it sometimes happens that a musician of long experience will suddenly about-face and challenge his own former assumptions, as well as everyone else's. This was certainly the case in the '60s, when musicians like John Coltrane and Eric Dolphy set aside their bebop groundings to help father a "new thing," and it's even more true of the past decade.

For all that, Ronald Shannon Jackson, at forty-two, seems an unlikely pacesetter. After playing drums in New York for a decade, he managed to achieve almost total obscurity. Then, during a period of three or four years with Ornette Coleman, Cecil Taylor, and James "Blood" Ulmer, he became the most talked-about drummer in town. Today, quite without warning, he looms as a bandleader and composer of unmistakable maturity and originality; his band, the Decoding Society, is one of the most electrifying in jazz.

I first heard Jackson play drums on Ornette Coleman's 1976 album *Dancing in Your Head*, but it wasn't until two years later, at a Cecil Taylor recording session, that he impressed me as someone to be reckoned with. Taylor's band was working through the final take of an album subsequently released as *3 Phasis* when Jackson, holding each stick in a tight overgrip, suddenly injected

into the music a volatile backbeat that transformed Taylor's free
rhythms into a sort of barrelhouse euphoria. Here was a drummer whose notion of freedom did not preclude a devotion to
dance-beat rhythms—who transcended the strictures of countable time without vitiating his determination to swing. With the
Decoding Society, he makes his sidemen swing as hard as he does.

Jackson—a tall, lean, disarmingly relaxed man who lives with
his family in a comfortable Manhattan high-rise and braids his
hair with nuts, bolts, beads, and subway tokens—credits his late
blossoming to his conversion to Nichiren Shoshu Buddhism; like
Herbie Hancock, Buster Williams, and other well-known musicians, he chants every day, and he insists that chanting plugged
him into the rhythms of life. On a secular level, his breakthrough can be traced to a broad range of musical experiences
that he has thoroughly absorbed and ingeniously synthesized.
Jackson's career supports the argument made by an Edward Albee character that it's sometimes necessary to go a long distance
out of the way to come back a short distance correctly.

He was born and raised in the uncommonly musical community of Fort Worth, which also produced Ornette Coleman, Dewey
Redman, Julius Hemphill, and John Carter. Two conditions that
nourished so much local talent, Jackson feels, were a powerful
Methodist tradition and a strong economy, manifested in the
availability of band instruments in the schools. Even before school
he was exposed to a variety of music: his mother played piano in
church, and his father stocked jukeboxes and operated a record
store. There Jackson first heard his father's favorite bluesmen,
Howlin' Wolf, B. B. King, and Charles Brown, and such jazz musicians as Charlie Parker, Erroll Garner, and Dave Brubeck.

After studying the rudiments of music on piano, Jackson
switched to drums, the instrument that had first caught his fancy,
and by age fifteen he was working professionally. By the time he
acceded to the drummer's chair in the high school band, all the
influences were operating. "In the morning you'd wake up and
hear hillbilly music on the radio," he recalls. "In school we'd play
Lohengrin, and at night we'd hear Bo Diddley or Bobby 'Blue'
Bland. On Sunday we'd hear gospel. It was a total black com-

munity, and music wasn't categorized as jazz or pop—nobody told you you weren't supposed to like something."

In 1958, he matriculated at Lincoln University in Jefferson City, Missouri. It was a good place to be; his freshman-year roommate was pianist John Hicks, and his peers in the school band included Julius Hemphill, Lester Bowie, and Oliver Nelson. But Jackson was more interested in playing and listening to music than in studying. When Dizzy Gillespie and John Coltrane were scheduled to perform in St. Louis, he left school for the concert and never returned. He tried college again, though—this time at Texas Southern University—but lasted only a couple of weeks because he wore himself out playing a supper club until midnight and then an after-hours gambling joint. Returning to Fort Worth and his father's jukebox business, he was exposed to the adventurous, young jazz labels—Blue Note, Prestige, Riverside—that were pressing 45s for the jukes. Jackson credits two events of the late '50s with straightening him out; the launching of Sputnik, which inspired him to launch himself, and the release of Miles Davis's *Kind of Blue*, which gave him the direction—away from the late-night gamboling, drinking, and dope smoking. When he enrolled at Prairie View A & M in East Texas, it was for two years of history and sociology—a cooling-off period. And when he transferred to the University of Bridgeport in Connecticut, he was so absorbed in those subjects that he intended not to play music at all.

Happily, his resolve was short-lived. He began sitting in with local groups and was reinspired when he visited New York and found his old roommate John Hicks playing at Slugs. In 1967, a scholarship from the New York College of Music enabled him to move to New York to work in various community stage bands. In no time his schedule was once again filled to bursting.

Ironically, his first recording session—with saxophonist Charles Tyler—came about through the unknowing auspices of his future mentor, Ornette Coleman. Charles Moffett, Coleman's drummer at the time, had been hired for the record, but when Coleman asked him not to play with other musicians, Jackson was brought in as a sub. Albert Ayler, one of the most controversial

and virtuosic figures in the avant-garde musical movements of
the '60s, was present and offered Shannon a berth in his band.
All the pieces seemed to be falling into place. When Ayler wasn't
working, there were gigs with Betty Carter. Even Charles Mingus was willing to take him on as a second drummer concentrat-
ing on timpani. Yet a combination of bad habits and economic
considerations prompted Jackson's decision to move to Queen's,
where he buried himself in lucrative socials—weddings, bar mitz-
vahs, local bars.

Jackson was in his early thirties and, despite all his experience,
utterly unknown except to a small nucleus of musicians when, in
1974, pianist Onaje Allan Gumbs initiated him into Buddhist
chanting: the phrase *nam myoho renge kyo*, repeated for an hour
at a stretch. A year later Shannon was having breakfast in a
Greenwich Village restaurant when who should walk in but Ornette Coleman—in search of a drummer. Coleman was prepar-
ing a European tour, and Jackson rehearsed with him every day
for a month before they embarked on a journey that would cul-
minate in the recordings of Coleman's *Dancing in Your Head* and
Body Meta. It was during this time that Jackson was introduced
to Coleman's ideas about playing and ordering music—ideas that
are generally subsumed under what Coleman calls his Harmolodic (a contraction of harmony, movement, and melody) Theory.

When I asked Jackson to explain this much-bandied-about term,
I was surprised by the good-humored candor with which he con-
fessed, "I couldn't." Yet he warmed to the subject as it assumed
a general or philosophical, as opposed to specific and musicological, meaning. "Harmolodics is a system to train people away
from what's been done. I can tell you one thing—it's not free. It
has to do with everyone playing in different keys and yet being
equal." Coleman never spoke about harmolodics at rehearsals, but
he wrote out a series of scales for Jackson to practice on flute,
based on the relationships between keys and on the mechanics
of overtones. He encouraged Jackson to write down his own melodic ideas and to think in terms of the highest and lowest pitches
of an instrument rather than the confinement of a single key.

At bottom, Coleman was goading Jackson into thinking of musical sounds first and traditional harmonic rules second, if at all. As Jackson puts it, "Most musicians were thinking in terms of chord changes, which meant that there wasn't much music being written. The problem today is to get musicians to stop thinking in terms of standard chords and keys." Yet total freedom is not necessarily the answer: "Albert Ayler said play everything, fill in every hole. But when I got to Cecil Taylor and Ornette Coleman, I realized it wasn't like that at all. The thing I'm trying to do is organize the music, and you have to rehearse constantly, because we're talking about putting together all the musical ideas of the past 30 years. It's got to swing—swing is the egg in the meatloaf—but it can be bop, reggae, rock, classical. It has to be a total experience for everyone involved, like going to a Buddhist meeting, where we deal in our energies, not in egos or who we are and what we do." That's why his band is called the Decoding Society—it decodes, finds a common denominator, simplifies, and brings together.

A period with Taylor, whose music is freely yet fastidiously organized around the energies of his musicians, followed; then a stint with Blood Ulmer furthered his interest in combining electric and acoustic instruments. These were the final elements in bringing Jackson the short distance back correctly. The next step was to assemble a group of musicians to rehearse the music he had been writing.

Several qualities of Jackson's music impress the ear immediately—his gift for evocative melody, his insistence on swing, his penchant for counterpoint, and his distinctive voicings for reeds. He tends to compose in the high-piccolo register, which creates difficulties in writing for lower-pitched brass instruments and in mixing the sound. As a result, he concentrates on saxophones, guitars, violins, and vibes. And because he works with a select group of musicians, he has developed a knack for getting the most from them; Byard Lancaster, Charles Brackeen, Lee Rozie, Vernon Reid, Melvin Gibbs, and others have never been heard to better advantage.

At the center of his alternatively rocking, swinging, contrapuntal, serene, and exotic, but always colorful, maelstrom are the drums. Jackson employs a three-beat figure—two sixteenth notes followed by two eighth notes, or the reverse—as his foundation, but he layers it in a broad canvas of rhythms. For several years he kept a diary in which he figured out the numerological quotient of each day and practiced only the equivalent rhythm. The result of this obsession with time is a staggering fluidity. His rhythms change with kaleidoscopic unpredictability, yet he always presents the illusion of balanced meters. His melodies and structures are kaleidoscopic, too.

The highlight of his first album, *Eye on You* (About Time 1003), is called "Apache Love Song": it begins with two guitars playing the same doleful melody in different keys; then the saxes enter with an extension of that melody, while guitarist Bern Nix introduces a new theme. During the intense middle section, Nix improvises off the melody he introduced, violinist Billy Bang improvises off the part for the saxes, alto saxophonist Byard Lancaster plays freely within the context of the primary melody, and tenor saxophonist Charles Brackeen improvises with total freedom. "Nightwhistlers" combines a moody, wistful tune, played out of phase, with a storming rhythm recalling Gene Krupa's drumming on "Sing Sing Sing."

Nasty (Moers 01086) contains Jackson's two most euphoric swing anthems: the title piece, with saxes voiced high over a shuffle rhythm, and "Small World," a superbly crafted theme that underscores the rich intensity of Jackson's rhythms. The most ambitious piece is "When We Return," which begins with a melody stated twice—originally by flute, sopranos, and vibes, and then on drums. After the theme is repeated at a faster tempo, Vernon Reid embarks on a long, textural solo, while the three saxes and the vibes repeat the melody. Unfortunately, the composer's intention of having the improvisation and melody feed each other is nullified, since the sound mix all but swamps the ensemble.

His third album, *Street Priest* (Moers 01096), employs his current working band—Reid, Rozie, Gibbs, Zane Massey, and "Reverend" Bruce Johnson. One cut, "Chudo Bey," is a backbeat extravaganza with a horn arrangement that suggests the off-pitch sonorities of a rhythm & blues band but with a fullness, spirit, and complexity quite beyond anything in the genre. The ear may make connections between the simultaneity of events, but the total effect on the listener is constant submersion and surprise. "Sperm Walk" is a witty montage of angular melodies that showcases Jackson's ability to wrest new sonorities from familiar instruments while keeping the undercurrent rhythmically jubilant.

That his work is confined to small labels that are all but unobtainable in this country and have neither the facilities nor the financial wherewithal to record his music properly is an indication that, however healthy the state of music may be, the industry that should be documenting it is racked with disease. Twenty years ago the adventurous labels that competed for space in Jackson's father's jukeboxes would have leapfrogged one another to sign on a band so accomplished and well received. Jackson's music is innovative because it achieves old goals in new ways: it is not afraid to be noisy one moment and rigidly controlled the next. For all its debt to Coleman, Taylor, Ayler, and who knows who else, it speaks in melodies that are immediately recognizable as Jackson's own and moves with the knowing grace that only a great bandleader can impart.

(March 1982)

Songs Your Mother Never Sang

Now that jazz composers are routing the Cult of Improvisation, easing the guilt of erstwhile fans who wearied of marathon sax-

ophone solos, they are turning increasingly to words. True, the
voice played a role in free jazz almost from the beginning, what
with George Russell's "You Are My Sunshine," Mingus's orchestrated groans, Coltrane's mystical chants, Shepp's polemical poetry, Leon Thomas's visionary yodeling, and much more. But
taken together, those instances remained peripheral—recitation
was less likely to control the design of a musical work than serve
as a prelude to an hour of the usual bravura harmonics. In a
number of recent recordings, however, voices give shape and
impetus to instrumental fervor; the vocalist, removed from the
traditional relationship of singer (or poet) plus obbligato, is a
theatrical entity at the center of the maelstrom. Significantly, none
of these vocalists *sound* like jazz singers.

Mike Westbrook, the English composer and pianist, who (not
unlike Carla Bley) blends the disciplined revelry of Kurt Weill
with the ecstasies of free jazz, unveils his most ambitious work in
The Westbrook Blake (Europa JP2006). The idea of setting famous
poetry to music is, generally, as unappealing to me as allowing
song-plugging lyricists to attain the podium at the 92nd Street Y.
And that goes double for the poetry of William Blake, partly because the deceptive simplicity of his lyrics inspires simplistic composing, and partly because musical interpreters tend to put all
levity aside when dealing with a man who saw God. Blake himself set his poetry to music (he illustrated it, too), but his melodies haven't survived, and I like to think that they weren't as earnest as his angry words, balance being all things to a good song.
As Eliot pointed out, Blake's honesty is terrifying. Westbrook, too,
is divertingly honest, flaunting his influences even as he assimilates them, parading his passions. Though flush with earnest-
ness, he balances his six selections with so much stylistic variety,
color, and melody that even his solemnity is tolerable. But as Eliot
also pointed out, Blake is a crank (damned autodidact!), and had
Westbrook remembered that, he might have told his singers to
lighten up.

If Phil Minton and Kate Westbrook tend to bellow and weep,
respectively, they are undoubtedly responding to the composer's
sense of mission—a sense underscored for the listener by his un-

usual choice of material. No *Songs of Innocence* here, but rather three choleric *Songs of Experience* ("London Song," "A Poison Tree," "Holy Thursday"), two celebrational excerpts from *Jerusalem*, and a make shift disputation on slavery that combines excerpts from *America: A Prophecy* and *The Four Zoas*. Excepting the last, the settings are a heady brew, full of fire and song and wit; they complement each other like parts of a suite. As the singers sing, making the most of Westbrook's ear for rowdy melody, the instrumentalists illuminate his recognition of the link between Blake's pain and Coltrane's. Richard Williams, reviewing Westbrook's Blake concert for the *Times* of London, justifiably suggested that someone hearing "the techniques of post-Coltrane jazz" for the first time "might easily imagine that they had been invented specifically for the project." In parsing those techniques to amplify the songs, the composer gives them new dimensions of expression.

Phil Minton declaims the poetry forthrightly—exercising his extraordinary range with precision, suggesting not only theatrical hardiness but the informality of a pub-crawler moved to spontaneous song. He's a real discovery, and I wonder what he'd do with American songs. In "The Fields" (the final quatrain of five in Westbrook's version, incidentally, comes much later in the original poem than the first four) and "I See Thy Form," Minton navigates the lines amid martial airs, explosive saxophone solos and duets, brass alarums, and menacing tympani. The primary melodies are simple, effective, and memorable, though not entirely free of operatic pomposity. But the problem is alleviated by the master stroke of introducing a children's choir from the Gospel Oak Primary School; its august harmony provides an eerie correlative to Blake's euphoria. Minton is most impressive on "Let the Slave," intoning the first four lines of the *America* excerpt a cappella, and shading subsequent high notes with fury and grit. Westbrook himself reads the *Four Zoas* section, and though he reads quite well, the stagnant voices chanting behind him underscore the general impression that his musical ideas have bottomed out, overwhelmed by seriousness.

The best arrangements are the three *Songs of Experience*, sung by Kate Westbrook, who is as overwrought as Minton is four-square. Since I don't hear maternal weepiness in Blake, some of the dramatics she brings to the poet's bitter observations in "London Song" and "Holy Thursday" seem to me misplaced. "London Song" opens with free-jazz effects, assuming real dignity in the expert melody statement by saxophonist Alan Wakeman; the rhythm and piano chords are compelling, and very English. As the singer sobs the dark images, however, the pianist bangs with sound and fury, and the interpretation suddenly gets so pensive it's funny. A little Brechtian irony would have done wonders—something Westbrook must have realized, because the ensuing "A Poison Tree" is a hilarious vignette. Westbrook bites her words like a pouting child, Wakeman plays stripper's sax, and the ensemble sustains a Weimar bacchanal, going Latin just long enough to quote a lick from *Carmen*.

By far the masterpiece of the album is "Holy Thursday," a 15-minute elaboration on Blakean bile that stands with the finest scores I've heard in recent years. Excepting the histrionics of the vocal, the excecution is flawless. The performance begins, appropriately enough, with forlorn blues piano. The singer appears and is joined midway by a cellist (Georgie Born), who soon moves center-stage; the smooth transition from blues piano to Bachian cello and back is arresting. There are wonderful solos by Wakeman on tenor and Chris Biscoe on alto clarinet, as well as a tenor and arco-bass duet, a modal free-for-all, and a passage of driving swing on familiar chord changes, before a blistering tenor solo brings the thing to an abrupt halt. Westbrook individuates each role (there's hardly any unison playing on the whole record), and keeps the episodes moving fast; not a measure is self-indulgent or excessive. Nor is Blake forgotten in the pitch of excitement. Having underscored the lyric with strong melody, Westbrook allows the musicians to augment the poet.

If Hannibal Marvin Peterson were to tackle Blake, he'd undoubtedly go for the innocence. Peterson's lyrics are almost ingenuous in their sincerity and simplicity, and it's characteristic that the angry note struck in his liner comment for *The Angels of At-*

lanta (Enja 3087) is not heard when the Harlem Boys Choir sings his dedication to the murdered children. Nor does the horror that inspired the record vitiate the optimism that sustains the other selections. There are some obvious similarities between the Westbrook and Peterson projects—children's choirs, singing relations, borrowed Coltrane—but the real link is an expressive honesty that, for all the compositional ambition, is muted very little by fancy artifice. Hannibal sticks closer than Westbrook to a contemporary jazz format, reserving for his trumpet any intimations of darkness. Pointedly, the album's one traditional song, the dolorous "Sometimes I Feel Like a Motherless Child," is not sung.

Hannibal's most carefully chosen melody is sung by the Boys Choir on "The Angels of Atlanta." The long, energetic solos that follow relate to the recitation much as an ebullient blues shouter relates to a sad blues lyric: by transcending it. The soloists—George Adams, Kenny Barron, and Peterson, who has removed some of the impersonal gloss from his sound—are very good indeed. A concluding duet by Peterson and Dannie Richmond goes on too long to make the point, but the permutations are logical and the embers are fanned. Cecil McBee, who may be the fastest bassist alive, is so responsive and quick-witted (especially during Barron's solo) that he never sinks below the surface of the front line. "The Inner Voice" and "Mother's Land" are more telling attempts to take the voice into instrumental territory, with Pat Peterson's melismatic phrases intertwining with the musicians—never reducing them to accompanists, or herself to an isolated soloist. But the grip of Coltrane's modality is wearing. As a trumpeter, Peterson has adapted Coltrane to brass much as Roy Eldridge adapted the tenors of the '30s, and in both instances the result is a fast, virtuosic style capped with stratospheric flourishes. On "The Story Teller," he even captures the broadsword intonation of Coltane's *Meditations*. What I miss is more of the structural diversity of his earlier work (especially *Children of the Fire*). Still, he manages to keep Coltrane's pyre burning bright, when others are simply anointing themselves with the ashes.

(March 1982)

Art Pepper, 1926–1982

It was no surprise to hear that Art Pepper died of a stroke June 15. The surprises were his annual appearances in New York since 1977, when he made his belated debut here. He was living on borrowed time, and he knew it. You could hear it in every note he played. The last time I saw him, at Fat Tuesday's a few months ago, his face was bluish white, and his lower legs—he pulled up his trousers to demonstrate—were as bloated as beer barrels. He told me he couldn't shake hands because he'd cut himself that afternoon and, not feeling any pain, didn't know it until he saw the streaming blood. He was obsessed with the miracle that he was still ambulatory and breathing; difficult to be around. How, I wondered, did his amazingly patient wife Laurie, whom he'd met at Synanon when he got out of jail in the late '60s, who'd put together his powerful autobiography, *Straight Life*, and kept him on the road and working—how did she put up with it?

Well, there was, as she once said in a moment of candid desperation, the music. Pepper had achieved the most ragingly expressionistic music of his career, and he made so much depend on the integrity and substance of each chorus that watching him play was an eerie sort of adventure. When the proof was in, when the payoffs rained—for example, in ballad performances as his alto stuttered a few clipped strained phrases and then suddenly found the wind and inspiration for a long, looping, richly evocative melody—you couldn't help but be impressed. Other musicians could play as well from beginning to end, with little fuss.

But it was part of Pepper's art that he didn't let you take anything for granted. His solos were a series of small victories. You
paid for them, couldn't turn your head from them; they had suspense. Listen to the ballads, especially "Good-bye" and "Cherokee," on the three records he made at the Village Vanguard in
1977 (Contemporary); in their own tenuous, occasionally un-
pleasant ways, they are as nerve-shattering as the unholy cries of
late Coltrane. John Coltrane was living on borrowed time, too.
Perhaps it's only in the recognition that we all are that the un-
pleasantness of their music becomes meaningful, acceptable, and
even beautiful.

Coltrane's influence transfigured Pepper when he resumed his
career after 20 year of hospitals and jails. In the early years, Lester Young, Zoot Sims, Lee Konitz, and Charlie Parker had been
his models. He had a lithe, dry-ice sound, and though his playing was always intense, he knew the values of bebopping profi-
ciency. By the early '50s, he was the sharpest white player in California—a qualitative and racial distinction that remained
profoundly important to him. Crazily competitive, in his later years
he wanted nothing less than to be the first white player to loom
as "the inspiration for the whole jazz world"; in the 1950s, however, he was content to prove his originality in a series of brilliantly realized Contemporary albums—+11, Art Pepper Meets the
Rhythm Section, Intensity—that were occasionally recorded in a
junkie haze so complete that he listened to the results in amazement: am I that good? The Coltrane influence was tortuous at
first—The Trip, Living Legend—but it resolved itself into a harsher
version of the old Pepper, as witness the Galaxy albums, Straight
Life, Today, and the nervously wistful Winter Moon. Finally, there
were two Peppers—the supple and professional recording artist,
and the neurotically emotive concert performer. If he was never
going to be at the center of jazz, he was nonetheless a center of
sorts. You couldn't file him in a category. He wasn't L.A. cool,
white bop, hype, '50s, or '80s, but an impassioned musician with
an alto sax and a rhythm section that never completely satisfied

him. Despite the facile clichés of the music he mastered, he made
you know that, facility and clichés notwithstanding, no one else
could ever play like that.

(June 1982)

Sonny Stitt, 1924–1982

Sonny Stitt's passing on July 22, three weeks after he was called
in to replace Art Pepper at the Kool Jazz Festival, ends one of
the most prolific and frustrating careers in jazz. Stitt played well
that night, trading choruses with Richie Cole; it wasn't one of those
performances where time stops and the arpeggios never land
where you'd expect them, but he steadfastly undermined the
changes with fresh ideas and generally avoided those tag endings that signaled he was on automatic pilot. And of course he
swung like mad. The most intense number of the concert was
the opening blues, when Stitt, feet planted squarely and eyes
staring ahead, played something like two dozen choruses. Cole
glanced nervously at his watch or offstage and tried politely to
get Stitt's attention, but there was no diverting him.

There never was. Stitt had long since become a lone wolf, traveling ceaselessly from city to city and studio to studio, usually
employing pick-up rhythm sections. One of the most recorded
musicians of all time—as a leader, not a sideman—he sometimes
seemed indifferent to the music he was playing. Not that he was
likely to disappoint his audience, who, he knew, couldn't detect
for the most part when he was on and when he was coasting;
after all, he could coast with head-spinning virtuosity. But there
was a touch of cynicism. A record session, finally, was just an-

other gig—a fast taste, no royalties. The blues, "I Got Rhythm,"
a couple of standards. Still, he countered that cynicism with the
conviction, shared by numberless jazz musicians about their own
work, that the knowing audience, however, small, *would* recognize the diamonds, *would* distinguish what was great from what
was merely professional.

For example: 10 years ago, in the midst of a relentless and
largely undistinguished recording regimen including tenor-organ
dates and a brief flirtation with electronic sax, Stitt made a superb album called *Tune Up* for Cobblestone. There isn't a rote
note on it. One reason for its success was producer Don Schlitten, who has a magical touch with bop saxophonists, and another
was pianist Barry Harris, a catalyst for some of Stitt's best playing since 1957 (their 1961 "Koko" for Cadet is one of Stitt's masterpieces). Heady with success, the three returned to the studio
four months later to cut *Constellation*, which is measure for measure probably the best LP Stitt ever made. When it tied McCoy
Tyner's *Sahara* for first place in the *Down Beat* critics' poll, some
colleagues were dismayed that what appeared on the surface to
be an ordinary six-hour quartet date, leader plus pick-up rhythm,
should win the prize from more fashionable doings. But I continue to think it was one of *Down Beat's* more privileged moments, recognizing a veteran player's reclaimed inspiration.

Edward Stitt was born to a musical family in Boston; his father
was a music professor, his mother a piano teacher, and his brother
a concert pianist. Stitt started on piano, then switched to clarinet
and alto. Like many altoists of his generation, he took up tenor
to avoid comparisons with Charlie Parker, whom he first met and
jammed with in 1943. Stitt was easily riled by people who labeled
him a Parker disciple. The issue is moot, since Stitt's style was
immediately recognizable. The consistency of his licks, mannerisms, intonation, and rhythmic habits over a 37-year recording
career proves that he was less than impressionable. Parker may
have provided some initial clues, but Stitt was his own man early
on. By 1945, he was firmly situated in New York, recording with
Dizzy Gillespie for Musicraft (see *In the Beginning* on Prestige),

Fats Navarro on Savoy *(Fat Girl)*, and Gene Ammons, J.J. Johnson, and his own groups on Prestige *(Genesis,* including the exhilarating "All God's Chillun" with Bud Powell, is the best anthology of early Stitt). The stomping give-and-take in a series of
tenor "battles" with Ammons encouraged confrontations with
other saxophonists—among them Sonny Rollins, Eddie Davis, Zoot
Sims, Paul Gonsalves, Red Holloway, and Ricky Ford. Stitt had
the qualities essential to a tenor battler; he was implacable, indefatigable, inventive. The dramatic climax of Art Pepper's autobiography is his description of going up against Stitt.

Yet in later years those competitions—that's what the audience
wanted them to be—seemed to bore him. The graceful, athletic,
almost ravenous saxophonist who took on all comers in the 1950s,
teaming triumphantly with Dizzy Gillespie and Sonny Rollins—
he wrote the enduring classic from one of their sessions, "The
Eternal Triangle"—and with Roy Eldridge and Oscar Peterson
(both on Verve), turned bewilderingly inconsistent by the mid-
'70s. There remained many nights of startling inspiration, when
the phrases unfurled like streamers, chorus after chorus, when
the ballads—he was insufficiently appreciated as a ballad player—
unfolded in melodic paraphrases and double-timed interludes. He
was in peak form for the Giants of Jazz tour with Gillespie and
Monk (recorded for Atlantic) and *The Bebop Session* on Sonet.
Other nights, he just turned on the motor; the intonation was
weaker and the fast phrasing, the millions of notes, spilled me-
chanically from his instruments, a dubious payoff for his having
so completely mastered bop's legerdemain.

The cause of his death was diagnosed as cancer, but as far as
I can tell nobody knew he had it—some people think Stitt didn't
know. He'd been ill for some time, though. When a musician
embraced him backstage at Kool, he howled in pain, explaining
that every part of him hurt from arthritis. Yet he kept moving,
making every festival, every city, all the recording dates. For his
admirers, it was often less a matter of hoping for a good night
than for good moments during an uneven night, but when you're
watching a master that can be enough. And Stitt was a master.

His best work, those diamonds, will live as long as anything in jazz.

(August 1982)

Woody Herman

1. Off the Road

Woody Herman must be one of the least disliked persons on earth. It isn't just sentimentality. Herman's name is a quality brand, representing craftsmanship, integrity, and receptiveness to new ideas. So when it was announced that Herman—who has been a traveling performer since the age of eight and a bandleader since 1936—was coming off the road to settle in a room of his own (opening night: December 27, 1981), there was considerable hoopla. It was widely assumed that Herman would be delighted to plant his feet on one patch of earth. But Herman is of another school, almost another world.

In the '30s and '40s, musicians roamed the land in herds. Crisscrossing a grid of interstate highways and back roads, corralled in buses, billeted according to celebrity status and race, and developing a collective, arcane wit to complement the music and to fight fatigue, they moved from town to town, ballroom to ballroom, glad for the ocacasional two-week stay but always ready to pack up after the gig for another long trip. Swing bands, fifteen to twenty strong on the average, were one of the Depression's more unlikely phenomena. Although many were sickly sweet or bland and derivative, more than a few were hot, impetuous, energetic, inventive, and inspired. These were the bands that combined strong leaders, brilliant soloists, adventurous writers, and the best songs of a golden age of song writing. Individual in their style of presentation as well as in their music, they coexisted in an atmosphere of friendly, if sometimes tension-ridden, competition. The stubbornest road musicians probably got to know America better than any of its other citizens, certainly than any of its other artists. But few were either stubborn or strong enough to survive the social and economic changes that followed World War II. And only two—Count Basie and Woody Herman—were also both gifted and lucky enough to survive into the '80s. They are as obsolete as buffalo, and just as grand.

Woody Herman's, as his new club is called, is located in the Hyatt Regency complex in New Orleans; thirty-six weeks a year, six nights a week, two shows a night, Woody can walk to work. Yet when I visited with him half a year after he was ensconced, he was grazing restlessly. He loves New Orleans and is grateful for the security, but . . . "if I told you I wasn't looking forward to doing dates again on the other weeks, I'd be lying." At sixty-nine, he's not entirely ready for the reservation. Maybe it's something in the blood.

Herman was born in Milwaukee in 1913 and was on tour singing and dancing in a kids' troupe eight years later. In four months he earned enough money to buy a saxophone and a clarinet (he was soon billed as "The Boy Wonder of the Clarinet"), thinking it was kind of childish for him to do vaudeville in a Ted Lewis hat when he could be a jazz musician. At seventeen, Herman dropped out of high school to join Tom Gerun's band at the Granada Cafe in Chicago, a front for the Capone mob. (This first job with a band was nearly his last. One night, a couple of Capone's thugs invited Woody for a joyride; when he demurred, they shot him in the leg.) After three years with Gerun, Herman went home to Milwaukee, hoping to start his own band. That plan failed, however, so he returned to Chicago to play with Harry Sosnick's radio band, then went on tour with Gus Arnheim's orchestra.

Woody was in Pittsburgh with Arnheim when some friends

recommended him to Isham Jones, the bandleader and song-writer. Jones asked him to meet his band in Denver and to return with it to New York, where they'd be working at the Lincoln Hotel. Because of union regulations, Herman couldn't play for three months, so he sang. And when he wasn't singing, he'd crawl under the piano and play clarinet in the shadows.

Two years later, Jones quit the business, and Woody recruited the key sidemen for a new orchestra, which debuted on Election Eve 1936. The Band That Plays the Blues, as it was known, was actually a cooperative: "I was made leader because of my performance experience," Herman says. "All I was was a coach, and that's all I still am. But I'm a helluva coach. I watch pretty good musicians grow better from second to second." Working in a quasi-Dixieland style with soloists of limited ability and a book overloaded with novelties, the band was nonetheless popular with dancers—not least for the husky, guileless warmth of Herman's singing. The band made dozens of records, but recording for Decca at a time when the label assigned the best songs to Bing Crosby, Louis Armstrong, and Ella Fitzgerald meant that Woody was all too often stuck with the likes of "I Wanna Be in Winchell's Column" and "Big Wig in the Wigwam."

By keeping the accent on jazz (a credo from which he's never wavered), Herman built a loyal following—especially when, in 1939, he recorded a simple blues instrumental that he'd written with trumpeter Joe Bishop. "Woodchopper's Ball" took off slowly at first but eventually sold well over a million copies and became the calling card with which Herman was welcomed into countless communities; it's still the piece by which he's best known. Not too long ago, Woody and a few guys in the band finished a concert-dance in a small town in Iowa and repaired to the only late-night eatery. A grizzled Walter Brennan type hobbled in, leaned against the bar, surveyed the room, and noticed Woody and his men seated around a table. He couldn't take his eyes off Woody. He sat down at a neighboring table, never averting his stare from the bandleader, who continued to eat while his companions started elbowing one another. Finally, he dragged his chair to within inches of Herman's, straddling it backward and gazing right into his face. Woody put down his fork and said, "Can I help you, bud?" The old codger stood up, eyes lighting now with recognition, a conspiratorial smile transforming his weather-beaten face, and—socking Woody in the arm—shouted, " 'Woodchopper's Ball'!"

The draft killed off the Band That Plays the Blues, but in 1944 Herman organized a new band, his own; he says, "It was like coming into a new world." George Simon, a chronicler of the Swing Era with an ear for alliterative sobriquets, dubbed it Herman's Herd, perhaps trying to capture the quality that Herman described as the band's "wildness and blatancy." The First Herd was, for all its unbridled excitement, an ambitious, sophisticated organization, with advanced arrangers (Ralph Burns, Shorty Rogers, Neal Hefti), distinguished improvisors (Bill Harris, Sonny Berman, Red Norvo), a swaggering rhythm section (propelled by Dave Tough), an internal chamber group (the Woodchoppers), and the easygoing, immensely likable leader-clarinetist-alto sax-ophonist-singer. It sounded like no other band before or since, mixing swing conventions with Ellingtonisms and European orchestration techniques.

During this period Herman made a record with Ellington, "Cowboy Rhumba," and performed with him—"one of the highlights of my life"—at the 1946 Esquire Awards broadcast. Ellington was—and still is—Herman's greatest influence. "The joy, the abandon, the madness in our band—that's Duke's influence," he says. They became friends; Ellington especially liked hanging out with him at the house that Woody and his wife, Charlotte, bought from Humphrey Bogart in 1946 and still live in. Another friend was neighbor Igor Stravinsky, who, long before meeting Herman, wired him: "I have listened to your orchestra and I wish to write a piece for you as a Christmas gift. It will be delivered on . . ." Stravinsky's subtly orchestrated *Ebony Concerto,* complete with a very tricky clarinet part, was introduced at the First Herd's last major concert. In 1982 Herman was invited to play it at the Stravinsky centennial at La Scala.

Fearful of losing touch with his family, Herman decided to leave the road for a while in 1946. Seven months later, though, he was back with the Second Herd, an entirely different kind of band, reflecting the insurgency of bop and as distinctive as its predecessor. The hallmark of its sound was a four-man reed section consisting of three tenor saxophones and a baritone. After Jimmy Giuffre wrote a piece called "Four Brothers" to feature the reeds, the band became known by that name; among the Brothers were Zoot Sims, Stan Getz, Serge Chaloff, Al Cohn, and Gene Ammons. Although it is regarded today as one of jazz's most distinguished orchestras—several of its compositions are still requested nightly of Herman—it was a financial disaster at the time. When he folded the band in 1948, Herman had lost $175,000. But a year later he was back with a Third Herd, and there have been countless unnumbered Herds since.

Herman occupies a unique place among the handful of great bandleaders who survived the era that gave them life. Ellington is beyond time, and Ellingtonia is a language unto itself; Basie employs a variety of writers (including a few Herman alumni) but invariably stamps them with the Basie signature. Herman's Herds, however, have served in the role of a Greek chorus, commenting on, interpreting, and reworking the changes in jazz. Herman keeps up with fashions yet refuses to succumb to their excesses. His bands have been as distinct from one another as they have been from other outfits, but they've all been governed by Herman's sense of taste, proportion, and adventure. He disdains fusion and is appalled when gifted musicians leave his band to play sound tracks and jingles or compromise their individuality to play trash. He didn't stay on the road 46 years to compromise.

"I have faith in the music," he says. "It's no business. As a business, it's a big pain in the ass. You're victimized before you start, and it never lets up. There is no life time, there is no home. My biggest worry is that we mustn't reach a point of boredom." in this regard, he's in constant deadlock with his audience, which is forever demanding the old stuff; gauging each audience on its own, he decides on the bandstand how many classics he'll have to mix in with the new arrangements that are constantly turned out by the youngsters in the present band. "I guess I still see the public as the great unwashed from vaudeville days. If you don't bring the audience up by its bookstraps, it'll never come. So I play the old book for the people who come to hear it, but I prefer the new and experimental. I remember when Glenn Miller was playing the Pennsylvania Hotel, and I'd drop by and I'd notice the tempos were getting brighter and faster, so I asked him about it. Now this was Glenn Miller, a smart guy about business. He told me, 'Yeah, I don't want those mothers to dance, I want them to listen.' That says it all. Did you notice where the dance floor is here?" At Woody Herman's, a plush, Vegas-style room, the dance floor is off in a corner.

He first came to New Orleans in 1932, with Tom Gerun's band. "We played the Club Forest in Jefferson Parish, and Sidney Arodin, the New Orleans clarinetist, would take me on the bayous in his boat and we'd drink home brew and talk about music." Two years ago Woody became the first white Honorary Grand Marshal of the annual Zulu parade during Mardi Gras. When Louis Armstrong was asked to be Grand Marshal in 1949, Herman was touring with him, and he remembers how Armstrong was criticized for accepting because appearing in blackface is required. Times have changed. Woody's whole band was in blackface, and the sensation they caused was entirely favorable. As a result, he was asked to make his home in New Orleans, and the city fathers have done much to make him feel welcome. Still, Herman will keep his house in Los Angeles and tour during the summers. He's prouder of his 46 years of marriage—"a world's record for a jazz musician"—than of his 46 years as the Knute Rockne of Jazz, and he's not at all sure that time on the road hasn't been a contributing factor to his marital success.

2. A Fan's Fan

The bond I feel for Woody Herman has less to do with his plenary abilities as a musician and bandleader than with his constancy as a fan. As one fan listening to another, I sometimes feel presumptuous enough to imagine that I could do what he does—bring together a handful or more of good musicians, edit arrangements, program diverse sets, sing the blues, play some clarinet, and leaven it all with dry wit. But then I wonder if I'd have been willing to risk everything I'd achieved with swing 45 years ago on a tempestuous romance with bop; and I marvel at the energy and discretion with which he returned from a pool of red ink to take on every wave, musical and otherwise, that jazz could hurl at him during the next four decades.

There are few enough fans who've been able to crest jazz's furious mutability with anything resembling confidence, and even fewer musicians. Name another living bandleader who can in one set play completely idiomatic pieces that draw on swing, bop, balladry, third stream, and modality—pieces that the bandleaders themselves made famous. Nothing musical fazes Herman, except fusion, which he tinkered with briefly and then rejected adamantly. For every Herman record I love, there are two or three I'd be happy to forget, and it's true that some of his bands suffer the sterility one associates with college lab recruits. But somehow he always cuts through the glossy sheen, and the things he believes in—freshness, spontaneity, swing, humor—he sticks to. What's more, he charms his audience without catering to it; knowing that most of his fans would be satisfied with his golden oldies, he lulls them into submission with one or two only to knock them bolt upright with a half-crazed confection that some 23-year-old third trumpeter came up with.

These are troubled times for Herman. Within one week in November, he lost both the New Orleans nightclub that was meant to be a lifetime respite from roadwork, and, more tragically, his wife of 46 years. Yet somehow he managed to summon the spirit to bring a rollicking sextet into Fat Tuesday's last week, plying every trick he ever learned or invented to make his music completely absorbing measure for measure. In the last few years, he's added a tagline to many of his performances; after playing a piece with which he's been associated for ages, he says with irreproachable finality, "That's the way it was." He led the band handily through the various shadows of his past, bopping "Lemon Drop" ("I got hung up with [bop] because I thought if everyone could sound like Bird, there ain't nothing wrong with that"), crooning "Laura," stomping the blues, cleaning up the minstrelsy of "Caldonia" (no vocal until the coda), and egging on his splendid cohorts. From the earlier bands, he had Jake Hanna, probably Herman's best drummer ever after Dave Tough, and Sal Nistico, an indefatigable roof-raising tenorist. From the current Herd, he had pianist and arranger John Oddo (who wrote some of the charts for Dameronia), bassist Dave Shapiro, and trumpeter George Rabbai, who convincingly combines aspects of Armstrong and Clark Terry in his style though he is unfortunately allowed to do a very bad Armstrong vocal impression.

Herman was in good humor, listening and cheering more than he played. In a small group like this it's especially evident how much he instigates and inspires the action. For me, the most surprising aspect of his performance was the credibility of his singing on a blues and on "Laura" ("If you're an old alcoholic," he said after the ballad, "that's the way it was"). Herman made his best vocal album in tandem with Erroll Garner about 30 years ago, but he doesn't sing much anymore, and the steely glint in his voice was unexpected. It's time for another vocal album. The only disappointing element in the set was that Nistico, playing well when he had the chance, seemed subdued; when Nistico plants his feet and starts hammering choruses at you, there's no looking away. Rabbai proved adept with Harmon and plunger mutes; Shapiro strummed the bass ("He thinks he's Freddie Green," Herman said); Oddo introduced versions of "Have You Met Miss Jones" and "After Hours" ("You don't sound like Avery Parrish," Herman told him, "but you sound good"); Hanna, who gets a marvelously elegant sound from his ride cymbal, floated them all; and Herman was sufficiently encouraged to take up his alto for a wistful chorus of "Early Autumn."

A new record, *Live at the Concord Jazz Festival* (Concord Jazz

191), tells part of the tale. There are guest performances by Al Cohn and Stan Getz, solid new charts by Oddo and the veteran Bill Holman, a smattering of Ellington and bop. Only a workmanlike arrangement of "You Are So Beautiful" suggests academic glossiness. It's Herman's best big band album in several years, brightly performed and recorded, and—like the set at Fat Tuesday's—additional evidence that while everyone pays lip service to Louis Armstrong, Herman really learned something from him. "Make the people happy," Armstrong used to say, "that's all we're trying to do." Think that's corny? Not me. A good fan is hard to find.

(September/December 1982)

Clarinets on Top

Let us now praise rehearsals, those dreary rituals frequently avoided in jazz, where men are men and spontaneity disguises disorganization. During the recent Clarinet Summit concert at the Public Theater, Jimmy Hamilton remarked that he'd played more in the preceding four days than in the 14 years since he left Duke Ellington and turned to teaching in the Virgin Islands. It showed, it showed. A quartet of clarinetists performing together for the first time and representing three generations of a music in which their instrument peaked 45 years ago, brought off a strenuously ambitious program almost without a hitch. In fact, my quibbles can be dispensed with in three quick jabs: (1) tempos on some of the older pieces flagged; (2) the absence of solos in most of Hamilton's arrangements was regrettable; (3) the very long and complicated closing selection, by Alvin Batiste, would have seemed less enervating if placed earlier in the program—1:30 a.m. is time for lullabies.

The original intention of Hamilton, Batiste, John Carter, and David Murray was to include 30 minutes of original music by each. Compromises had to be made, but the concert was nonetheless a triumph of preparation; the players were heard in solos, duets, trios, and quartets, and the stylistic variety was consistently absorbing. Things went so smoothly that it was easy to forget that history was being made on two counts. To my knowledge and to that of the musicians, this was the first concert built entirely around a clarinet quartet. On a more parochial level, the collaboration of four such diverse jazzmen represented a triumph of pan-generationalism. Not once during 13 pieces and nearly three hours could I detect oil nudging water; Hamilton played Carter's and Batiste's music as authoritatively as Murray played his.

Excepting his surprise appearance with Mercer Ellington at the Kool Festival a couple of years ago, I'd never seen Hamilton other than with Ellington senior. For 26 years, he represented the most schizoid voice in the Ellington orchestra, playing ethereal clarinet (in contrast to his earthier bandmate Russell Procope) and, too infrequently, funky-butt tenor saxophone. Ellington seemed to feature his two clarinetists ever more persistently in the 1960s, when the instrument was otherwise neglected, and Hamilton recorded what was perhaps his most poetic statement in the 1966 "Ad Lib on Nippon." So it was fitting that Hamilton's contributions to the Clarinet Summit evening were largely Ducal—"Creole Love Song," "Mood Indigo," and "Jeep's Blues," as well as originals ("Waltz a Minute," "Night Mist Blues") richly colored by the Ellington palette. Somewhere along the way, he developed into a charming arranger, succinct and unpretentious, and his four-part harmonizations gave familiar melodies—including "Groovin' High" (a tribute to Hamilton's friend and bandmate in the 1930s, Dizzy Gillespie)—an engaging old-world lilt.

On most of these pieces, he eschewed improvisation. He compensated, however, with the wittiest playing of the evening in two

duets with Batiste, who rivals John Carter in his absolutely astonishing lack of recognition. They transcended and transformed two
of the moldiest of standards—"Honeysuckle Rose" and "Satin
Doll"—with follow-the-leader ingenuity, rephrasing and reharmonizing the themes, injecting jocular quotations, and trying their
damnedest to trick each other up. The emotional, ebullient Batiste noted that he'd always idolized Hamilton but had never met
him, and there was an air of respectful yet determined elation in
the challenges he threw down. During the evening's first piece,
which sounded like a Carter original, there were passages for a
Carter-Murray duet and for a Hamilton-Batiste duet, and the
latter suggested something of the Hamilton-Procope frisson in
timbre and feeling.

I've concentrated on Hamilton because his appearance was so
rare, but I'm being unfair to the others. Murray, who played bass
clarinet throughout (the others stayed with the usual B-flat instrument), demonstrated exemplary control in the written passages and contributed apt obligati to the Ellington themes. His
unaccompanied solo, opening and closing with tremolos that explored the clarinet's unusual system of partials, combined introverted fury with a melodicism that was in places almost girlishly
delicate; employing full range and dynamics, he achieved a rearing sort of majesty at the apex of his performance. Another
highlight was Carter's unaccompanied prelude to his "Ballad for
Four Clarinets," which began with a single pitch that, through
careful use of circular breathing, achieved broad coloration before exploding into multiphonics and then receding into the pastoral timbre reminiscent of a recorder. The four-part voicings were
handsomely conceived and executed. Batiste's aforementioned
finale combined pages of written music with solos and duets which,
at this point, seemed repetitive; yet his opening solo progressed
measurably from economic blues phrases strongly reminiscent of
Jimmie Noone to a feisty borrowing from Coltrane's "Chasin' the
Trane."

Other than Murray, these clarinetists have spent much of the
past decade teaching. Hamilton, of course, had a long public ca

reer, and Carter has managed to get a few records out; Batiste has rarely been heard outside of Louisiana since he briefly toured with Cannonball Adderley in the early '70s. It's a sign of the times that some of jazz's most accomplished thinkers are content to be stay-at-homes, no longer regarding New York as the Mecca that justifies their art. And it's a sign of these musicians' seriousness that when they do come to Mecca they are well prepared.*

(December 1982)

Virtuoso Entertainment

The inspired teaming of Jaki Byard and Eric Kloss at the Village West last week was more than a meeting of minds; it was a corrective. Kloss's most recent record, *Sharing* (Omnisound N-1044), is so steeped in narcissistic lyricism—one piece is actually dedicated to James Taylor—that it makes you want to cook brown rice and do good deeds. This is music for the monastery run by Keith Jarrett and bears little resemblance to such deliriously virtuosic inventions as Kloss's alto solo on the 1969 "So What" (to pick one of several examples). What it needs, in addition to rhythmic vitamins, is a sense of humor, urban irreverence, a thumbed nose—in other words, Jaki Byard, who on his current album, *To Them—To Us* (Soul Note SN 1025), radiantly transforms a song he dislikes, Mangione's "Land of Make Believe," because he reasoned with characteristic perversity that so popular a song ought to be made likable. Together at the Village West,

---

*Two years later, highlights from the concert were released on record as *Clarinet Summit in Concert at the Public Theater* (India Navigation IN-1062).

sparking each other with bravura and wit, they were like-minded and enthralling.

Byard is 27 years older than Kloss, who's been recording since he was 16, but they share some history. Between 1966 and 1969, they made three Prestige albums under Kloss's leadership: *Grits and Gravy, Sky Shadows,* and *In the Land of the Giants* (which includes Booker Ervin and the remarkable "So What"). Byard's fabled eclecticism, which by now must bore him to read about, has long since yielded an indigenous, insoluable style in which stride and bop and clusters are less bemused affectations than tools to make improvisations engaging and lucid. Kloss's immense technique enables him to exploit various jazz styles as well, and not by stealing a lick from this player or that, but by adapting the obvious aspects—harmonic and rhythmic—of those styles. On "C-Jam Blues," Kloss opened on soprano with some spacey flurries, preceding an orthodox swing statement of the theme, followed by a two-beat Dixieland episode, with Byard pumping some Jelly Roll bass figures. This was modestly clever. The performance achieved something special, however, when they began to alternate four-bar passages of free jazz (albeit not so free as to be uncountable) and the Dixie two-beat. The contrast between the beginning and end of jazz, rather than the rapprochement between the two that avant-gardists often aim for, enhanced both. To modernist ears, Dixieland lost the stigma of old-timeyness; to traditionalist ears, new music became accessible.

In somewhat similar manner, they enlivened all the material of the set. Byard used a Stevie Wonder ballad, "Send One Your Love," as the introduction to Coltrane's "Giant Steps," and managed to inject Harlem stride into the subsequent solo. He accompanied Kloss's searing variation on "You Don't Know What Love Is" with plush arpeggios out of a '40s cocktail lounge, then switched suddenly to brash dissonant chords that marched across the keyboard with the effect of a bass walk. Kloss's extraordinarily vivid projection gave "Sharing" an immediacy absent from the record; Byard's comping was a temperate zone, but Kloss sliced the air with slurs and cries.

Among the highlights were two unaccompanied numbers. Byard chose "European Episode," which he used to play at the opening of Mingus concerts; it's a funny montage of polka, stride, two-beat, swing, bop, and waltz rhythms, permitting apposite quotations and the-hands-are-quicker-than-the-ears transitions. Kloss made the "Cosmic Blues" a tour de force that never sacrificed emotion for technique—a cliché that means something when this much technique is employed, including circular breathing, split-tones, abrupt dynamics, hand-clapped cross-rhythms, and a chordal intonation that mimicked the sound of his voice (and reminded one listener of the fuzz-tone on Jimi Hendrix's guitar). Kloss has always had an original approach, but his affection for pop music—he's recorded songs by Donovan and Joni Mitchell—often brings out a sentimentality in his work that the presence of strong jazz personalities (Byard, Pat Martino, Hannibal, DeJohnette) mitigates. He and Byard should record together alone.

In the meantime, Byard's new album, his first solo date in a decade, is mostly splendid, including impressionistic originals, two Ellington themes, three contemporary pop tunes (even "Ode to Billy Joe" is freshened, though the tough ostinato and furiously whirling phrases that come just short of snapping the harmonic boundaries of "Land of Make Believe" are the real triumph in transcendence), and a blues older than he is ("Tin Roof Blues"). There's a new economy in Byard's music. Themes are reduced to their essentials; chords and modulations are dramatically emphasized; and the improvisations proceed logically from the written material. He never merely skitters through chord changes. No one else could think of the careful variations with which he rebuilds "Solitude," or manipulate the quietly lambent stride of "To Them—To Us," or get away with the jerky lockstep of "Tin Roof Blues." He gives entertainment a good name.

(January 1983)

Motor City Classicist

Ten years ago, Onyx Records reissued a 1961 Dave Bailey session as Tommy Flanagan's *Trio and Sextet*. The commercial wisdom of putting the pianist above the title is clearer now than it was then, since few people are likely to recall that Bailey, the president of Jazzmobile, Inc., was once an accomplished drummer, whereas everybody knows Flanagan. At the time, however, the decision had more to do with the producer Don Schlitten's determination to see that there was at least one record in Schwann listed under Flanagan's name—the only one recorded between 1960 and 1975. The pianist has more than made up for lost time, having released 14 albums as leader and many more as a sideman in the past seven years; each of his two current offerings is up for a Grammy. Last week, at Lush Life, he crashed another gate. With Rufus Reid and Billy Higgins, the Tommy Flanagan Trio played its first New York nightclub gig in more than 20 years.

Part of the reason for Flanagan's elusiveness is that he spent 10 years as accompanist to Ella Fitzgerald, and part of the reason for his reemergence is the renewed interest in bebop piano. Flanagan is one of five extremely gifted pianists who came out of the Detroit area spellbound by the music of Bud Powell. The oldest is Hank Jones, born in 1918, who absorbed the stylings of the key '30s pianists (Tatum, Wilson, Waller) before arriving in New York in 1944 and falling under the influence of Powell and Al Haig; the others—Flanagan, Barry Harris, Roland Hanna, and Hugh Lawson—were all born between 1929 and 1935. Each is a true stylist, easily distinguished from the rest; if they didn't share

similar background, I'd be no more disposed to labeling them—
the MC5, as it were—than I would be to call certain southwestern tenors Southwestern Tenors. Yet time even more than cir-
cumstance has given them a unifying aura; in the 1980s, they
practically monopolize classical bop piano. If you were looking
for a pianist for an all-star '40s or '50s ensemble, you'd almost
certainly choose John Lewis or one of the MC5. Of course, they
have a lot of playing experience in common, in addition to influ-
encing each other, reverencing Powell, Monk, Tatum, and Garner, and working with the modernists of their generation. Jones
and Flanagan accompanied Fitzgerald (and recorded duets with
each other); Jones and Hanna worked with the Benny Goodman
and Jones-Lewis orchestras; Hanna and Lawson served time with
Mingus; Lawson and Harris became known through associations
with Yusef Lateef; and Harris, Jones, and Flanagan were among
the preferred pianists of Coleman Hawkins.

Something else binds them: they belong to that species of musician that gets better with years. Granted, gauging whether or
not a musician's career is an ascending arc is often perilous. We
believe Bach, Mozart, and Beethoven got better, but their contemporaries weren't so sure; maybe in a hundred years people
will think Strauss, Stravinsky, and Copland got better too. The
verdict on jazz musicians is often modified, usually upwards. Still,
I don't imagine there will be much resistance to the idea that each
of the MC5 is a more exciting and deeper musician today than
he was 20 years ago. They haven't survived so handsomely into
the '80s simply because the ranks have thinned. Whereas once
they were merely (merely!) accomplished players trying to make
a space for themselves in the crowded field of modern jazz, they
now survive as comprehensive stylists with unusually large rep-
ertoires and decisive attacks. As unembarrassed by time as their
early work is (Hank Jones's solo recital for Savoy qualifies as a
masterpiece), each recorded a disproportionate number of his best
performances in the '70s and '80s. They are better not only for
accepting new challenges but for refining their proven skills.

They've chosen incisiveness instead of technique, melody instead of fashion, clarity instead of obscurity.

Flanagan took a midlife risk in the '70s, moving from the safe shadows of the accompanist into the vague spotlight provided by piano bars and foreign record labels. The 1975 album that signaled his return to leadership, *Tokyo Recital,* a tribute to Strayhorn and Ellington, demonstrated his remarkable perspicacity in choosing material. At Lush Life with his exceptional accompanists, he concentrated on jazz pieces that would be standards if more musicians were willing to tackle them. In one set, he remodeled Monk's "Pannonica" and "Friday the 13th," Strayhorn's "Chelsea Bridge" and "Star-Crossed Lovers," Coltrane's "Syeeda's Song Flute," Parker's "Barbados," and Ellington's "Single Petal of a Rose." I've never heard some of them played by anyone but Flanagan and the composer. In several instances, he sidled into the melody with a discursive introduction of the sort Erroll Garner invented; in every instance, he achieved that essential balancing act in which the composition and the embellishments enhance each other, and the improvisation emerges sensibly and forcefully. Billy Higgins emboldened him, and it will be hard to settle for hearing Flanagan with just a bassist in the future.

Of the two most recent Flanagan records, his homage to Coltrane, *Giant Steps* (Enja 4022), is a wholly compelling, lucid, and deeply considered tribute to the saxophonist, with whom Flanagan originally recorded four of the six compositions. The authority he exhibits here was only hinted at on the seminal 1959 album of the same name. Accompanied by George Mraz and Al Foster, his fingers fly through the blues choruses of "Mr. P.C." and "Cousin Mary," his harmonic imagination faces up to the daunting chords of "Giant Steps," and his deliberate, articulate way with a ballad demystifies "Naima" and "Central Park West." In demonstrating the sturdiness of Coltrane's writing, Flanagan also proves the versatility of bop piano. *The Magnificent Tommy Flanagan* (Progressive 7059), again with Mraz and Foster, is a congenial trio date highlighted by some characteristically resourceful ballad reassessments ("Good Morning, Heartache," "Change Partners," and "I Fall in Love Too Easily" are standouts). Still, not even *Giant Steps* is as consistently mesmerizing as the Lush Life set was. Maybe he's gotten better even during the past few months.

(February 1983)

Stan Getz's Transfusion

Fusion, like the common cold, is a debilitating illness for which the only certain cure is time. Although the physiological symptoms are well known (stuffed rhythms, runny intonation, bloodshot melodies), the psychological ones are even more piteous, as witness the gifted musicians who, during the plague years of the 1970s, donned funny hats to play unspeakable clichés. I'm referring, of course, not to natural fusions—American music is, at bottom, an alloy of hybrids—but to those sugary studio contrivances in which the victim succumbs first to such relatively harmless narcotics as a Fender Rhodes and later, in the final stages of the disease, to deadly doses of preservatives (usually injected through overdubbing). The saddest casualties were the mature musicians, since they had the most to lose, and one of the more unlikely of these was Stan Getz, a superb melodist who's sustained a popular following for almost 40 years. Getz's bout, culminating in the delirium of *Children of the World*, proved relatively mild, however, and his recovery in the '80s has the glow of a personal renaissance.

Fittingly, perhaps, the piece that best demonstrates his re-

newed powers, or at least his determination to perform in an idiom he trusts, is Billy Strayhorn's "Blood Count." He recorded it
for his current album, *Pure Getz* (Concord Jazz CJ-188), and played
it nightly at his recent engagement at Fat Tuesday's. "Blood
Count" is hardly an unlikely vehicle for Getz; it was composed
by one romantic, Strayhorn, for another, Johnny Hodges, and
Getz is as much a romanticist as they. Indeed, his deeply personal performance comes to some of the same conclusions about
the music as Hodges's, though not in a way that makes me sur-
mise direct influence. A little background may be helpful. Strayhorn, perhaps the most underappreciated songwriter in American music (only his first song, "Lush Life," has the currency of a
standard), was Duke Ellington's closest collaborator from 1939
until his death in 1967. "Blood Count," completed in the hospi-
tal during his last months, was the last in a series of dreamy yet
powerful miniatures designed to feature the alto saxophone of
Hodges. Apparently, it was untitled when Ellington first began
performing it, during a European tour in February and March
of 1967. He introduced it as "Manuscript," when the band presented the piece at Carnegie Hall in late March (a performance
subsequently issued on Pablo's *The Greatest Jazz Concert in the World*).
Strayhorn passed away in May, and in August Ellington recorded a memorial album, *And His Mother Called Him Bill* (RCA),
including a definitive "Blood Count" that is one of the period's
insuperable jazz masterpieces.

Jazz is no less collaborative than cinema, and credit for the
perfection of the August "Blood Count" can be passed around
to the writer (Strayhorn), the director (Ellington), and the star
(Hodges). Possibly because the performance *is* definitive, in emotional resonance as well as execution, the song was laid to rest.
Neither Ellington nor Hodges ever played it again, and the album—one of the band's best—disappeared so fast it became pre-
maturely legendary. Not until the '80s were the only two subsequent interpretations of "Blood Count" recorded. Jimmy Rowles,
a Strayhorn diehard, created an ingenious piano reduction for

his 1981 album, *Jimmy Rowles Plays Duke Ellington and Billy Stray-horn* (Columbia), and Getz followed several months later with his *Pure Getz* version.

Getz says that when he recorded the piece he had only a lead-sheet to go by, having been unaware of the recordings with Hodges. Considering the penchant both saxophonists share for extreme dynamics, it comes as no surprise to find Getz balancing his phrases with meticulous attention to intonation and volume. The most poignant episode is his forte-piano treatment of the release, which, unlike Hodges, Getz plays only once. It's a sub-lime exercise in equilibrium, an evenly calculated montage of roaring cries and quiescent moans. The phrases (each only two or three notes) couldn't be more economical as he alternates them loud and soft, concluding with a two-note figure that, repeated three times, makes for a seamless transition into the next epi-sode. Interestingly, Hodges opted for a forte-piano treatment of the release for the Carnegie Hall performance (which is marred by a slightly rushed tempo and insensitive drumming), but re-jected it for the more expansive studio recording. Hodges's de-cision was right for him, as it increased the songfulness of his interpretation. And Getz's was right for him, as it underscores the turmoil that animates his introspection. The other changes are also relevant. In the Ellington arrangement, "Blood Count" was 56 measures (AABABAC); Getz excised the second AB. Hodges consigned his intimations of the blues to subtle glissandi, whereas Getz uses vivid blues cadences as well as a two-note stut-ter phrase near the close.

With "Blood Count," Getz joins the relatively small group of jazz stylists who can lay personal claim to material by sole virtue of their interpretive integrity. Like Hodges, Ben Webster, Pee Wee Russell, Art Tatum, Miles Davis, and a handful of others, he doesn't have to improvise variations to make his point. He dem-onstrated this capacity to look at a song from the inside out in the first recording that made him famous, Woody Herman's "Early Autumn," but that was a fragment of a solo, and the ballad per-formances for which Getz was acclaimed in later years were as notable for the facility of his variations as the sensuousness of his sound. "Blood Count" isn't the only example of Getz's new economy. At Kool last summer, he stopped the concert tribute to Alec Wilder cold with his impassioned reading of another swan song, Wilder's "A Long Night."

On the other hand, he is no less volatile an improvisor. Nor is he any less volatile in his demeanor. At Fat Tuesday's, where Getz was reunited with Albert Dailey and Victor Lewis and joined by George Mraz, patrons at a ringside table persisted in talking through a couple of numbers. The saxophonist asked them to leave, which, in an obnoxious manner, they did. When Getz asserts his rights as an artist, he takes a stand, consciously or not, for all the musicians who aren't in as enviable a position of power. The audience applauded his truculence, and he calmed himself down with a vigorous performance of "Confirmation," righteous with stabbing glissandi and register-climbing broadsides; by contrast, Lewis's drum solo was entirely thematic. Getz has just recorded an album of duets with Dailey, and he allotted the pianist several unaccompanied features, of which the most notable was a richly chordal "Round Midnight." (Amazing how that tune continues to inspire fresh variations. Still, it's become Monk's "Lush Life"—his other ballads are rarely heard.) For the rest, Getz played uptempo standards, jazz originals, and an occasional bossa nova—exemplifying a *natural* fusion.

There is, in addition to *Pure Getz*, another new release by the tenorist. *The Master* (Columbia FC 38272) was recorded in 1975, but never released—not because it wasn't good enough, but because it was too good (no kidding). As I understand it, Columbia signed Getz to give him a shot of fusion, so rather than releasing a solid quartet session of considerable vivacity, they released *Captain Marvel*, a humdrum quartet session with Chick Corea's electric piano. *Captain Marvel* had been sitting in the vault since 1972. Soon he was encumbered with Brazilian guitars, synthesizer, and *Evita*, and soon he was off the label; his best work in this period was the lovely collaboration with Jimmy Rowles *(The Peacocks)* and, we now learn, a fine quartet session. It's probably a good thing

The Master (an unfortunate title) didn't come out in 1975, when it would have been taken for granted. Now that Getz has survived his tango with smart producers, we can treasure it as supplementary evidence to *Pure Getz* that the master was up and about even when we thought he had the fusion.

(February 1983)

Hard Again

Hard bop is a useful adjective, as in "he has a hard bop band" or "he plays hard bop tenor," but hardly anybody as a kind word for it as a genre. To many people, hard bop is simply music played by the bands of Art Blakey and Horace Silver or by any musician who ever apprenticed with Art Blakey and Horace Silver. Even in its heyday, the 1950s, it was regarded as ordinary mainstream modernism, limited in instrumentation, repertoire expressiveness, and ambition. The very word "hard" suggested something loud and implacable, and nary a tear was shed when hard bop was eclipsed first by avant-gardism and later by bebop revivalism. Oh sure, occasionally a couple of Silver alumni would get a gig and a few fans would mutter nostalgically, "gee . . . hard bop." But you've never heard anyone clamor for a hard bop festival; no one asks, "Will hard bop ever come back?" Yet lately, hard bop seems to have done just that—come back.

I report this phenomenon with some trepidation since I'm not entirely certain what hard bop is. When it was burgeoning, hard bop was more easily identified by what it wasn't. It wasn't cool or white or from California. As for cool, you might say that hard boppers seemed to think that healthy vibrato was a sign of virility. There were a few worthy white hard boppers (Pepper Adams, Joe Farrell, Joe Zawinul), but only a few; in fact, hard bop was even more solidly black than cool jazz was white. Cannonball Adderley never ceased proclaiming how black Zawinul sounded, and when, a decade later, Silver and Blakey began turning up with white front lines, it was taken as a sign of the genre's final death rattle. Hard bop was decidedly urban and industrial, the jazz of New York, Philadelphia, Detroit, and Chicago. It was as much a retort to the harmonic complexity and received ideas of bebop as it was to the enervating lyricism of West Coast jazz. It was a functional music at a time when the long-playing record was encouraging longer solos (hard boppers could go on all night), when rhythm and blues was tweaking jazz for its loss of soul (let's not forget that Ray Charles had one of the best hard bop bands of the '50s), and when bandstands were shrinking (a hard bop band almost always comprised trumpet, tenor, piano, bass, and drums, except when it added trombone or another saxophone).

For a while, it was assumed that any black East Coast quintet with a Sonny Rollins-influenced tenor and a penchant for funky blues was hard bop. (It might be useful to point out here that when Horace Silver popularized "funk" as a musical term he did not have George Clinton in mind.) Soon it became evident that there was hard bop and post bop. The distinction is fuzzy. Miles Davis's great quintet met all the implied and explicit definitions of hard bop yet transcended it; Jimmy Heath incorporated cool instruments (French horn, flute) in complicated compositions yet came up with fanciful hard bop. The Clifford Brown–Max Roach Quintet was too boppish to be hard boppish, but the High Priest of Bop, Thelonious Monk, suggested ultrahard bop in recordings like "Jackieing" and "Brilliant Corners." Charlie Mingus yelled at everybody to stop copying Bird, but since he didn't really mean it, he tended to rage to the right and left of hard bop. Cecil Taylor, who never bopped, took hard bop into the space age with "Bulbs." We could play this game all day.

By the early '60s, hard bop was often confused with soul jazz, which could usually be identified by food titles such as "Greasy

Greens," "Grits and Gravy," and "Cornbread." But the best soul jazz tunes—Silver's "Song for My Father" (which James Brown covered), Bobby Timmons's "Moanin' "—were substantive springboards for improvisation, and hard bop continued through about 1965 as a familial alternative to the New Jazz. Herbie Hancock never played hard bop with Miles Davis, but for his first date as a leader, he not only put together a hard bop quintet but composed the best-known food tune, "Watermelon Man." Freddie Hubbard, on the other hand, left Blakey to try his hand with Coleman, Coltrane, and Dolphy and proved that his soul would always be in mortgage to the Jazz Messengers. Even Sam Rivers flirted with hard bop for his Blue Note debut, but then Blue Note was to hard bop what Oxford is to dictionaries.

If there is one generating force in what appears to be a revival of hard bop it must surely be Art Blakey, who, since discovering the Marsalis brothers, has been enjoying his biggest roll in 20 years; he's probably graduated more good musicians in the '80s than Texas State. Whenever Hubbard descends from cloud-cuckoo land to play a joint, he's got a hard bop band. Now that Jimmy Heath has temporarily lost his brother to the reconstituted Modern Jazz Quartet, he's hooked up with fellow hard bop veteran Slide Hampton. I had hoped to hear them at the Highlights in Jazz concert last week, but Hampton had to cancel, and the resultant jam (with Red Rodney, Pepper Adams, Howard Johnson, Billy Taylor) leaned closer to bop than hard bop. It occurred to me that one reason hard bop has suffered as a recognizable genre is that its book has dwindled into obscurity, while the compositions of Monk, Parker, and Dameron (which dominated the program) were widely rediscovered in the '70s. Still, at the close of the first set, Billy Taylor made a little speech about one of the most underrated jazz composers by way of introducing Horace Silver's "Nica's Dream"—admittedly more bop than hard, but another sign of rediscovery. Jimmy Heath, Wayne Shorter, Cedar Walton, and Benny Golson, as well as Silver and Timmons, have written dozens of pieces that could withstand renewed scrutiny.

The most refreshing hard bop sound I've heard live in the past few weeks came from the reunited Jazztet, a band originally co-founded by Benny Golson and Art Farmer in 1959. At Fat Tuesday's, playing for an audience that still remembered "Killer Joe" and "Whisper Not," the sextet included trombonist Curtis Fuller and the first-class rhythm section of pianist Mickey Tucker (a preternatural hard bopping successor to Silver), bassist Ray Drummond, and drummer Albert Heath. Heath was the soul of the band, with his dashing ride cymbal and geometric precision, and the soloists were sufficiently diverse to remove the stigma from the inevitable string-of-solos that cheapen so much small-band jazz. The band had a keening momentum, a brute force, that now seems trim and clear compared to, say, McCoy Tyner, who debuted with the Jazztet and whose rise once made hard bop seem provincial. Farmer's pressence on flugelhorn injected simmering lyricism, and Golson made sure everybody paid attention to the details of his compositions.

A few current hard bop records have also come as a tonic. Ricky Ford has been a promising tenor player for so long that it's a relief to finally have an album, *Interpretations* (Muse 5275), in which his compositional ambitions are perfectly matched to his authority as a soloist. Ford has gone into the heart of hard bop structuralism, the AABA pop song, and like Monk and Silver he's expanded it to challenge the soloists. The three sextet selections are daring because each interpreter (Ford, John Hicks, Robert Watson, Wallace Roney) has to watch his footing or perish in the ongoing changes. "Interpretations Opus 5" has a 14-measure bridge that affects the players much as Monk's "Criss Cross" (with its six-bar bridge) would; every time the soloist gets to the end of the release, you think he's going to slip off the precipice. "Fix or Repair Daily" forces them to construct 19-measure choruses, and, if some of the resolutions are tenuous, how refreshing that tenuousness is compared to the eight-bar licks that a player like Ford could reel off in a coma.

Steppin' Into Beauty (SteepleChase 1158) is not the Hilton Ruiz revelation we've been waiting for, but the three quintet pieces have a splendid Silverian punch. Pharoah Sanders's "Origin" consists of two nine-bar phrases which Frank Foster and Ruiz negotiate with near-arrogant confidence, and "The Last Profit," by the former Silver drummer, Roy Brooks, is built on a Cape Verdean vamp and concludes with Brooks altering the pitch of his drums by blowing into a connected hose. The album was made in 1977, and trumpeter Richard Williams's stiff phrasing and lack of ideas is deadly, but Foster (very Tranelike) and Ruiz are juggernauts. Benny Powell's *Coast to Coast* (Trident 507) compares West Coast and East Coast proclivities; side one, recorded in Los Angeles, employs the same instrumentation as side two, recorded in New York, but the former offers polyphony ("Pennies from Heaven") and balladic expansiveness ("Infant Eyes"), while the latter combines teeming unison ("The Highest Mountain") with a brusque undercurrent ("Lifelong Dreams"). Powell's trombone glides effortlessly in both situations, but New York gave him sharper support in Clifford Jordan and Mickey Tucker. (Both drummers—L.A.'s Donald Bailey and N.Y.'s Vernel Fournier—are smashing.) Hard bop is probably as limited and relentless as its detractors always said it was, but at its best it feels like the right stuff, and with the neoclassicists sorting through every other facet of jazz history, I'm pleased to see the original funk coming into its own again.

(March 1983)

The Jazz Singer

Jazz singing, a specialized dimension of jazz for which my passion is generally unsatisfied, has brought me numberless hours of sheer masochism: the white girls who think Annie Ross is the quintessence of hip, the black girls who think Aretha Franklin's melisma will indemnify any expression of soul; the women of both races who perform in period costume because jazz singing for them is a show of nostalgia, a kind of Dixieland of the larynx. (The boys/men of the decade are hardly worthy of mention.) Jazz singing stopped regenerating itself about 20 years ago, and it's not hard to see why. The great jazz singers of the previous 40 years were as stylistically wedded to their eras as the instrumentalists who improvised alongside of them. Billie Holiday and Lester Young spoke the same language; so did Sarah Vaughan and Charlie Parker. In the '60s, jazz jettisoned Tin Pan Alley and didn't offer much encouragement to singers; in order to keep up, they had to yodel or bellow or chant about peace and love. No wonder most talented young singers joined Aretha's church.

The results in the '70s were dismaying. In theaters and cabarets, young singers interpreted Ellington and Waller, Ethel Waters and Eubie Blake as though their songs had been conceived for the liturgy. The authentic, winnowed tribe of jazz singers experienced a renaissance—with veteran Betty Carter emerging as the baby of the group—but produced no distinguished offspring, only Manhattan Transfers and soulful lounge lizards. Twice in the past decade, I thought I heard an exception. First, there was Dee Dee Bridgewater, who demonstrated with the Thad Jones–Mel Lewis Orchestra and on several diverse recording projects that she could sing anything, but who opted for disco. Then there was Bobby McFerrin, whom I've by no means given up on, though his debut album collapsed under the overweening desire to please everybody.* Dwight Macdonald used to complain that his every knock was a boost; for me, every boost brings a sell-out. So it's with some trepidation that I call your attention to an authentic young jazz singer named Carmen Lundy. Nevertheless: She's got it all.

*McFerrin's second album, *The Voice* (Musician 60366-1-E), released in 1984, so thoroughly fulfills his promise, that I take this opportunity to recommend it unreservedly. Lundy, however, had still not recorded by mid-'84.

I heard Lundy about five years ago at Jazzmania Society, shortly after she arrived here from Florida, and I left in the middle of her set. When I encountered her again several weeks ago, I was knocked out not only by her vitality as a singer and the variety of her repertoire, but by her startling authority as a performer. I went back to hear five or six sets—at Greene Street, Seventh Avenue South, and Swing Plaza—and I wasn't the only one; at twenty-eight, Lundy has picked up a cult on the New York circuit. She's studied long and hard, and the most significant indication of how much she's accomplished is that she obviates the most troublesome question associated with jazz singing in the '80s: how do you make it musically relevant and immediate? You don't ask that question watching her. From the moment she struts onstage, shimmying and smiling, she's in complete control of her material. There's a trace of Vaughan here and of Carter there (especially in her movements), but those influences have been assimilated. Lundy is a contemporary, a rocker (post-Aretha and post-Stevie Wonder), but in the sophistication with which she launches tempos, the harmonic inventiveness with which she improvises, and the unselfconscious brightness with which she projects her voice, free of excessive melisma and undistorted by glottal thrusts, she is thoroughly and enchantingly a jazz singer.

What's more, she has a terrific trio. Her Teddy Wilson is Harry Whitaker, who used to accompany Roberta Flack; he paces Lundy with spare, percussive chords, occasionally weaving them into contrapuntal phrases without getting in her way. The drummer J.J. Lewis and the bassist Stanley Banks, who uses his foot to swivel a tambourine against a floor mike, provide a full and heady scrim, not unlike Betty Carter's trios. Lundy, long-limbed and rangy, stalks restlessly before them, choreographing the beat, and selling the songs not to the ether but—here's an old-fashioned aesthetic—to the audience. The material includes revamped standards ("The Lamp Is Low," "I Got It Bad," "I Didn't Know What Time It Was"), contemporary pieces (Wonder's "If It's Magic," Al Jarreau's "We Got By"), and originals ("Love Me Forever" and "Perfect Stranger" are memorable). She has a forthright contralto that allows her to breathe vowels easily and intimately, and she sustains its purity when she switches from ballads to swingers, waving her long arms or grasping her hair. I could quibble about a couple of her songs, but I don't feel like it. Carmen Lundy is her own woman, and jazz has been looking for her for a good long while.

(April 1983)

Gypsy Soul

At the age of eight, a precocious Alsatian Gypsy named Bireli Lagrene decided that the music of the spheres was the music of his Gypsy forebear, guitarist Django Reinhardt. So diligently did he set about teaching himself Reinhardt's tunes and improvisations that when he learned about Reinhardt's mangled fretting hand (a fire had left his fourth and fifth digits paralyzed), he spent three years figuring out how the runs could be played with only two fingers—a secret that has mystified Reinhardt admirers for decades. Lagrene's first album, *Routes to Django* (Antilles), recorded in a German nightclub in 1980, was released here last summer with little fanfare. One of the most unusual debuts in jazz history, it captures to an unprecedented degree the elusive sound and idiosyncratic virtuosity of the fabled Django Reinhardt. When it was made, Lagrene was only thirteen. Yet even then he displayed a will to individuality that transcended his talents as a copyist.

Though of different tribes, Reinhardt and Lagrene were both born in Gypsy caravans near the northeast border of France, Reinhardt in Liverchies, Belgium, in 1910, Lagrene about 200 miles south in the Alsace community of Saverne in 1966. Both were self-taught musicians who were playing professionally at twelve and who drafted guitar-playing brothers as accompanists. When Reinhardt's brother, Joseph, heard Lagrene in concert, he enthusiastically announced that Bireli Lagrene had inherited Django's right hand.

By the time of his death in 1953, Reinhardt had long since been recognized as the one non-American to make a vital contribution to jazz. Duke Ellington, who cosponsored his only American tour, ranked him with Art Tatum and Sidney Bechet as one of the "inimitables." Guitarists of every stripe, from B. B. King to Julian Bream, acknowledged his inspiration; even Charlie Christian, whose influence in jazz superseded Reinhardt's, was known to entertain friends by playing Reinhardt's solos note for note. Yet today Reinhardt seems inseparable from the Swing Era. Not the least interesting aspect of Bireli Lagrene's promise is his determination to explore an older style with a contemporary sensibility and two good hands.

His first album radiates technical aplomb, almost to a fault. On most of *Routes to Django,* Lagrene is heard with his regular group, which includes his brother Gaiti Lagrene and his cousin Tschirglo Loeffler on rhythm guitars and the Czechoslovak Jan Jankeje on bass. The quartet is modeled on Reinhardt's Quintet of the Hot Club of France (which was completed by Stephane Grappelli on violin), and Lagrene plays the same guitar as Reinhardt, a Selmer Maccaferri, noted for an extra sound chamber in its large unamplified body. He doesn't play any Reinhardt compositions here, but two originals are worthy of Django: "Fiso Place," performed as a duet with his brother, and "Bireli Swing 1979," played by the quartet plus piano.

If a first listening to these selections is impressive chiefly for Lagrene's buoyant command of the Reinhardt style (the poised swing, minor-key lyricism, dizzying arpeggios, slashing chords, glissandi, bent notes, offhanded harmonics), subsequent listenings reveal his self-reliance. Bireli's harmonic grasp allows him to phrase seamlessly over the bar lines. He plays more notes than

Django, favoring breathlessly long figures that maintain lyrical interest despite the absence of even an eighth-note rest. Lagrene's playing suggests a speed demon's fury, unlike the more deliberate kind of violence one hears in Django; it also shows up his limitations as a melodist. Lagrene is not as comfortable at ballad tempos as he is at high velocity. It's extraordinary how many things he can think of to vary the content of his phrasing at top speed, but unlike Reinhardt, a master of piquant melodic improvisations that were never rushed or unbalanced, he is unnerved by the special demands of a ballad. Consequently, his best work on standards is taken at a medium clip—"All of Me" (on which he also plays the bass solo) and "I've Found a New Baby"— while slower tempos bring out the demon in him, determined to parade streams of notes over every beat. He begins "Wave" with pretty Wes Montgomery-style octaves, but as soon as he introduces the theme he undercuts it with a brilliant, double-time run; the rest of the performance is almost schizoid in its alternation of busy, rhythmically intense passages and calm releases. "Don't Worry 'Bout Me" (inexplicably identified on record and jacket alike as "Night and Day") is a tour de force, since he's none too sure of the chords and has to rely on the rhythm guitars for his cues. His phenomenal ears save him every time, but the three and a half choruses are precarious. Listening to him here is like watching someone do acrobatics in a minefield.

Because of its driving swing and instrumental bravura, as well as its refreshing confidence in reviewing and reviving a part of jazz's distant past, *Routes to Django* was one of 1982's most unexpected pleasures. But was Lagrene merely precocious, or something more? Two Austrian concerts last fall, in Salzburg and Gmunden, a few weeks after Lagrene's 16th birthday, provided ample reason for optimism.

In Salzburg one naturally thinks about musical prodigies. Aldous Huxley once noted that Mozart was "only the most marvelous of a small army of marvelous boys." Although child prodigies are not unusual in classical music, they've been relatively rare in jazz, perhaps because jazz places less emphasis on composition and interpretation than on spontaneous invention. In those few instances where a child prodigy achieved greatness in jazz (Bud Powell is a notable example), the early work was not recorded. By jazz standards, the teenage years—the years in which we first heard from Fats Waller, Benny Goodman, Billie Holiday, Miles Davis, Sonny Rollins, and Wynton Marsalis, among many others—are considered formative, and by those standards Charnett Moffett, who was playing bass in New York clubs a couple of years ago at eleven, and Bireli Lagrene qualify as authentic wunderkinder.

Lagrene is shy and somewhat diffident onstage. He speaks French, German, and a Gypsy dialect (Sinti) but never utters a word during a performance. Instead he smiles briefly to acknowledge applause but otherwise stares impassively at the ground or into the middle distance; he almost never glances at his spidery fingers. He has a chipmunk's features under a thatch of tousled brown hair, and he dresses indifferently: gray leather shoes, white socks, blue jeans, a yellow knit shirt, and a blue lumber jacket. Gaiti, who is twenty-six, and Tschirglo, who is twenty-five and looks a little like Django, have dark complexions and mustaches; Jankeje, the bass player, is thirty-two, blond and bearded, a bear of a man.

Lagrene opened the Salzburg concert with an improvised solo that employed natural and artificial harmonics, trills, and two-fingered glissandi. Loeffler joined him for "I'll Never Smile Again," which, after 16 bars, became "I Love You for Sentimental Reasons." Then the quartet assembled for "I've Found a New Baby," and the rhythm guitars geared into 4/4. Lagrene wound up the tempo like a propeller plane; he skittered across the fret board, picking melodies at lightning speed, sliding across the strings and beyond the frets, popping occasional harmonics, leaning into dissonances, soaring through the chords. And this was a warm-up. After a few more selections—including Reinhardt's "Django's Blues" and "Minor Swing"—the deep, furious quality in his music began to peek through. Using staccato notes and vibrato, he maintained a personal sound in the manner of

Reinhardt, but the fleet, heated arpeggios contained much that was his own.

The second set confirmed that he hadn't stood still in the two years since he first recorded; the harmonies were chancier and the technique richer. There are at least three aspects to Lagrene's guitar playing that make him special if not unique. First, he phrases horizontally on the fret board, in part a legacy of Reinhardt, who was forced to play this way because of his impaired hand. Whereas most guitarists finger the strings vertically in a single position, Lagrene's hand is in constant horizontal flight across the fret board. Second, his fluency with artificial harmonics is probably equaled only by Tal Farlow, if at all. This device, with which the guitarist can produce thin, belling pitches by gingerly plucking the string an octave above the stopped note, was a favorite of Reinhardt's, but even he was less relaxed about it than Lagrene; on "September Song," Lagrene played 14 bars of flawlessly intoned artificial harmonics. Third, his penchant for long phrases has reached new heights; the most exhilarating chorus of the evening was a 32-bar extrapolation of "I Can't Give You Anything but Love," which, notwithstanding the absence of a single rest, avoided rhythmic and melodic monotony and brought the audience to a roar.

There were other highlights, especially a moving recitation of Reinhardt's most famous melody, "Nuages," which suggested Lagrene's increased ease with ballads. Although Reinhardt usually began his improvisation on this piece with several measures of harmonics, Lagrene avoided the technique this time. He also improvised an unaccompanied blues, using only a familiar Basie vamp as his jumping-off point, and on a razzle-dazzle quartet performance of "Cherokee" demonstrated his awareness of bop licks and harmonies.

At the concert hall in Gmunden the following evening, the program began with a solo number, this time on classical guitar, and Lagrene's intonation was weak. Once again, the second piece began as "I'll Never Smile Again," but after 16 bars he and Loeffler switched to Django's jaunty "Douce Ambiance." With the quartet in place and the Maccaferri on Lagrene's lap, the magic started. Several selections were the same as the night before, but the treatments varied considerably. This time his bass solo on "Django's Blues" was played with a bow, and this time he played "Nuages" more slowly and with a full chorus of ghostly harmonics. The strangest performance of the evening was "I Can't Give You Anything but Love," played by Lagrene and Loeffler on one guitar, with the latter seated and playing chords and Lagrene standing behind him and picking the single notes. Reinhardt's "Daphne" seemed to stump Lagrene, and he ended it abruptly after a chorus. But a dramatically designed performance of Reinhardt's "Manoir de Mes Rêves," including a surprisingly fast chorus of false harmonics and a climax of smashing octaves, illustrated Lagrene's ability to combine pet techniques in cogent musical form. In contrast, he turned "After You've Gone" into an uproarious series of single-phrase choruses—his face impassive, his lumber jacket finally unbuttoned.

A member of the Sinti Gypsy tribe, Lagrene shares a caravan with his mother, an older sister, and a cousin, in Soufflenheim, a village near Strasbourg and about 40 miles from Saverne, where he was born. Brother Gaiti is married and lives nearby; Tschirglo, also married, lives in a caravan about a mile away. Lagrene's father, Fiso, who died two years ago, played guitar and led a band for a few years in the 1940s; when Lagrene was four, Fiso taught him the rudiments of the guitar and told him to listen to Reinhardt's records. Other than that, Bireli Lagrene is entirely self-taught on guitar, bass, violin, and zither. He began playing professionally five years ago in Strasbourg, where he won a prize at a festival and met Jan Jankeje, who was so impressed with Lagrene that he asked to join him.

Like Django, Lagrene is an avid record collector, and though he tries not to copy the styles of other musicians (excepting Reinhardt), records provide a means of learning songs, since he doesn't read or write music. After listening to a piece two or three times, he knows it. Today, he listens to Reinhardt mostly to inspire himself, but he insists that he no longer plays like Django and that, in any case, it would be impossible for him to duplicate Reinhardt's sound. He listens to classical music and to old rock 'n' roll, which he played in a dance band for two years, but his allegiance is to jazz because, as he says, "There's so much feeling. Every performance is totally different from concert to concert." His favorite guitarists are Joe Pass, Pat Martino, B. B. King, Wes Montgomery, and Charlie Christian, but, unlike them, he avoids the electric guitar, because he cannot get from it the sound he wants.

Americans have begun to discover Lagrene, who is especially proud of having played with Betty Carter in London and with Benny Goodman in Antibes. This year he will visit the United States,* where an increasing interest in acoustic string instruments—as witness the success of mandolinist David Grisman and others, and a renewed awareness of Django Reinhardt's music, spurred in large measure by Stephane Grappelli's frequent tours—should guarantee a receptive audience not entirely rooted in jazz. His appearance will be further heralded by the American release of his second album, *Bireli Lagrene 15*, which shows marked gains since the first one. Recorded early in 1982, it suggests a continued awkwardness in his ballad playing, but his seven blues choruses on "Solidarnosc" are marvelous—fast, spiky, and full of arresting details, with each chorus built on a riff that smoothly jets into the next, ending in a consummation of high notes.

Still, while some people will find the swaggering authenticity of his quartet irresistible, others will undoubtedly be disconcerted by a style of music that blithely ignores contemporary fashions. There's a lot of weathervane thinking in jazz, despite the occasional inroads made by jazz repertory companies and the familiar lament of critics who complain of various styles' being jettisoned before they are fully explored. Lagrene's great accomplishment is that instead of playing Django, he used Django to

*The visit was postponed until June 1984, at which time he made a triumphant appearance at the Kool Jazz Festival.

unlock his own voice and to demonstrate the freshness with which the swing style can still speak to us. Whatever he may achieve in the future, he makes that point superbly now, at sixteen.

(May 1983)

Jolson's Greatest Heir

Several years ago, I got tired of having to jump the needle every three or six or nine minutes whenever I binged on my long out-of-print Jackie Wilson albums and wanted to skip the gross excesses that even the staunchest Wilsonians acknowledge with shame. So I made a tape of about 30 favorite cuts. Gregg Geller and Joe McEwen have just done the same, but because they work for a record company everyone gets the benefit. Actually, they've chosen nineteen of his best performances and added five more that they like better than I do. My quibbles will be modest, nevertheless. Wilson has been hospitalized since a 1975 heart attack, but his career had been slackening ever since a woman paid her respects with a bullet in 1961. *The Jackie Wilson Story* (Epic EG 38263) is the first comprehensive look at one of popular music's most exhilarating performers. As someone who at the age of twelve intuited more about the vitality of American rhythms and the paradox of racial divisions from watching Wilson than it was possible, then or now, to satisfyingly articulate, I'm delighted at the long overdue homage.

My memories of seeing him in action are so vivid that I no longer trust them; after more than 20 years, you begin to embroider. Recent conversations with someone else who haunted the Brooklyn Paramount, the Hillside in Queens, and the Apollo reminded me that I may even have grafted some of the moves of his imitators—especially the Isley Brothers, who in 1960 stormed the stage like Wilson in triplicate—onto Wilson himself. On the other hand, my memories are buttressed by kinescopes and films. To begin at the beginning, there was the matter of his entrances. He didn't walk on stage. His motor had started in the wings so that he was in full dancing motion when he glided from behind the curtain, waddling at the waist, snapping his fingers, and radiating energy. Then there was his costume: a tailored tuxedo with a huge black satin cummerbund, lots of lace, and a buttoned tie that he invariably sacrificed to the audience. One specific glimpse: at the climax of a furious rocker, he tosses the microphone four feet into the air, pirouettes while leaping into a split, and deftly rising, catches the mike inches before it would have hit the stage floor; the timing is impeccable, the audience is screaming. Did it really happen that way or have I made this up? I'm no longer sure. I do know that from the time he strutted out, I was sitting on the edge of my seat, like the mostly black teenagers all around me, and feeling about as good as I'd ever feel.

Wilson's rock and roll arrogance had nothing to do with the rebelliousness of the rockabillies or the narcissism of their bullshit imitators in Philadelphia. His was the arrogance of a consummate performer. He didn't threaten anybody; he pleased everybody, and was visibly pleased with himself for being able to do so. I remember my grandmother watching him with me on Dick Clark's Saturday night show with the same fascination I imagine she brought to Eddie Cantor. He was the kind of schvartze no Yiddishe mama could resist. But then, no aspect of American life undermined the habits of racism as much as the thirst for entertainment. Maybe it isn't possible to appreciate the galvanizing effect black rock and rollers had on white middle-class kids unless you recall the late '50s and early '60s as a brief lull before civil rights consciousness set in (on the part of the kids, that is). I've no doubt that our devotion to the black rock and rollers triggered in many of us a far more emotional commitment to that

issue than we could later muster for Vietnam (which was em-
blematic of a more distant type of racism).

If Wilson makes me raise those ghosts now, it's because in those
days he triggered—in an all-Jewish playground—hard questions
about the matter of blackness. No, he triggered a desire to *be* black,
and to have a tuxedo, as if only that combination of mask and
costume could enable one to express that much raw emotion. In
other communities, a similar kind of transference was taking place
between kids and rock stars with perfect Aryan features, pom-
padours, and leather jackets. Our attachment to Wilson had
something to do with the presumed mutuality of outsiders, black
and Jew, but it also reflected our bourgeois security. Wilson, in
his ingenuous exuberance, was a bourgeois performer from head
to toe—in a way that Elvis and Chuck Berry, at least early in their
careers, were not. They were more alienated than he was. Their
sexuality was down and dirty; his was stylized and moot. It's interesting to recall that, while ghetto Jews were best able to adapt
the pose and expressiveness of blacks in the 1920s, when burnt
cork was still an acceptable gesture, no Jewish performer came
close to the fundamentalist rockabillies or the working-class Brits
in assimilating the black rhythm and blues of the 1950s.

Still. Render unto Elvis the things that are Elvis's; but, please,
a little respect also for Jackie Wilson. If Elvis represented the dawn
of a new style, Wilson represented the apotheosis of an old one.
In the mere five years in which he was a full-force presence in
pop music (1957–61), he embodied the ambitions of that last
generation of entertainers who grew up thinking of show biz as
a kind of well-paid exercise in heart-on-sleeve altruism. It's a
mistake to think of Jackie Wilson in terms of the other church-
reared soul singers of his generation. With his operatic voice,
mania to perform, and patience with sentimentality, it's no surprise to learn that he idolized Al Jolson. The only liner note he
wrote was on his homage to Jolson, *You Ain't Heard Nothin' Yet:*
". . . the greatest entertainer of this or any other era. . . . I guess
I have just about every recording he's ever made, and I rarely
missed listening to him on the radio. . . . During the three years

I've been making records, I've had the ambition to do an album of songs, which, to me, represent the great Jolson heritage. . . . This is simply my humble tribute to the one man I admire most in this business. With the sincere hope that my contribution will in some way keep the heritage of Al Jolson alive. . . ." Lord, have mercy. Maybe Wilson didn't actually write those words; maybe his producer wrote them and Wilson signed them. But one can hardly listen to the album or, more pointedly, to his own masterpieces without recognizing the relevance of the sentiments. Wilson loved show-biz kitsch; as a graduate of Billy Ward's Dominoes, he had no trouble making the connection between church and stage.

It's often argued, usually by people who didn't see Wilson live, that his recordings are compromised by his producer's meretricious designs. Ken Emerson, in a recent Boston *Phoenix*, complained that Wilson didn't have "vision," that he made good on his potential only when he began recording Motown arrangements. I don't doubt the meretriciousness of his producer, but as is the case with many other Top 40 acts, calculating avarice produced memorable results. Wilson's soul records from the 1965–75 period are rarely first-rate; he often sounds a little like Stevie Wonder. During his glory years, he didn't sound like anyone but himself, and his meticulously crafted rockers are unlike any other records ever made. You didn't have to see him live to appreciate them. The white shooby-doo choirs, mechanical rhythmic figures, and bloated arrangements are dated, to be sure, but they animate Wilson, inspiring him to the full measure of his self-mocking virtuoso power. I am no more embarrassed by them than I am by the Guy Lombardo-like reeds on Louis Armstrong's 1929–31 recordings or the strings with which Charlie Parker was saddled. In each instance, banality jolts.

Which is not to say that Wilson is always at odds with the arrangements. He was at his best with material especially created for him, and the very effusiveness of Dick Jacobs's arrangements complements his keening opulence of style. The only selection on *The Jackie Wilson Story* that I hate as much now as I did when it came out is "Night," a bathetic steal from Saint-Saëns's *Samson and Delilah,* and one of several commercially successful attempts to turn Wilson into the black Mario Lanza (it's original LP appearance was on *Jackie Wilson Sings the World's Greatest Melodies*). Considering its popularity, Epic could hardly have left it off. On the other hand, the 1965 flop "Danny Boy" is splendid. With the fourth note, he departs from the melody and never fully returns. The uncredited arrangement smacks of Dick Jacobs's eclectic approach, with its mooning strings, tightly voiced trombones, honky tonk piano, and prominent bass. Wilson is all over himself, turning the word "down" into a falling glissando, swooping into a sustained falsetto, and closing with a cadenza that instead of floating to earth, as expected, goes out on a high note.

There are other characteristic ballads in this collection. "To Be Loved," with his yodeling of "truly," was a big hit. "Please Tell Me Why" finds him borrowing Clyde McPhatter's trademark sobbing; compare Wilson's singing here—his rhythm, humor, and histrionics—with the unswinging choir, especially at the coda, and you get the impression of two different records grafted together. The disparity is even more apparent on the blues, "Passin' Through," where the horrid choir seems to be doing the stroll while Wilson struts 10 yards ahead of it; Wilson turns the kitsch chart to his own advantage, no alibis necessary. "The Tear of the Year" started life as the highlight of an album of mostly standards, *Body and Soul;* it's a terrible song, probably the worst on the original LP, but the arrangement, expertly tailored to Wilson's pipes and penchant for melodrama, coaxes from him a solid performance, while the album's good songs—"Body and Soul," "I Got It Bad," "I'll Be Around"—were vulgarized beyond reparation. The finest of his ballad recordings was also his biggest hit, the 1960 "Doggin' Around," another example of the tension generated between the blisteringly dramatic Wilson (listen to the way he phrases, "I don't mind yourself having a real good time") and the insensible choir; but the arrangement is effectively spare, and the stop-time gambits—also heard in "A Woman, a Lover, a Friend"—are brilliantly executed.

Wilson's best records, however, were the rockers, a unique group of wildly exciting performances that are entirely sui generis. The arrangements, most of them by Jacobs, incorporate old jazz riffs (one lesser performance not included on this anthology, "Shake! Shake! Shake!," is a catalog of Basie licks), stodgy white choirs, triplets, stop-time, and various instrumental surprises. Through it all, Wilson rides herd with unperturbed authority. His phrasing is as winged as his voice is agile, and it's hard for me to listen to these performances and not mentally choreograph his moves. Wilson's timing is amazing, allowing him to apply nuance—not just falsetto flourishes, but growls and sighs and rolled r's—to specific words in spite of the roaring tempo.

On his first hit, "Reet Petite," he was supported by a choir, expert drumming, an orchestra with a conspicuously bright trombone section, and a good chart. The song is a 12-bar blues with an 8-bar refrain, but the difficult lyrics, taken at a demanding tempo, and the sheer number of people involved make the performance a tour de force; Wilson rolls the r in "reet," articulates every word, groans at the right places, and closes with a falsetto flourish. The follow-up, "Lonely Teardrops," supplanted the orchestral riffs with a stiff chorus, but Wilson remained undismayed and his breaks and the closing minor-key chant are triumphant. "That's Why" is rock and roll Jolson, complete with piccolo and tag ending; Wilson exhorts and the chorus plods. He rebukes the chorus with his growl notes at the outset of "Talk That Talk" and goes on to one of his best performances despite the most compromising of all these arrangements; when he lays out, the record dies. "Baby Workout" is a mess that works out. The chorus is laughably out of tune; the orchestra plays Basie figures; Wilson shouts. Somehow the record swings like mad, and when Wilson breaks into his second vocal with a falsetto cry, he sounds like a saxophone. "You Better Know It" is especially effective, since the entire performance alternates breaks with call-and-response chants. It has the kind of footloose energy you can imagine Wilson sustaining in concert for an additional several minutes. "I Just Can't Help It," with a member of the Dixie

Hummingbirds singing bass, is a throwback to the secular gospel pieces Wilson recorded with the Dominoes. On "I'm Comin' On Back to You," the orchestra rises through the intervals of a major seventh (rock and roll's answer to the "Mephisto Waltz"), at which point Wilson comes gliding in a la falsetto. If I had to pick one selection to represent this side of Wilson it would be "Am I the Man," a 12-bar blues with a 16-bar release and a sustained celebration of self at a brutal tempo, with every note made to count.

The Motown selections that close the album are well chosen, expecially "Your Love Keeps Lifting Me (Higher and Higher)" and "Whispers." Yet in those performances the glitzy irreverence is gone. Wilson is trying to measure up to the soul industry's new serious image of itself, and the awful truth is that he thrived on the white/black paradox of the late '50s, when he could parade his chops over a lavish background without worrying about the meaning. On "Higher and Higher," he was singing someone else's song and singing it superbly. On "Reet Petite," "Doggin' Around," and "Am I the Man," he was singing himself. The totality of these performances was kitsch then and it's kitsch now, but by God it's kitsch for the ages.*

(May 1983)

Kind of Miles

The weird stick figures on the cover of Miles Davis's *Star People* may or may not be eponymous, but they look happy to be there,

*Wilson died in 1984, at 47.

and they're decked out in happy colors. In case anyone thinks they don't represent Davis's current state of mind, a credit on the liner reads, "All Drawings, Color Concepts and Basic Attitudes by Miles Davis." Released just a couple of weeks before his 57th birthday, this is one of the mellowest records Davis has ever made. It's a blues album, almost pure if rarely simple. The six selections total nearly an hour in playing time, and if Miles's chops aren't what they once were, his brain is still buzzing with ideas; he rings several surprises on the most fundamental of jazz songs, and demonstrates even more conclusively than on *We Want Miles* that he's effected a rapprochement between the Basic Attitudes of his classic period and those that followed *Bitches Brew.*

The first thing that hits you is how coherent the band sounds. As far as trumpet playing is concerned, there are a couple of solos on *We Want Miles* that I prefer to anything on the new album, yet, conceptually, that was a concert recording given largely to strings of solos; *Star People* uses the band in ways that obviate most of the questions about Davis's choice of musicians. He knows he's never going to have a mainstream band as good as those he had in the '50s and '60s, and he's not comfortable with the post-avant-gardists some people think he ought to be nurturing. So he's built himself a sextet of young players with a jazz bias; by means of tape editing, demanding chord patterns, and the ardent coloring of his keyboard work, he's orchestrated them into a genuine unit. The guitar duties are divided between Mike Stern and John Scofield, neither of whom has ever sounded this convincing before; Bill Evans's sax is limited to ensemble figures and brief interludes (he solos only twice, for seconds at a time); the rhythm section is practically fastidious.

The immediate attention-getter is the 18:44-minute title cut—Davis's first traditional 12-bar, three-chord slow blues recording in ages. The first time I heard the album, I was startled to hear him looking backward so fearlessly, but after living with the record for a while, I find "Star People" less absorbing than some of the other cuts. There's no head; instead, Davis recorded two rubato keyboard-guitar passages that were subsequently edited into

the performance, one at the outset and the other about two-thirds
through. Other contrasts are provided by a chorus for bass and
guitar and one for tenor, but most of the time is marked by Davis,
soloing lyrically and at length, and Stern, playing what Davis calls
his "B. B. King thing." As moving as Davis's work often is (note
the passing reference to *Sketches of Spain* in his second chorus),
it's only intermittently effective.

When a long slow blues is successfully pulled off, it seems like
the simplest thing in the world. This one occasionally plods. The
shuffle rhythm is disfigured by Al Foster's double-bashing on the
two and four, and Davis sounds tinny and unsure at moments.
His comments on the blues, quoted in Leonard Feather's notes,
suggest an ingenuous rediscovery of an idiom of which he is his-
torically one of the supreme masters, but his solo hardly stands
comparison with those on "Walkin'" or "Blues Changes" or
"Freddie Freeloader." For that matter, he achieves less drama than
Muhal Richard Abrams did in his slow blues of last year, "Blues
Forever." The somewhat less tradtional pieces, however, withstand closer scrutiny.

"It Gets Better" is also built on a 12-bar progression, but the
execution is looser, the form almost elastic. Davis says he took
the highly melodic harmonic cycle, with two tellingly placed minor chords, from Lightnin' Hopkins, and it provides a firm underpinning for him and Scofield as they exchange deft and imaginative choruses. The rhythm section sustains a lazy shuffle, and
bassist Marcus Miller closely shadows the protagonists. "It Gets
Better" is spliced directly to the preceding cut, "Come and Get
It," which has the most acerbic trumpet playing on the record.
The theme is just a two-bar vamp (Davis credits it to Otis Redding), and Davis uses it as a launching pad for an impassioned
matrix of staccato blasts, ascending arpeggios, tremolo swirls, and
razor-sharp high notes. The drumming—Foster on traps, Mino
Cinelu on percussion—is vivacious, and the leader totally governs the mood with his dark keyboard chords, even while he's
also playing trumpet.

"U 'n' I" is as jocular as the cover art. The theme, perched atop a witty vamp, is an eight-bar blues fragment that the soloists take turns embellishing. The improvisation is minimal, yet every departure from the melody, which is repeated more than two dozen times, is keenly felt. "Star on Cicely," another eight-bar blues, and "Speak" are more challenging, and on these selections the hand of Gil Evans is most apparent. During the recording of *Star People,* rumors abounded that it represented a reunion between Davis and Evans. It seems, however, that Evans was solicited less as a collaborator than as a consultant, and it's impossible to gauge exactly what he did. He isn't listed in the formal credits. In the notes, Davis is quoted as saying that Evans wrote some parts, and that Davis consulted him on tempos. (I'm shattered to learn that Miles Davis, who all but invented modern medium tempos, would ever have to solicit advice on this matter, but never mind.)

In any case, the unison passages on "Speak" and "Star on Cicely" smack more of Evans's pen than Miles's. The former comes off as something of a mini-concerto for Scofield's guitar. There's no trumpet until the last couple of minutes, and Davis's improvising is perfunctory. His stamp is everywhere, though, usually in the form of closely voiced organ chords. The combination of Davis's Oberheim and the unison riffs played softly behind Scofield creates the illusion of a much larger group. About five minutes into the piece the riffs become as aggressive as those in a swing band. For "Star on Cicely," the theme is no more than a four-bar unison figure that goes by in a flash, and sets Davis off for the first of three solos, interspersed with a written episode that Evans apparently transcribed from a guitar solo played during a warm-up and subsequently voiced for guitar and soprano sax. I wish Evans had also been asked to write real endings; four of the six pieces end with fade-outs. But that's a small point. The big point is that the orchestration on these pieces, the loopy melodicism of "U 'n' I," the tempo variations throughout the album, the refreshing exploration of familiar turf, the shifting colors, the tight unity of the band, and the relentless energy of the leader offer

bewitching evidence that the Miles Davis story isn't over yet.
Probably not by a long shot.

(May 1983)

Wynton Marsalis and Other Neoclassical Lions

The future of jazz looked splendid at the 1982 Kool Jazz Festival, in New York, where more than two dozen of the best young
players were included, most of them for the first time, in the
largely mainstream series of concerts arranged by the impresario
George Wein. At one concert, the World Saxophone Quartet, a
neoclassical collective in its fith year, opened for the Four Brothers, a reunion of star saxophonists who first became famous in
Woody Herman's orchestra in the late 1940s. The insurgents—
Hamiet Bluiett, Julius Hemphill, Oliver Lake, and David Murray—took the stage in tuxedos, juggled a variety of saxophones,
clarinets, and flutes through a program of original pieces that were
either entirely notated or mostly improvised, and stole the show.
There were lurching free passages that settled into fastidious,
generally romantic melodies; earthy rhythm-and-blues ostinatos;
and contrapuntal mazes. Individually, the soloists conjured up five
decades of jazz saxophone, from the sweetness and light of Johnny
Hodges and Benny Carter to the banshee cries of Albert Ayler
and Eric Dolphy. They were funny and sure, outrageous and
suave. The part of the audience that came to hear the Herman
alumni—Stan Getz, Zoot Sims, Al Cohn, and Jimmy Giuffre—
seemed at first puzzled and then delighted. I don't think they

could have realized how impressive the WSQ was until the veterans, dressed in motley and accompanied by an inchoate rhythm section, finished their familiar if occasionally inspired set. Many of those who came to hear the modernists of the 1940s must have gone home thinking about the eclectics of the 1980s.

At another concert, 17 musicians billed as The Young Lions* presented compositions that ranged in instrumentation from solo to full orchestra. Most of the stylistic options open to the jazz neoclassicist seemed to meld in a pastiche of received and modified influences, including tailgate trombone smears, swing-band dynamics, bop's harmonic labyrinths, modal simplicity, and avant-garde chaos, with frequent allusions to African and European music, as well as to American pop. The balance between avant-gardism and influences from the mainstream resulted in a kind of show-and-tell, as musician after musician demonstrated what he had heard and what he could do with it. Craig Harris relied on African rhythms and repetitions to buoy an orchestration called "Nigerian Sunset," which employed voicings for oboe, cello, and wordless singing, in addition to the usual big-band instruments, and provided solo space for such noteworthy young players as the pianist Anthony Davis and the flutist James Newton. The climax was Harris's trombone solo: its barrelhouse energies were derived almost solely from the premodernist rips, snorts, and glissandi of swing trombonists such as J. C. Higginbotham and Dickie Wells. African music also permeated a hypnotic recital by Jay Hoggard, who played recurrent pentatonic riffs on a bala-phon (a mallet instrument with wooden bars and hollow resonance) while seated cross-legged on the floor, and then moved to the vibraphone, where he developed them into lush melodies. John Purcell, who plays all the reed instruments and flutes with conservatory precision, conducted an orchestra work that combined traditional big-band voicings, free episodes, Latin rhythms, improvised polyphony, rubato, and vocal grunts; he called the piece "It's a Joy," and much of it was.

*Much of this concert was subsequently issued on records as *The Young Lions* (Musician 60196.1).

But if any one of these young lions shows off most of the replenished energies in jazz, it is Wynton Marsalis, a 21-year-old
trumpet virtuoso from New Orleans. He is the first major trumpeter raised in that city since King Oliver, Louis Armstrong, Henry
Red Allen, and other trumpet kings of the '20s. Other jazz musicians have played and recorded the classical repertoire, but
Marsalis is the first ever recruited by a major record company
(Columbia) as a jazz player and as a classical player. At fourteen,
he performed the Haydn Trumpet Concerto with the New Orleans Symphony, and at seventeen he was cited as the Outstanding Brass Player at the Berkshire Music Festival in Tanglewood,
where he auditioned with Bach's Second Brandenburg Concerto. ("Do you really want to try that?" the conductor Gunther
Schuller asked him. Schuller says he "soared right through it and
didn't miss a note.") A year later he was studying at Juilliard,
subbing in a Broadway pit band, and touring with Art Blakey and
the Jazz Messengers.

Wynton's father is the distinguished New Orleans pianist Ellis
Marsalis, who impressed on Wynton and his brother, Branford
(a rising tenor saxophonist, older by one year), the necessity for
complete instrumental mastery, reverence for the complexities of
jazz improvisation, and sartorial elegance on the bandstand. These
lessons, almost incredibly, have had a chastening influence on some
older musicians, too. The pride that animates Wynton's music is
reflected in candid interviews that make clear his preference for
jazz and his familiarity with its history; his advocacy is a welcome
response to the jazzmen who have complained bitterly of the de-
meaning implications of the word "jazz." The fastidiously tailored Marsalis even looks like a performer from jazz's glory days.
With his husky arms supporting the trumpet at about 30 degrees
short of a right angle and slightly right of center, his stance re-
sembles that of the legendary King Oliver.

Marsalis hasn't found his own style, but his instincts are aston-
ishingly mature. For one thing, his solos have poise: he phrases
in an unhurried, thoughtful manner, and is not afraid—as young

musicians often seem to be—of using long rests. He rarely falls back on his virtuosity as a substitute for sound thinking. At recent concerts, including the evening of Young Lions, he used dynamics ingeniously, allowing long phrases to sink almost inaudibly beneath the volume of the rhythm section and then emerge with blinding brilliance. His projection is so sure that he can change tone midstream, suggesting a flugelhorn one moment and a trumpet-with-straight-mute the next. Like Rex Stewart, he is proficient at snarling, half-valved effects, and like Miles Davis, he favors angular, fragmented phrases shot against the rhythm. Davis's playing is an obvious influence, but Marsalis affects little of its pain and mystery, preferring a more robust and rounded attack. There are areas for improvement: his music is almost cubistic in its calculatingly aggressive attack and driving rhythms, and his ballad playing is occasionally awkward and given to preening.

His first record as a leader, *Wynton Marsalis* (Columbia FC37574), was recorded before he turned twenty. It's impressive, if uneven, and not the least impressive aspect is the fact that Marsalis's original compositions are far more invigorating and imaginative than the pieces written by Herbie Hancock (a tiresome pastel) and Tony Williams (chi-chi funk). One of the best selections is "Hesitation," which, notwithstanding its 4/4 meter and "I Got Rhythm" harmonies, is a homage to Ornette Coleman, complete with a five-note Coleman lick for a coda; the meat of the performance is a series of galvanizing exchanges between the Marsalis brothers. The brothers' dramatic duet against a rousing bass/drums figure on "Twilight" and the smears, register-hopping, and decaying notes of Wynton's solo on "Father Time" are equally memorable. Still, his playing isn't always as relaxed here as it was with Art Blakey (Blakey's *Album of the Year*, on Timeless, is a good example), a fact that bespeaks the perils of being a bandleader.

•

Think of One . . . (Columbia FC38641), Marsalis's second quintet recording, is better, not least because it shows his ability to organize a first-rate band with compatible personalities and a challenging repertoire. Each of his collaborators is impressive: Branford Marsalis on tenor and soprano saxophones, Kenny Kirkland on piano, Jeff Watts on drums, and Phil Bowler and Ray Drummond alternating on bass. The material includes five originals, a standard ballad ("My Ideal"), a piece by Thelonious Monk ("Think of One"), and a Duke Ellington piano solo ("Melancholia") transcribed for trumpet. Some of the material is derivative, but all of it is interpreted with verve and imagination. "What Is Happening Here (Now)?" for example, sounds like something Wayne Shorter might have written, but the polyphonic camaraderie between trumpet and tenor gives it a sterling freshness. Most impressive is "Think of One," a thoughtful recasting of Monk, built on a playful use of dissonances and dynamics.

Playfulness is a constant in Marsalis's music. His trumpet playing is varied by his ability to sculpt each note; in the course of an improvisation he will growl and flutter and purr (as on the blues "Later"), or bounce between registers, alternating long and short phrases (as on "Knozz-moe-King"). At times his fussy manipulation of tone gets the best of him, and the result (as in the coda to "My Ideal") is lots of show, some wit, little feeling. But ballad playing often comes late to a jazz musician—it was the one area that still troubled trumpeter Clifford Brown at the time of his death—and Marsalis's overall control is on an ascending glide.

The album of trumpet concertos—*Hayden, Hummel, Leopold Mozart* (Columbia IM37846)—makes a handsome package, a kind of essay in the development of the eighteenth-century style from the sagacious Haydn to the proper Leopold Mozart to the guiltily romantic Hummel. Marsalis's preening tone occasionally mars the Hummel, especially his overripe low notes, but he shines in the Andante, negotiating the register jumps beautifully, and attacks the Rondo with fervor. The Mozart is an exercise in high notes, and Marsalis meets the challenge with impeccable finesse. His best performance is saved for the best music, the Haydn Concerto in E-flat Major; here, Marsalis is as supple and dashing as in a jazz performance, the rhythmic momentum thoroughly idiomatic but individual. No jazz enthusiast can listen to his cadenza in the Allegro without being reminded of the cadenza Louis Armstrong improvised on "West End Blues."

As eagerly as I anticipate watching the careers of Marsalis and his contemporaries develop, I don't expect much in the way of innovation. My intuition tells me that innovation isn't this generation's fate. After the turbulence of the past 20 years, however, with the avant-garde rooting out clichés only to be followed by fusion mercenaries and their middlebrow posturing, the neoclassicists have a task no less valuable than innovation: sustenance. Not unlike the popularizers of swing in the 1930s and soul in the 1950s, musicians such as Marsalis are needed to restore order, replenish melody, revitalize the beat, loot the tradition for whatever works, and expand the audience. That way we'll be all the hungrier for the next incursion of genuine avant-gardists, whose business is to rile the mainstream and keep it honest. Until then, a conscientious neoclassicism that revitalizes the jazz tradtion and makes it accessible to a new audience should be seized greedily.

(November 1982/July 1983)

The Latest Scat

Louis Armstrong put scat singing on record in 1925 with "Heebie Jeebies," claiming later that he accidentally dropped the sheet music with the lyrics and had to improvise nonsense syllables to save the take. He didn't expect people to believe that story, but the fact that he invented any story at all suggests how weird the

notion of scat must have seemed. Within a few years, everyone
was doing it, though rarely as imaginatively as Armstrong, who,
to choose one example, used the technique on "Hotter Than That"
to sing crossrhythms that would have daunted most instrumentalists. Bing Crosby went bu-bu-bu-boo on a Paul Whiteman record ("Because My Baby Don't Mean 'Maybe' Now"). In the mid-
1930s, George Gershwin (inspired by Cab Calloway) institutionalized scatty-wahs in *Porgy and Bess*. Soon, Ella Fitzgerald energetically affirmed the case for scat as a means of improvising jazz
rhythms and melodies without the hindrance of words.

Scat singing is not universally embraced. Some of the best jazz
singers would have nothing to do with it, among them Bessie
Smith, Billie Holiday, Jimmy Rushing, and Dinah Washington.
Others do it at their own peril: Sarah Vaughan and Betty Carter,
for all their harmonic ingenuity, are generally more persuasive
improvising with words, and Anita O'Day's scat is sometimes rid-
den with cliché. Pop singers who try to scat almost always sound
like idiots. It might be argued that all the sighs, moans, shouts,
slurs, and gasps that are part of every jazz singer's vocabulary
constitute a kind of scat; in some of Armstrong's recordings ("Star
Dust," "All of Me"), real words sound like scat—that is, the
meanings are so completely subordinated to his musical impulses
that they have no meaning.

The vocabulary of scat, which is growing, appears limitless, from
Armstrong's biting consonants (bop-ba-du-ZET) to Sinatra's wan
shoobie-doobie-do. Leo Watson used scat and words almost in-
terchangeably, and Slim Gaillard could fashion an entire scat
sonata around his favorite word, avocado. Watson and Gaillard
flourished during the war years, when lyricists put pen to paper
to laud Flat Foot Floogie's floy-floy and three little fishes in an
itty bitty poo; they used scat to underscore the irrepressible,
childlike quality that had circled the outskirts of jazz ever since
Cab Calloway first induced audiences to chant hi-de-hi-de-ho.
They were funny and inventive and irreverent, and they suggested a barely restrained lunacy, which may be why they could
get away with anything. Gaillard's send-ups of Latin crooners and

his pig-Chinese were devastating, and Calloway regularly transported unsuspecting swells to Minnie the Moocher's coke den.
Watson must have seemed completely unhinged, singing whatever phrases leaped into his mind, as though a musical work were
really a Rorschach test.

In recent years, that lunatic edge of expressiveness has taken hold
of various musics. Contemporary scat singers have gone beyond
the scat syllables popularized by swing and bop, borrowing additional phrases from the sounds of electronic music. The jazz
singers who were most responsive to the new music of the '60s
and '70s had little choice—it was either innovate new sounds of
vocalese or sing songs about love and peace and flying away. Some
memorable compromises were effected: Leon Thomas sang about
love et al. but also made a sport of yodeling; Sheila Jordan sang
standards but opened them up with scat lingo of her own invention. Most of the younger modernists, however, concentrated on
new sounds, often simulating the beeps and whirrs of the electronic age, sometimes with the aid of electricity (Urszula Dudziak), sometimes not (Jay Clayton). Bobby McFerrin has gone in
the other direction entirely, simulating the sounds of acoustic
string instruments. But these are relatively sober citizens. The edge
of lunacy is in them, but its often stifled.

The heirs to Leo Watson and company are those who use their
voices and the parlance of scat to support the illusion of a ram-
paging id. Although they are obviously mining a virtuosic field
with great control, they give the appearance of impetuousness,
of frazzled nerves. They seem to have no inhibitions, and they'd
almost certainly be embarrassing if they didn't know exactly what
they were doing. Of no little interest is the fact that these strangely
unrepressed singers are all women. The best-known example, at
least in New York, is Meredith Monk, whose classical training and
compositional abilities tend to place her childlike babble in ironically punctilious settings. But jazz has lately revealed its own inspired psychic-scatter in Lauren Newton, who also was classically
trained (she has performed works by Schoenberg, Webern,
Pousseur, and others), though her affection for jazz rhythms and

improvisation provides the fulcrum of her unusual talent. Because she records for Hat Hut, which provides nothing in the way of biographical material, little is generally known about her, except that she was born in Oregon and has lived in Germany for the past nine years, performing with the Vienna Art Orchestra since 1979. She appears on two VAO albums, the 1980 *Concerto Piccolo* (hat ART 1980/81) and the current *Suite for the Green Eighties* (hat ART 1991/92), and on her own *Timbre* (hat MUSICS 3511), and she is pleasantly unsettling.

The VAO is a 14-piece orchestra under the leadership of the composer and arranger Mathias Ruegg. With the first album, the band gave the impression of ragbag eclecticism on the order of the Willem Breuker Kollektieff; the usual tango, carnival theme, military march, and swing band ingredients were wittily blended, and one could only marvel at the incongruity of an ensemble that was named for the most musically blessed city on Earth yet finds most of its inspiration on our humble shores. The oddest element in the orchestrations was the inclusion of Lauren Newton's voice, which edged out over the brasses. Her frenetic, winged scat improvisation on the title selection is one of the double-album's highlights.

Suite for the Green Eighties isn't as lively, though the various influences abound (the Paris fleamarket provided some of the instruments) and Newton's voice adds the expected frisson. Here, the arrangements sound more like a combination of lab band orthodoxies and avant solos—the music of the Art Ensemble of Chicago as interpreted by Woody Herman. The soloists are uneven—saxophonist Harry Sokal is best (he invokes Rollins on "Blues for Two")—and the writing is occasionally heavy-handed. Ruegg favors background riffs that are all elbows and knees, yet shape the terrain for the improvisors; his rhythms blend a gallimaufry of American and European influences, and are generally convincing. But, again, the most ingratiating presence is that of the singer, who shades the ensemble and comes into her own on the third part of the *Suite*. Her scat language sounds Germanic or Dutch, with its accent on d's and harsh, repeated phrases. Lots of ka-do-dat-do-da-do and seh! seh! seh! or da! da! da! Once, she seems to be singing about Sal-Ni-sti-co, and more than once she recalls the sounds Cecil Taylor has been known to sing at the start of a concert.

The real breath of her work is revealed on *Timbre*, where she sings six pieces mostly of her own devising, accompanied by a trio that commands a lot of sonic space; David Friedman plays vibes patterns in the treble sphere, Thomas Stabenow bows darkly in the well of the bass, and Manfred Kneil navigates midstream on drums. Newton is everywhere, building glowing crescendos, tumbling in a sudden cascade of notes, leaping octaves, dilating her vibrato, and gliding high like a hip Yma Sumac. Her scat is frequently jokey, but it always intimates a willingness to stand out on the ledge of her own feelings, and so the tension she ultimately builds is inseparable from a kind of voyeurism she inspires in the listener: will she sustain her musicality or will she collapse in a gargle of funny noises? The cleverest selections are "Conversations," in which she makes use of Clark Terry's Mumbles routine and manages to sound like a scold, a flake, a maid, and an extortionist, and Manfred Kniel's "Cross Rhythms," in which her constantly changing timbre and use of hard syllables (chika-tiki-da) are more daringly expressive than most lyrics. Although "Run of the Mill" has a motif (a chromatic doo-doo-doo), the performance is infused with a serendipitous whimsy, as though she didn't know where she were headed. And on "Who's Blue," she comes on like Bea Lillie, admits "I really don't have the blues," and goes out parodying a diva.

If Lauren Newton is at all reminiscent of the crazed scat singers of the Watson-Gaillard generation it's because, separated from the Vienna Art Orchestra, she doesn't seem to have a pompous bone in her body, and because, even with the VAO, she seems willing to sing anything that comes into her mind. Her larynx is in the service of her intelligence. She's that rare thing—a jazz wit. I wonder if she knows "Body and Soul."*

(July 1983)

*She does.

Return of the Organ Grinder

In 1975, Jimmy Smith, who was then and probably still is the most famous organist in the world, released a rather logy record (pointedly titled *Paid in Full*) on his own label, toured Europe, and announced his semi-retirement. He opened a nightclub in North Hollywood, where he occasionally played on weekends, but refused to tour or record until last year, when he brought a group into Fat Tuesday's and organized an uninspired "all-star" album (George Benson, Stanley Turrentine, Ron Carter) for the Musician label. If neither of these episodes was likely to produce a clamoring for his return to active duty, Smith's reappearance at Fat Tuesday's last week, with Kenny Burrell, his best collaborator, will do the trick.

Smith and Burrell are, each on their own terms, masterful blues players, and never more so than when they are working together. They seem to temper each other, Burrell bringing out the lyricism in Smith, and Smith forcing Burrell to a stark lucidity of purpose. And yet they make the most of the extreme contrasts in their sounds. Smith, plays a torrent of notes in the right hand, sustains bass walks and/or a drone in the left, and frequently sparks his solos with glissandos that vary as much in speed (some are in excruciatingly sensuous slow-motion) as they do in texture—a consequence of his peerless ability to use and combine all the stops and pedals. The hallmark of Burrell's guitar is cool economy and a tone that is autumnal and shrewd. They work off each other rather than trying to blend.

It's a tribute to Jimmy Smith that, even though he bears almost singlehanded responsibility for the organ-guitar lounge trios that proliferated in the '50s and '60s, he is rarely held account-able—no more so than Erroll Garner is blamed for the tribe of cocktail tinklers he unleashed. Yet from the time he began re-cording in 1956, at thirty-one, Smith not only popularized an in-strument that had previously been the province chiefly of rhythm and blues and skating rinks, but established the instrumentation (organ, guitar, drums, possible tenor) and stylistic parameters (blues and ballads) that still hold sway. For a self-appointed crowd pleaser, he has superb taste as a soloist, and a flair for building excitement without succumbing to it. He manipulates his audi-ence. Smith is a great blues player—it is astonishing how many thousands of 12-bar cycles he has tread without losing interest—and although it's tempting to compare him to the best blues pi-anists, from Jimmy Yancey on down, what he achieves as an or-ganist could hardly be translated to any other instrument. He is not, after all, a distinguished pianist.

Burrell first recorded with Smith in 1957, which may explain the ease and slight irony he brings to their collaborations today. At one set at Fat Tuesday's, George Benson and Stanley Turren-tine sat in, and although it was a pleasure to hear Benson's twangy sound put to elemental use, even the ferment that accompanies an impromptu jam session by excellent players couldn't match the easy electricity that flowed between Smith and Burrell. Fanned by the drummer Tommy Campbell, they played the usual organ lounge set, but with startling freshness. The themes included "Mack the Knife" (jocular, chatty organ sonorities broken by swelling keyboard rolls), "The Days of Wine and Roses" (a lithe organ cadenza and breezy guitar chords), and any number of blues of diverse tempos. With Smith controlling the design of every chorus, the trio waxed and diminished, swung and rocked, tight-ened and relaxed.

As noted, Smith's new record, *Off the Top* (Musician 60175), is less than the sum of its personnel, catching fire only on "I'll Drink to That." The new Burrell album, *Listen to the Dawn* (Muse 5264), was recorded in 1980, and is merely proficient. However, Poly-

gram has recently reissued two Verve sessions from 1965 that
capture both men at their best. Smith's *Organ Grinder Swing* (Verve
UMV2074), with Burrell and Grady Tate, is a flawless set despite
what promises to be a program of deadly material ("Green-
sleeves" and "Satin Doll" as well as the title cut); on "Blues for
J," Smith pulls out the trick—a sustained drone while he's soloing—that used to get concert audiences screaming. Burrell's *Guitar Forms* (Verve UMV2070), a collaboration with Gil Evans, remains his masterpiece; each of nine tracks explores a different
genre, allowing Burrell to parade the variety of his interests, and
giving Evans the chance to indulge his penchant for obscure fin-
de-siècle composers (Cecil Scott's "Lotus Land") and to refurbish
a couple of first-class songs (Arlen's "Last Night When We Were
Young" and Wilder's "Moon and Sand"). Judging from the energy at Fat Tuesday's, and the attentive crowds that packed the
room, Smith and Burrell should be making records that good now.

(July 1983)

Technicolor Repertory

A superior entertainment called *Regeneration* (Soul Note 1054) goes
a long way toward tying up loose ends between two idiosyncratic
and ingenious composers of the post-bop era, Thelonious Monk
and Herbie Nichols, and their two most devoted interpreters in
the free-jazz movement that followed, Steve Lacy and Roswell
Rudd. Lacy and Rudd organized a quartet in the early 1960s to
explore their mutual obsession with Monk's music; they managed to land recording dates at Columbia and Verve, but the results were never released. The band's only legacy was an ama-

teurishly recorded tape made in a coffee house in 1963 and not issued until 1975 (by a small label called Emanem).

During the past 20 years, Lacy, an endlessly cagey soprano saxophonist who could never quite find his footing in the United States, blossomed in the capitals of Europe as an all-purpose modernist, recording as prolifically as Sonny Stitt and gliding effortlessly over the murky boundaries between new music and old, free music and—what? imprisoned music? Lacy luxuriates in dissonance and surprise, and enjoys a good ruckus as much as anyone, but no one is more preoccupied than he is with form and function, with the strictest Euclidean demarcation of point, line, and plane.

Roswell Rudd, a robust trombonist whose apprenticeship in Dixieland, affection for Bill Harris (the eccentrically sensuous Woody Herman trombonist), and training with Herbie Nichols somehow landed him in the cauldron of the avant garde, where his lovingly elaborated tailgate smears were mistakenly interpreted as satire, similarly wandered homeless between the old and new; Rudd, however, has recorded relatively little. As *Regeneration* makes clear, he also thrives on formal precision. His and Lacy's interpretations of Nichols and Monk are authentic in every detail. But perhaps because they are estranged from bop's received solutions to labyrinthine harmonic problems, they are able to skirt cliché. Challenged by the material, they poke at it, embellish it, and finally inhabit it with inspired resolve. This is the sort of homage that honors mentor and student alike.

The myth that makes jazz the exclusive domain of the performer probably reached its apex in the boozy environs of the 52nd Street era, with its countless choruses of blues and "I Got Rhythm." By 1960, the shibboleth that made every performer a composer resulted in countless recordings in which improvisations of various quality were wedded to tired and often ponderous "originals," usually based on familiar chords. Renewed respect for the genuinely gifted composer/arranger appears in cycles, and we are passing through one now, as witness Dameronia, Sphere, various repertory projects, and, above all, the large number of jazz standards appearing on current albums. Of course, nothing spurs revival like death, and the passing of Ellington, Mingus, and Monk has encouraged numerous reinvestigations of their music. Lacy and Rudd, however, are riding nobody's bandwagon. Rudd's early experiences with Nichols, and Lacy's with Monk, were catalytic, and, with admirable loyalty, they've kept the fires burning. The selections on *Regeneration* are played with great good humor, substantiating Rudd's liner comment, "We all grew up on this music and finally, after all these years, we can begin to play it like it was our own."

The Herbie Nichols side is especially rewarding, since his music is so much less well known than Monk's and has rarely been played by wind instruments. "Blue Chopsticks" and "2300 Skiddoo," excellent examples of Nichols's geometric art, are performed here as technicolor extrapolations of the original piano trio recordings. In true Nichols style, drummer Han Bennink and bassist Kent Carter state the beat while the irrepressibly ironic pianist Misha Mengelberg and the winds take, with each chorus, ever larger steps away from the intoxicating themes. The formal structure remains absolute. The third Nichols selection, "Twelve Bars," heard here for the first time, is a capriciously funny blues, interpreted with daring barroom braggadocio (duck before Rudd clips you with his slide). The Monk selections are less successful, partly because they are so well known, and partly because Mengelberg's cleverness, so effective when he reharmonizes "Blue Chopsticks," is merely facile when he tries to out-Monk Monk on "Monk's Mood"; his interpolations and subsequent solo are comically broad, but weightless. Far better are "Epistrophy" and the delightful "Friday the 13th," a song whose time has come. Monk recorded it in 1953, and Lacy tried it in 1969, but it was generally ignored. In recent years, it became a permanent staple in the repertories of Tommy Flanagan and Gil Evans, and is now a candidate for standardhood. Rudd turns the vamp, played by Monk, into a blowzy trombone figure.

Regeneration is billed as a collaborative effort, with all five musicians sharing the same typeface, and this seems fair. There are ties between Lacy and Rudd that go back more than 20 years; during the year that their quartet dissolved, Mengelberg and Bennink (Dutch musicians and founders of the Instant Composers' Pool) were introduced to American audiences on Eric Dolphy's *Last Date,* and a year later Lacy began his association with Carter. *Regeneration* doesn't sound like a one-shot, and at this stage, it shouldn't be. It should have been subtitled Volume One.

(August 1983)

The Education of David Murray

At twenty-eight, David Murray might be considered the representative jazzman of the 1980s. Since his arrival in New York, in 1975, he has succeeded not only in staking a claim for himself as a major tenor saxophonist, but has emerged as the kind of bandleader who can impose a contagious respect for form on a music that seems to itch for anarchy. Although he is every inch an original, he is very much a neoclassicist, having rejected the arrogance of total expressionism no less than the blandishments of pop-jazz. His playing has been compared to that of reed men from every period in jazz, from Sidney Bechet and Johnny Dodds to Ben Webster, Paul Gonsalves, Sonny Rollins, Albert Ayler, and Archie Shepp. His composing has been likened to that of Ellington, Mingus, and King Oliver. Murray encourages these comparisons with specific homages in his music, but such references merely underscore his own resourcefulness and the success with which he's assimilated his influences. His music is in constant transition, but as his three dozen or so albums attest, it is also consistent. Murray's position at the very center of the new generation in jazz is suggested by the fact that he is at present a member of five distinguished ensembles: the David Murray Octet and Quartet, the World Saxophone Quartet, James Blood Ulmer's funk band, and Jack DeJohnette's Special Edition.

If he never played another note, David Murray's accomplishments of the past eight years would ensure him a vital niche in any accounting of the present period in jazz. And yet he is only now on the threshold of a real breakthrough. Since 1980, he has proven himself a forceful bandleader and a singular arranger. As an instrumentalist (he now plays bass clarinet as well as tenor saxophone), he has learned to edit his improvisations and sharpen his rhythms. Without sacrificing its emotional power and drive, he has made his music more approachable, even alluring. Before 1980, Murray often gave recondite if persuasive recitals for unaccompanied saxophone; today, he's more likely to immerse himself with disarming modesty in arrangements he's written for some of the best of his contemporaries.

Born in Oakland, California, in 1955, David Murray comes from a musical family, albeit one that distinguished between music made for the greater glory of God and music that reflected the sinfulness of man. The Murray Family Band—mother on piano and directing, father on guitar, three sons on reeds and percussion— played four nights a week and all day Sunday at the Missionary Church of God in Christ. A faculty member in the Berkeley school system introduced Murray to jazz, and had him play the alto parts in the school's stock arrangements. But he was forbidden to practice the Devil's music at home—a stricture that was relaxed only after his mother died. Murray was thirteen at the time, and his father permitted him to play with a local group, the Notations of Soul. One of the arrangements he worked on for that group found its way onto a hit by the Miracles ("I'm Just a Love Machine"), though he wasn't credited. Around the same time, he fell under the spell of Sonny Rollins at a jazz festival and decided to switch from alto to tenor.

By the time he had matriculated at Pomona College, Murray had listened long and hard to such classic tenor saxophonists as Lester Young, Coleman Hawkins, Webster, Gonsalves, and others, though he remained especially enamored of Rollins. Initially, he was less enthusiastic about the avant-gardists of the 1960s; he admired Archie Shepp's tone, but he considered Albert Ayler's music "a bunch of noise." He concentrated instead on the saxophonists who had influenced them—in effect, he wanted to study the masters and find his own route to modernism. While at Pomona, he was encouraged by his teacher, the trumpet player Bobby Bradford, who emphasized the practical problems of music making, and the writer Stanley Crouch, who raised what Murray calls philosophical considerations and made him take another look at Ayler.

Murray was twenty when he arrived in New York, on leave from Pomona to research a paper on the development of the tenor sax since 1958. Hungry for action, however, he dropped out of school and started playing in the Bowery lofts that served as alternatives to the city's established jazz clubs. Crouch served as something of an advance man, and though his claims for his friend and former student were great, they weren't undeserved. At that time, Crouch occasionally played drums in Murray's trio, and the two briefly shared a fourth-story Bowery walk-up that they grandly named Studio Infinity. Intrepid fans sat cross-legged on the floor while the trio (Mark Dresser played bass) soberly delivered itself of painstakingly constructed and rehearsed originals that made reference to classic jazz styles yet sounded unmistakably new. At one of the earliest of these performances, Murray introduced three of his best-known compositions, "Dewey's Circle," "Low Class Conspiracy," and "Flowers for Albert," an evocative tribute to Ayler. Yet Murray defused much of Ayler's bluster by developing his ideas thematically in the middle and upper-middle registers. There was a sighing, almost whimpering quality to his work, and he tended to phrase way behind the beat.

Murray appeared at other lofts, occasionally with the Ted Daniel Energy Band, and proved his mettle in blowing bouts that were structured on little more than the energy levels of the participants. But that kind of playing was a detour for him. Murray had a rarer kind of talent: he could improvise on predetermined harmonic patterns, yet sustain the illusion of playing free. During the peak of the loft era, the summer of 1976, he recorded his first two albums, *Flowers for Albert* (India Navigation) and *Low Class Conspiracy* (Adelphi), both with his preferred rhythm section at that time, Fred Hopkins and Phillip Wilson; "novice efforts" (in Murray's words), these nonetheless demonstrated his penchant for melodic understatement and thematic development. In 1977, Murray married the poet and playwright Ntozake Shange, a union that lasted only three months but resulted in a theatrical collaboration that brought him to the attention of producer Joseph Papp. Papp, who had recently initiated a series of weekend new-music concerts at the Public Theater, commissioned Murray to assemble a big band from the pool of first-rate musicians that flooded New York in the middle 1970s. Murray wrote the arrangements, and Butch Morris, another ingenious musician from California, conducted. Although the orchestra performed only three times and set Murray back $3,500 in recording fees, the event was an overwhelming succès d'estime— not only among critics, but among musicians who now saw Murray as someone capable of shaping a music that had become flabby with self-indulgence. Moreover, it proved to Murray that he could handle a large ensemble; the vital octet he presently leads was a direct outgrowth of that experience.

But first, another important ensemble involving Murray was born. The World Saxophone Quartet originated with an offer from Ed Jordan, the chairman of the music department of Southern University in New Orleans, to four of the most gifted saxophonists of the day. Julius Hemphill, Oliver Lake, Hamiet Bluiett, and David Murray were invited to perform at Southern with a local rhythm section. After that concert, they decided to stick together, but without the rhythm section. Back in New York, they performed at the Tin Palace (now defunct) as the Real New York Saxophone Quartet. When a lawyer for the no less real New York Saxophone Quartet threatened suit, the musicians enlarged their territory. At first, the WSQ was a ragtag outfit that depended upon the good will of a coterie audience accustomed to indulgent improvisations. Within months, it grew into something disciplined and deep. The musicians began appearing in tailored tuxedos, not unlike the Modern Jazz Qartet of an earlier generation, and incorporating subtle shtick—a shuffle-rhythm entrance, dance steps, comic turns—to pace the music, most of it composed and orchestrated by Hemphill. The WSQ's progress, traceable on four albums, from the inchoate *Point of No Return* (Moers), in 1977, to the lustrous and cosmopolitan *Revue* (Black Saint), in 1980, is remarkable. In Murray's words, "We used to sound like four people blowing against each other; every improvisation would sound the same. Then we became a group—now we're immaculate." The immaculate *Revue*, at bottom a blues and ballads affair, is dominated largely by Hemphill's arrangements, but Murray's contributions are prime. He wrote the Ellingtonian ballad "Ming" for the photographer Ming Murray, his wife of three years. His rocking cadenza on "David's Tune" is a glossary of saxophone techniques conjoined with stunning authority. The WSQ is occasionally described as a reed section, or a band without a rhythm section, as if it were somehow incomplete; in fact, it is built along the traditional lines of a chamber group. The altos of Hemphill and Lake are the violins; Murray's tenor is the viola; and Bluiett's baritone is the cello. Yet its collective sound, not to mention its rhythmic vitality, is thoroughly original.

Murray's own albums began to mature along with those of the WSQ—his landmark octet date, *Ming* (Black Saint), was recorded only three months before *Revue*. His previous recordings document, in numbing detail, his development as a saxophonist, and include at least five volumes of unaccompanied saxophone solos. Taken a few tracks at a time, most of these tours de force remain admirably lucid. It might even be argued that the copiousness with which he improvised on his compositions prepared him to exercise the compression that characterizes the octet versions of the 1980s.

Like so many jazz composers of the past 25 years, Murray's

persistent desire has been to write music for a big band. The main obstacle, of course, is that ever since the decline of the Swing Era, big bands have been economically unfeasible. Murray's compromise, like that of Charles Mingus before him, was to organize a midsize group, in his case an octet with three brass, two reeds, and three rhythm instruments. Even the octet has trouble finding work in clubs, but has recorded three albums for the Italian Black Saint label—*Ming* (1980), *Home* (1981), and *Murray's Steps* (1982)—and these have brought David Murray more attention than all his previous work combined. In demonstrating his gifts as bandleader and arranger, they are exceptional showcases for some of the strongest soloists of the day, including Henry Threadgill, Butch Morris, Olu Dara, George Lewis, Anthony Davis, Curtis Clark and Craig Harris. Murray, like Mingus or Miles Davis in the 1950s, is undaunted by competition. He uses the best musicians available to him, and declines to hog the spotlight.

It's fascinating to compare Murray's sundry versions of the same tune; several of his pieces have traveled the route from unaccompanied saxophone to richly colored octet. The nostalgic lament "Home," for example, was meditative when played solo (on *Conceptual Saxophone*), mischievous when kibitzed by a quintet *(The London Concert)*, and ominous as a dialogue with bass *(Interboogieology)*; as interpreted by the octet, it blossomed into a cogent, churchy blues with muted brass and sumptuous flute *(Home)*. Significantly, the latter performance is half the length of its predecessors, and Murray doesn't solo on it. "3D Family" started life as a rubato tenor solo (on *Solomon's Sons*), took shape as a vivacious waltz for tenor and rhythm *(3D Family)*, and metamorphosed into a joyous, polyphonic octet arrangement, climaxing with call-and-response exchanges between brass and reeds *(Home)*. "Dewey's Circle" once had bebop connotations (on *Low Class Conspiracy*); now it combines a shuffle rhythm with a riff that would not have been out of place in a King Oliver recording, and features a duet by Threadgill and Dara that retains all the textural idiosyncrasies one associates with jazz of the 1920s *(Ming)*.

If the octet performances recall a world of jazz tradition, they never come off as ersatz. Murray's eclecticism is too personal for that. The more he borrows, the more individual he sounds; his influences—the church, Ellington, Rollins, Mingus, *et al.*—are so guilelessly embellished that no one could mistake the authorship of these pieces. He strikes just the right balance between writing and improvising, employing a matrix of homophonic flurries, unison riffs, elliptical swing themes, and motley timbres to set off and complement the pungent solos. The title selection of his current album, *Murray's Steps,* is exemplary. Murray's model was John Coltrane's "Giant Steps," though instead of using traditional harmonic turnbacks, Murray inserted major seventh chords in a pentatonic cycle. The written passages combine dissonance with consonance, swing time with long meter, and control the shape of the solos while allowing freedom of interpretation. Thus, the trombonist Craig Harris ripples through the theme with slurs and tremolos, the pianist Curtis Clark follows with exuberant bebop, and the trumpeter Bobby Bradford (Murray's old mentor) concludes with graceful melodic warmth. The most impressive soloists, however, are Threadgill, whose acrid and inspired alto strangely recalls that of Cannonball Adderley in the late 1950s, and Murray, who swings furiously (by *any* standards) and enunciates the so-called false register of the tenor with startling aplomb. This is new jazz for people who think new jazz has nothing to say to them.

Appropriately, the final selection on *Murray's Steps* is a new setting for the piece that first earned Murray attention as a composer, "Flowers for Albert." In this version, with the band paraphrasing the original melody over an undulating Afro-Cuban beat, one hears few traces of the aspirate respectfulness that Murray invoked back in the loft days. This is a comic rendition, a rendition for dancing. And Murray's tenor saxophone improvisation is a triumph, a montage of trenchant riffs that chortle through every register of the instrument with confident articulation. Still, to appreciate the range of Murray's emotional bravura, you have to see him live. During his week at New York's Sweet Basil in May, he made "Flowers for Albert" alternately tender and raucous, a balladic lament one night and a pulsating swinger the next. Since the octet is financially unmanageable, Murray usually appears these days with a quartet consisting of pianist John Hicks, drummer Ed Blackwell, and either Dr. Art Davis or Reggie Workman on bass. This band made its debut as Lush Life in the spring, and will soon record; its repertoire includes Tin Pan Alley standards as well as originals. Murray also appears with Jack DeJohnette's Special Edition from time to time ("I love it because I get to play some standard forms and traditional stuff," he says) and with the "harmolodic funk" band of James Blood Ulmer ("We have a special thing together, pure energy"). He'd like to record the music he wrote for a string ensemble he organized in 1982, and he'd like to record and sustain the kind of big band he debuted at the Public Theater. Yet Murray, like most adventurous jazz creators, operates as an outlaw. He is known in a few key cities here and abroad; his records have started to sell respectably (the recent Black Saint albums have sold in the area of 10,000 to 12,000 copies each); major musicians are eager to work with him; his star is clearly on the rise. But jazz remains so isolated by the virtual blackout in the mass media that the hardest question raised by the appearance of a David Murray is: What must an exceptionally gifted American musician whose art falls between the shores of the academy and the Top 40 do to get the hearing he deserves?

(September 1983)

Illinois Jacquet

1. Flying in Place

During his first set on opening night at Sweet Basil, the philistines were so noisy that Illinois Jacquet made a plea for discipline in the audience—a strange turn of events. Used to be that critics demanded discipline of Jacquet, whose chilling bellicose riffs taught fans how wonderfully rude jazz could be. He didn't exactly invent the honking tenor, but at the age of nineteen, in the few minutes it took Lionel Hampton's orchestra to record "Flying Home," he put it on the map. Jazz was now finally as erotic and vulgar as the *Ladies' Home Journal* had always warned, and the crowds that came to hear Jacquet with Hampton, Jazz at the Philharmonic ("Blues"), and Basie ("Mutton Leg") expected nothing less than a shot to the glands. He spawned generations of rabble-rousing tenors (none as gifted or rounded as he), and went his own way, mastering ballads, slow blues, and—of all unlikely instruments—the bassoon. He started the Sweet Basil set seated, essaying a polite "Robbins' Nest," a punchier "Port of Rico," and a nostalgic "All Too Soon." Then, maybe because his feelings were hurt by the chattering, he stood up for "Jumpin' at the Woodside," and though his choruses weren't very imaginative, the raspy conception and energy were explosive enough to warrant his saying at the finish, "I guess you saw me sitting down and thought I forgot how to do that."

Still, music is a lot louder now than it was in the 1940s, and it takes more—maybe more than it's worth—for a swing saxophonist to rouse an audience numbed by megaton sound systems. Nor is it entirely the fault of the philistines if Jacquet's introspective side seems less commanding than it should. At sixty, Jacquet is hardly an old man; he plays with as much technique and concentration as ever. But his book is old, and remnants of vaudeville date him more than his music does. For example, it's a mistake for Slam Stewart, a superb pizzicato bassist, to sing and bow a solo on every number. (While dining in a restaurant where a trio was playing, Duke Ellington once remarked to Stanley Dance, "These bass solos keep coming up like commercials on TV.") And after 45 years, surely it's time to retire "Flat Foot Floogie" except for rare séances, say when Shriners are present. Richard Wyands plays orderly on-the-beat solos with occasional block chords, but the center of tension in the band is Michael Carvin's crisp, pressing cymbal, which animates the beat and—more than the others—keeps Jacquet honest. When Jacquet communes with him, the whole quartet glistens. When he doesn't, the music is so cool you can almost sympathize with the talkers.

Any set without Jacquet's bassoon is wanting. He gets a noble, worldly sound from the instrument, especially in the lower register—almost an analagous sound to Harry Carney's on baritone. His most celebrated interpretation on bassoon is " 'Round Midnight," which he first recorded in 1968; on "Caravan," he switches between the two reeds, and, as is the case with most multi-instrumentalists, finds different melody patterns on each. Given his technical aplomb, especially the variety of timbre he can mine on a ballad, it seems wasteful for him not to expand the number of tunes he plays on the instrument.

The Cool Rage (Verve VE 2-2544), a new compilation of Jacquet's Verve recordings from 1951 to 1958, is, though arbitrarily selected and programmed, a winning sampler of his more refined playing. Jacquet's first session for the label produced—thanks to King Pleasure's subsequent addition of lyrics—his most famous ballad solo, "All of Me," and there's no better example of his ability to expand a melody motivically through supple and diverse variations. He's as convincing but less inspired on "Mean to Me" and "Talk of the Town," though "Somewhere Along the Way" underscores Jacquet's tendency to compensate with boudoir coloring for a conspicuous lack of ideas. Except for two moderately impassioned jams with Ben Webster, all of the selections were originally produced for release on 45s, and their jukebox brevity is almost always satisfying, especially two organ-tenor dates that were milestones of their kind. With Count Basie or Hank Jones on organ, a certain lightness was guaranteed, and Jacquet's barbed solos prove he never had to screech to make a point. Even a remake of "Flying Home" is relatively but not disappointingly subdued. Some performances have an ersatz quality, Jacquet's most frequent failing, as if the weight of his pitch-perfect sound wedded to a few deft riffs was enough to make an improvisation, but the rest show that even 30 years ago Jacquet knew there was more than one way to please a crowd.

2. Jacquet Expands

Although Illinois Jacquet's age—he'll be sixty-one in October— should place him squarely in the first generation of bebop, his precocious accomplishments with Hampton, Calloway, and Basie (after an apprenticeship in Southwestern rhythm-and-blues outfits) clinched his destiny. He is the youngest of the great swing saxophonists, a bridling dinosaur who, notwithstanding frequent contact with advanced thinkers of all sorts (Fats Navarro and Miles Davis sat together in one of his big bands), holds proudly to the rhythmic verities. He swings from the gut. So news of Jacquet bringing a big band to town, as he did last week at Fat Tuesday's for the first time in many years, promised more than could fairly be expected of an opening night performance—i.e., an orchestra that would swing from the gut.

Yet Jacquet and company often delivered. The opening salvo— a Jimmy Mundy arrangement of "The Birth of the Blues"— touched all the bases. The gears interlocked with stout precision, and as the riffs parted Jacquet's tenor saxophone came scudding regally across the melody and into the chords. It was a revealing moment; an orchestra like this competes only with records, which can never duplicate the experience of hearing an authentic swing band in the flesh. Basie and Hampton, long may they wave, are stylized by time, and Panama Francis's Savoy Sultan's is half a big band. Jacquet's got 16 pieces, and the ability to steer a course that pays homage to his former employers without mimicking them. Given the reach of its soloists, the sturdiness of its rhythm section, the fund of available arrangements, and the rough and ready potential of its leader, this could even be a first-class repertory ensemble.

But that takes more than rehearsal; it takes years of playing together, and what amounts in these times to an almost unima-

ginable degree of ambition. Still, Jacquet has got this far, and by
the end of the week the band sounded even more confident than
on that opening number—enough, presumably, to make him want
to go further. Meanwhile, there is room for improvement on other
counts. The sets, not surprisingly, were autobiographical, though
I'm pleased to report that there was no "Flying Home." They began with true Apollo-era slickness, the reeds crooning "Robbins'
Nest" as the leader dramatically attained the stage. Jacquet's other
standard, "Black Velvet" (or "Don'cha Go 'Way Mad"), soon followed in a somewhat perfunctory Mundy arrangement.

Two Wild Bill Davis arrangements illustrated the group's merits and shortcomings. Yes, it was able to play "April in Paris"; no,
it wasn't able to breathe life into it. Leave this fussy showpiece to
Basie, especially the "one mo' time" stuff. Jacquet was incandes-
cent on the first chorus of "Sweet Georgia Brown," but the subsequent solos, excepting those by Eddie Barefield (puffing energetically) and Richard Wyands (clever and spare) dragged. Hugh
Brodey featured his own soprano saxophone on a Horace Silver-
like original called "Who's On First" that, while appealingly sinuous in its melody and changes, was self-consciously protracted.

A splendid full performance of "Robbin's Nest" found Jacquet
in his romantic Hawkins mood and confirmed the fact that, however rough the band might be, its very presence inspired the
leader to heights of rococo lustiness all too infrequent in his usual
nightclub appearances. He swaggered on Mundy's "killer diller"
version of "Ol' Man River," while the brasses exclaimed every first
and third beat, but a drum solo (by a good timekeeper, Nasyr
Abdul Al-Khabyyr) vitiated the effect. Then, apparently because
he had just spent a residency at Harvard, he introduced "Harvard Blues" and sang George Frazier's dreadful lyric from a
leadsheet as though he thought it hilarious; in compensation the
reeds played Don Byas's solo from the Basie recording. Jacquet,
facing the audience, hummed the final riffs along with the band,
as if transported. I doubt he really was.

Jacquet's usual closer, "I Want To Blow Now," introduced several soloists, including trumpeters Irvin Stokes and Richard Wil-

liams, saxophonists Norris Turney and Barefield, and Wyands, who was in good form all evening. The band needs fewer show-business ploys than Jacquet has always thought necessary. It needs better and more varied arrangements; above all, it needs time to grow. Swing rhythms may seem as natural as breathing, but they aren't naturally engendered—not these days. Jacquet has his work cut out for him if he wants a big band, and I hope he does.

(January/September 1983)

Life After Death

A short while ago Peter Lowry, who is esteemed by blues enthu-siasts for his (presently dormant) Trix record label, came across a cut-out album of unusual interest and sent me a copy. It's be-come my favorite blindfold test, and I mention it here with mild regret at relinquishing the chance to fool the friends and col-leagues who will now swear that they would have known right off what I was playing for them. The selection I used begins with a few percussion figures, and billows luminously with the en-trance of a mostly-brass ensemble playing a spiritual-like theme; the centerpiece of the performance is a clarinet solo that stretches the pitch of key notes into rainbows of aching microtones.

One listener guessed David Murray's Octet, another Henry Threadgill's Sextet. Everyone—five or six dupes in all—knew it had to be a new release by some contemporary hot-shot eclectics. Needless to say, everyone was wrong. The piece was indeed a spiritual, "Lead Me Savior," and the performance was recorded in New Orleans in 1958 as part of the only album ever issued by the Young Tuxedo Brass Band (*Jazz Begins*, Atlantic 1297). The band was recorded by Ahmet Ertegun and his splendid engineer Tom Dowd as one of many Atlantic Records designed to capture the traditional music of New Orleans—that is, before modernists like Louis Armstrong and Jelly Roll Morton tricked it up. I suspect that even among those who are profoundly moved by Bunk Johnson, only two of the musicians are widely known, and they were not members of the Young Tuxedos: Paul Barbarin, who sat in on snare drum (Emile Knox played bass drum), and trombonist Jim Robinson.

From a historic point of view, *Jazz Begins* may be unique in its preoccupation with New Orleans burial rituals. The subtitle reads, "Sounds of New Orleans Streets: Funeral and Parade Music," and these sounds, recorded outdoors with the highest fidelity, are far removed from the usual funeral bit you find on traditionalist albums: a three-minute medley of "Flee as a Bird" and "Didn't He Ramble." These guys, weekend musicians for the most part, aren't shy about wrong notes. When clarinetist and leader John Casimir hits a bad note, he doesn't rush to make it right. On the contrary, he wallows in it, making it badder and badder until he's legitimized it through sheer stubbornness. In New York in 1983, John Casimir would be a star, as welcome at CBGB as at the Public Theater.

At least one critic in 1959, however, was not amused. In his one-star review in *Down Beat,* Richard Hadlock placed the Young Tuxedos at "the musical level of contemporary high school Dixielanders." The specific terms of his displeasure will be familiar to all avant-gardists: Casimir plays "a squealing clarinet solo with noise accompaniment"; Jim Robinson is "excruciatingly shallow"; the general result is "esthetic puerility." Yet I don't think Hadlock was necessarily wrong, not 25 years ago, when Ornette Coleman had yet to effect his "change of the century." I hope I would have been as discerning. So what does it mean that I can enjoy and recommend a sizable portion of this music—the dirges—now?

Well, it doesn't mean that musical standards have come undone, though it may mean that a quarter-century of free jazz has made it possible to hear with greater generosity the inspired idiosyncrasies of our musical forebears. I'm no longer certain just how mistaken or deliberate Casimir's pitch-problems or pitch-fancies are; I do know that his "squealing" has a vitality and gameness that have nothing to do with "high school Dixieland-ers," and that the dark, crinkled ensembles have a texture no repertory company could easily duplicate. Nor would I argue that the amateurishness of the Young Tuxedos (who, of course, weren't young at all; the average age was over fifty)—the con-gested ensemble passages, sloppy homophony, discursive solos—is characteristic of the idiom. I'm still amazed at how many awful records have been touted by traditionalists who mistook Bunk Johnson for the messiah—records I would not have thought could be admired by anyone even vaguely aware of the existence of Armstrong and Morton, Oliver and Bechet, Noone and Dodds. No, this record has a quality of its own, and judging from the less enchanting parade music on side two, I assume that quality has to do with the bleat potential of a heavy dirge.

Death is a subject that hasn't been given much play by the civ-ilized jazz of the North. There are dozens of homages to the dearly departed (Ellington wrote enough to people a smaller Spoon River), but few works about death itself: Morton's "Dead Man Blues," Ellington's "Black and Tan Fantasy," Mingus's "The Chill of Death," John Lewis's "In Memoriam," and how many others? Massive requiems are not part of the idiom, perhaps because the most insightful commentary on death offered by the jazz culture is that mixing of memory and desire made manifest in the New Orleans ritual. So it's fitting and proper that Henry Threadgill should take up his New Orleans instrument, the clarinet, for "Cremation" on his beguiling new record, *Just the Facts and Pass the Bucket* (About Time 1005).

This is the second album by the septet mysteriously known as the Henry Threadgill Sextet, and its ostensible subject—sug-gested by a cover photograph taken in a cemetery—made me at-tach new significance to the buried bones on the cover of its pre-decessor, *When Was That?* (About Time 1004). Threadgill is at work on a trilogy about the death of a computer; the first part was a selection on the previous album called "Soft Suicide at the Baths"; "Cremation" is the second part of the uncompleted work. Another new piece, "A Man Called Trinity Deliverance," also has a funereal theme, while other selections veer off into different directions: "Gateway" celebrates the St. Louis arch, and "Black Blues" is a blues that repudiates standard blues changes and form. It's always a mistake to indulge in programmatic description, yet the changeups between bright and melancholy passages throughout succeed in conjuring the deep dirges and second-line euphoria of New Orleans. The important point to make is that the music is almost consistently prepossessing.

Like the Young Tuxedos, Threadgill leads off (on "Gateway") with his two percussionists (Pheeroan Aklaff and John Betsch), and the soloists are never permitted to depart for more than a few measures from the ensemble. Although there are wonderfully tempestuous moments on the first album that are never equaled on the second, Threadgill's writing has progressed markedly in the year between the two. *What Was That?* combined selections in which the ensemble was always center stage with others in which the ensemble merely accompanied a succession of solos. With *Just the Facts and Pass the Bucket,* Threadgill the composer is ubiquitous. The contributions made by every member of the septet are heightened by the ensemble textures. To pick one example out of seven, I don't think I've ever appreciated the authority of Fred Hopkins's time quite so much.

Yet the music isn't directly connected to the sounds of New Orleans. Threadgill makes his own way to tradition, avoiding pastiche and superficial reference points. The music is understated and formal; the harmonies are rich with fourths and fifths and minor thirds. In fact, notwithstanding the muted work by the brass players (Craig Harris and Olu Dara), there is far less pitch-play here than on "Lead Me Savior." On the other hand, many of the techniques that make the record most rewarding are as old as Bunk: stop-time is used frequently, riffs are played with a breath-like naturalness and grace, thematic ideas are employed and developed in the solos. The title of the album underscores the fact that it was made without the usual studio devices, including earphones and postoperative mixing. The idea was to produce a natural acoustic sound ("just the facts"), and engineer David Stone gets some of the clarity I associate with Tom Dowd. Threadgill's bold and reverberating flute has never sounded more solid than on "Cover," an attractively voiced performance in which the role of each musician is scrupulously defined (the interplay between Hopkins and cellist Deidre Murray is especially well worked out).

The pieces, however discrete in motivation and material, are intelligently integrated. In addition to the musical ploys mentioned earlier, there are motifs that connect the selections, especially a rat-a-tat phrase that can be traced from "Gateway" through the closing "A Man Called Trinity Deliverance," and a fund of riffs that spark the soloists and vary in character from the revival-house hollering of "Black Blues" to the canonical figure in "Cremation." "Cremation" starts off where the preceding "Just the Facts" leaves off, and the whole record is made symmetrical by a conclusion that features the two percussionists.

Bob Moses's new record, *When Elephants Dream of Music* (Gramavision 8203), is also impressive for showing how traditional elements can be juxtaposed to give life to a music that is presently less concerned with coming up with something new than with finding new ways to be traditional. Death touches this album as well, in a memoriam to Trevor Koehler ("Trevor") and a homage to Billy Strayhorn ("Black Orchid"), and is counterbalanced with a celebration of Miles Davis's return to music ("For Miles") and a jolly Dixieland send-up called "Everybody Knows You When You're Up and In." The colors are entirely different from Threadgill's, dependent as they are on synthesizer, electric contrabass clarinet, and voices, but the venture is generally successful for many of the same reasons. Moses has crafted settings that heighten the contributions of several of the two dozen or so participants without letting them run away with his music. Two selections don't work for me. "The River" begins with a ragalike rhythmic pattern that leads to mostly unintelligible singing, though someone is clearly repeating the word "Buddha"; why American musicians who can pull off lively and indigenous performances on the order of "For Miles," "Trevor," and some of the others would want to pretend a studio was an ashram is beyond me. "Lava Flow" was "inspired by the magic and power of Hawaii," but the cawing birds and ooo-ing voices don't mesh with the rhythm-and-blues vamp, and the free stuff is too equalized by the mix to have any bite.

On the other hand, "Black Orchid" is a gleaming ballad, even if it does seem less Strayhorn than Carla Bley, and Jim Pepper's tenor solo is sinewy and fine. Moses brightens the colors with a whistle (it serves as a kind of bridge between the first two pieces), David Friedman's vibes, and Howard Johnson's electric contra-bass clarinet. His "Disappearing Blues" has the usual form and changes, with a difference; the thematic content is altered slightly during three choruses. A particular highlight is "Happy To Be Here Today," in which Sheila Jordan, in excellent voice, sings a negligible lyric a cappella and then with rhythm; ignore the lyric and attend to her cantorial ardor.

Threadgill and Moses are among the few musicians—David Murray is another—to pass through bouts of expressionism and come up composers, organizers. I suppose either of these albums might suggest a list of au courant techniques going round the jazz world. But their real significance is that the leaders have found ways to order their music so that all of the participants are brought to levels of cooperative playing rarely encountered outside of working bands. Of course, this ability is very much a part of the New Orleans tradition. In fact, if you want something further out, I suggest you search the cut-out bins for the Young Tuxedo Jazz Band.

(September 1983)

School for Moderns

Red Rodney and Ira Sullivan have been friends since 1955, when they worked together at a celebrated Chicago jazz club, and Sullivan's stomping ground, called the Bee-Hive. Rodney had played in several important swing and bop bands and was best known as the trumpeter who replaced Miles Davis in Charlie Parker's quintet; but although he wasn't quite 28 at the time, a series of personal calamities had all but demolished his once prodigious career. Sullivan, four years younger, was one of Chicago's premier young modernists, with a growing reputation as a multi-instrumentalist (trumpet and saxophones). Rodney's only recording with the Bee-Hive group, *Modern Music from Chicago* (Fantasy OJC-048), has just been reissued as part of Fantasy's Original Jazz Classics series. Arriving almost simultaneously with the latest Rodney-Sullivan Quintet album, *Sprint* (Musician 60261-1), it helps to place in perspective one of the more anomalous bands of the 1980s.

Recorded shortly after Parker's death, *Modern Music from Chicago* is a neglected gem—a glittering bebop period piece by three Chicagoans (Sullivan, pianist Norman Simmons, and bassist Victor Sproles) who accompanied Parker during his visits to their city, and two members of Parker's 1949 quintet, Rodney and drummer Roy Haynes. The fact that jazz still had a birthright on radio in 1955 is attested to by the short playing times of the 12 selections as well as the three dedications to disc jockeys. Simmons prepared several fanciful heads (notably a reworking of "Indiana" called "Dig This"), Sullivan unveiled his tenor sax (and

an approach surprisingly beholden to Sonny Rollins), Haynes
addressed himself to an old Chick Webb showpiece ("Clap Hands,
Here Comes Charlie"), and Rodney, lyrical and sure, navigated
the rhythms with nearly Baroque intensity (for example, his second chorus on "The Song Is You"); he even felt giddy enough
to sing Billy Eckstine's "Rhythm in a Riff." Dual trumpets were
brandished on one selection—"On Mike" according to the label,
"Trumpet Juice" according to the notes—and already the contrast between Rodney's fluent melodicism and Sullivan's calculating designs was unmistakable.

Rodney and Sullivan made a better album in 1957 (still available on Onyx as *The Red Arrow*), but Rodney, after leaving music
altogether, eventually wound up in the pit bands of Las Vegas,
and Sullivan settled in Florida and refused to budge. Only in 1980,
when Rodney once again played on Sullivan's turf (Bubba's in
Fort Lauderdale), did they decide to organize a working quintet.
What at first promised to be an exercise in bebop revivalism,
however, quickly turned into a school for moderns. Young musicians contributed new pieces in contemporary styles, largely at
the insistence of Sullivan, who had no interest in reliving his past.
Instead of "Donna Lee" and "Groovin' High," they were playing
modal frames by Jack Walrath, and elaborate themes by Jeff
Meyer and the group's pianist, Garry Dial. With Rodney concen-
trating on the mellow-hued flugelhorn, and Sullivan switching
among brass, reeds, and flutes, the quintet achieved refreshing
zeal as the leaders tackled material that increasingly challenged
their complacency as bravura technicians. But it also succumbed
on occasion to ponderousness.

For contractual reasons, the first two of the band's four albums were released under Rodney's name ("featuring Ira Sullivan"). *Live at the Village Vanguard* (Muse) is overwritten, and
Rodney sounds unsteady at times, but the follow-up, *Night and
Day* (Muse), with three impressive Jeff Meyer originals and a
couple of standards, is a stout, frequently stunning example of
what this band can do when the compositions and improvisations
are in just proportion. *Spirit Within* (Musician) sounds like a sop

to radio, as if radio weren't soppy enough; Dial's pedantic, un-swinging pieces overwhelm the interpreters, who come alive only on Meyer's "Crescent City" and especially Sullivan's "Monday's Dance," in which the two brassmen—Rodney warm and natural, Sullivan expressive and intellectual—intertwine over a resolute rhythm.

With *Sprint*, though, everything comes together. Dial has gone beyond the textbook and, in "How Do You Know," written a convincing and pretty melody that begets three yeoman cho-ruses apiece by the leaders (Sullivan on alto). His "My Son the Minstrel," a duet for Rodney and piano, combines fey stride with cool, dense harmonies. Best of all, his Ornette Coleman-inspired "Sprint" forces the soloists to navigate without chords—some-thing they do with elan—until the resolution, which is pinned down with chromatic blues tonality. "As Time Goes By," the only standard by the mysterious Herman Hupfield (his other titles in-clude "When Yuba Plays the Rumba on the Tuba" and "My Lit-tle Dog Has Ego"), usually seems too cloying for jazz (Billie Hol-iday excepted), but Sullivan's sense of drama (Dial's piano trembles in response) and Rodney's after-hours glow transform it into a blues ballad. On the other hand, "Speak Like a Child," by the no less mysterious Herbie Hancock (his other titles include "Hang Up Your Hang-Ups" and "Shiftless Shuffle"), is belabored by lengthy scene-setting before Rodney announces the central theme. After 12 minutes of such prim beauty, a concluding bebop rouser would have been a relief. Throughout the album, bassist Jay An-derson and drummer Jeff Hirschfield ably underscore the unity of this mildly daring, often surprising, and usually captivating 25-years-in-the-making quintet.

(September 1983)

Gunslinger, Phase Two

The legend of the jazz musician as gunslinger—the guy who ar-
rives in New York, uncases his instrument, bests the locals, and
establishes himself as the number one man—proliferated in the
1920s, but pretty much died out by 1960. The last widely known
tale of that kind concerned the appearance one night in the mid-
'50s of an overweight Florida schoolteacher who wanted to sit in
on alto sax with Oscar Pettiford's band. Next day, everybody was
talking about Cannonball Adderley; he was promptly given a recording contract and sent on the road. Something similar occurred in 1972, when Jon Faddis appeared as an emergency replacement for Roy Eldridge at a Charles Mingus concert.

Faddis was an 18-year-old trumpet player from Oakland, California, and word of his bravura high notes and glimmering sound
spread with remarkable rapidity—there hadn't much been new
talent, earthshaking or not, in the five years since Coltrane died.
What's more, as Mingus immediately perceived, Faddis's style was
a blend of Dizzy Gillespie's conception and Snooky Young's sound,
refreshing points of reference when most young trumpeters with
technique were aping Miles Davis or Freddie Hubbard, and most
without were justifying their shortcomings with homages to Don
Cherry. Within a week or two, he was ensconced in the Thad
Jones–Mel Lewis Orchestra, while also sitting in with Gil Evans,
Buddy Rich, and his idol Dizzy Gillespie.

The recording contract, however, took a few years, and when
Faddis began appearing on Pablo the disappointing results (all
flash, no bite) accelerated debate over whether he was a genuine

talent or just a virtuoso. Confirming those of the latter opinion, he did something that would have been unheard of for a young black musician in a previous decade. He found a lucrative place for himself in the studios. Members of the elite studio clique pay a lot more taxes than most artists, but not all of them are artistically worthless. There are few more musical trombonists in the world than Carl Fontana, who has spent much of his life playing riffs for Paul Anka. Hank Jones and James Moody replenished their spirits after a spell in studios and pit bands. Some musicians with superlative reading skills and an unlimited threshhold for trash have discovered that studio work has replaced big bands as an opportunity for apprenticeship or subsidization.

Faddis did not completely immerse himself in jingles, of course. He also established himself as quite simply the best lead trumpet player in New York. Having him in the band was like getting insurance on your brass section. Faddis is one of those rare section players—Snooky Young, Al Porcino, Bill Watrous, Marshall Royal, and the late Bobby Plater are others who come immediately to mind—who seem to coat ensembles in their rich and opulently textured sounds. At the same time, he appeared almost without fail at every engagement Gillespie played in the area, and it was in these encounters that he began to emerge as a distinctive soloist. Returning last summer to the scene of his Mingus triumph, Avery Fisher, he stunned musicians and audience alike with compellingly restrained and original readings in a re-creation of the Miles Davis-Gil Evans collaborations. And now he's finally organized a quintet to brave the club circuit.

It's a good post-bop band, with a high level of musicianship and an infectious spirit—precisely the kind of band you'd expect Faddis to have. His playing is fiery and exact, with the preponderance of high-register skeins so neatly executed that they suggest a genuinely comfortable range for him, not a facile trick to increase tension. This is not, however, a distinctive band, and its very congeniality could work against it. When America feels good about itself, it appreciates Dizzy; when not, it needs Miles. In this Milesian period, Faddis's music may be too good natured and too forthright, especially given the predictable instrumentation of rhythm plus a trumpet-alto sax or, less satisfyingly, flugelhorn-soprano sax front line. He needs to attend more carefully to pacing and repertoire—a slow blues, a deep ballad, tricky constructions, forgotten gems. Indeed, the undoubted highlight of the set I heard was a sparkling version of Benny Golson's multi-thematic "Whisper Not," limned over a sashaying groove with a coquettish muted trumpet solo, played tight and fast. By contrast, the originals shared similar tempos, Latin rhythms, and familiar changes.

More difficult matters are already taken care of: the rhythm section—James Williams, Anthony Cox, and Kenny Washington—is fine, and the band generates effortless authenticity in meshing the blues and swing. Williams, a Memphis-born former member of Art Blakey's Jazz Messengers, is an unfailingly lyrical pianist whose heated, broadly colored, improvisations could lift the most mechanical piece of music out of the doldrums. The band's newcomer is saxophonist Greg Osby, from St. Louis, and he fits well into the ensemble, though he's still working his way through a Wayne Shorter infatuation. With this level of playing talent, Faddis's band could develop into whatever he wants it to be.

(November 1983)

Eclecticism:
Ancient to the Future

Fifteen years ago, I attended a college lecture by sociologist Charles Keil, whose *Urban Blues* remains a pioneering study. Considering the aura of apocalypse in the air, with every prophet—from McLuhan, Marcuse, and Fuller to various defendant groups (pick a city, pick a number)—promising some kind of revolution, the semiradical students Keil addressed should not have been surprised that he too peddled a provocative fantasy. As I recall, he envisioned a not-too-distant future in which the nation would be divided into city-communes that would produce and attract traveling musicians. These artists (he gave Aretha Franklin as an example) would spread the news and accompany dancing, not unlike the fiddle bands that toured the Dust Bowl in the 1930s. The punch line was this: records would soon become outmoded. They couldn't contain or do justice to Aquarian music, and would probably get in the way of a truly communal experience.

Maybe I'm being unfair. After all these years, it's certainly possible that I've misremembered. Yet it's not my intention to ridicule the pipedreams of 1968, but rather to offer a wary amen. In the space of a week recently, I've attended two of the best concerts I've ever seen or ever expect to see, and recordings would do little justice to either. One obvious reason is that the performances—by the Art Ensemble of Chicago and the Willem Breuker Kollektief—were extravagantly visual. So is opera. Still, I'm certain that an experienced listener with a good stereo could approximate for himself a more faithful experience of *Tosca* than of those concerts. The plot would help you get through, whereas the seeming randomness of the AEC's and Breuker's visuals are part of what keeps you on the edge of your seat. I say "seeming" because you realize, on reflection, that little has been left to chance. And I say "on the edge of your seat" to suggest the suspense generated by music so eclectic and discursive that the battery of contrasting elements makes complacency impossible. There is no place to hide, for the listener or the musician—no easy grooves in which to nod off, no extended solos to support meditation. Yet at the same time it's all very easy to take, and although it was fashionable for many years to discuss each of these collectives in terms of the jazz avant garde, those terms now seem peculiarly inappropriate.

The term *avant garde* is simply wrong. The AEC has been around for about 16 years and the Kollektief for 10. Even at their inceptions both approached modernism less by attacking the fundamental elements of music than by rethinking modes of presentation, and they've long since concentrated on refinement. The term *jazz* is less simply wrong, since definitions tend to focus on whatever passed for jazz when the definer was approaching the age of consent. The Art Ensemble, which has always sported the slogan "Great Black Music: Ancient to the Future," underscores its ecumenical ambitions by surrounding itself with dozens of primitive instruments (from traditional Latin percussion to streetcorner noisemakers) and occasionally dressing and painting their faces in accord with African custom (not Chicago custom, anyway). That most of their source material can be traced to the various phases of jazz is unquestionable, but even if this material outweighs the considerable borrowings from rhythm and blues, European atonalism, and African rhythms, the result is a modern American selectivism that would seem to offer much to classical and rock audiences. It may be that the jazz audience adopted the Art Ensemble out of superior taste and a sense of adventure, but that doesn't explain why other audiences have ignored them. Race and instrumentation are probably more to the point. When the AEC appeared at the Brooklyn Academy of Music on October 22, the occasion was a series that also included *The Photographer/Far from the Truth* (music by Philip Glass), *The Way of How* (by the George Coates Performance Works), Trisha Brown Company, and Lucinda Childs Dance Company. The audience consisted mostly of subscribers who, excepting a handful of early walkouts, were captivated. They couldn't have asked for a better introduction.

The AEC specializes in vignettes. Its best performances consist of either contrasting tableaux or accumulated details assembled around a single motif; in each case, a large-scale work is constructed of fragments. In early years, the band occasionally indulged itself in the petulant demands symptomatic of avant-gardists—that is, they took their time getting to easy payoffs, blooping and beeping aimlessly and then falling into step with a rousing unison anthem that was supposed to make the dull stretches forgivable. The five musicians would amble through textual forests before stumbling upon a specific idea; then, quite suddenly, they all fell into line and you had a shuffle band or the Hot Five or an indolent blues group. The AEC played the Five Spot in 1975, the only time I saw them negotiate several sets in a jazz club, but it wasn't the best setting for them. They could almost always engage and hold your interest by their conceptual vigor and intonational variety, and it was fascinating to watch them stretch and contort their materials so that one set was all exultant shouting and the next studied restraint. But the most compelling episodes tended to come as relief from the overworked tinkling of little instruments.

At the Brooklyn Academy, and at several performances during the past couple of years, the AEC has been nothing if not precise. They begin with a moment of silence, facing stage left, and as soon as they turn to their several dozen instruments, they proceed in a frenzy of certitude. For 90 minutes, they altered the kaleidoscope with unerring taste and conviction. Every gambit was the right length, and every contrasting episode was ideal. They were funny and witty both. During one spasm of rocking and rolling, Joseph Jarman, his painted face in a peaked hat, grimly waved a blue flag and a moment later leeringly waved a red one. He also tossed handfuls of confetti. It is impossible to convey the effect of his pantomime, which, however abstract, provided visual correlative to the music's momentum while acknowledging the satirical edge to its digressions.

During another episode, each of the musicians except drummer Famoudou Don Moye congregated before various congas and, in African style, built complicated rhythmic structures out of simple individual contributions. Moye, who had been pounding gongs and blowing into pipes and whistles, worked his way over to the percussion melee and played a masterful solo that combined American traps wizardry with ancient instrumentation. Here, perhaps, was the evening's epiphany: just when you think

they're going nowhere or biding time, they demonstrate their
virtuosity—in the strictest academic sense—with a supreme
flourish. The keening saxophone solos of Jarman and Roscoe
Mitchell, the sassy behind-the-beat trumpet lead of Lester Bowie,
the bright and impeccably played bass figures of Malachi Favors
Maghostut, and the endlessly busy machinations of Moye were
articles of faith. It was partly our confidence in them that kept
the plot racing, one vignette blending into the next with scrupulous illogic, as they deftly (and collectively) mimicked and par-
odied various musical schools while obliterating the putative
boundary lines between them. This is an exhaustively great band.

And so is the Willem Breuker Kollektief, a nine-piece Art Ensemble of Holland. Four years ago, I wrote at length about several of Breuker's records (see *Riding on a Blue Note*), but although he had been to New York once before that, I never saw
his band in concert until its appearance at the Public Theater on
October 28. I still admire the records but, by God, this too is a
band you've got to see. The jazz tag is even less meaningful here,
and a sociologist could probably do as well as a musicologist in
explaining why Breuker has been introduced to Americans exclusively through the jazz press. Most of his pieces are written
out and executed as precisely as chamber music. Jazz plays a sufficiently important role in the music to justify the claim that
without jazz precedents there could be no Kollektief, but that same
claim could be made for marching band music, tangos, the Yid-
dische folk tunes that gave Kurt Weill his inspiration, Tin Pan
Alley, a capella pop groups, and romantic classical music—some
of which plays a more important part in their overall conception
and all of which they plunder shamelessly and daringly.

The audience at the Public Theater reacted like the one at
BAM—hesitant at first and then, when it was established that you
could trust these guys absolutely, wildly enthusiastic. Breuker no
less than the AEC is determined to keep you on the edge of your
seat, but while it's easy to draw connections between the eclectic
bravura of both bands, a more significant difference intrudes.
Breuker and his music are of Europe—he addresses American

music insofar as American music has conquered 20th-century
Europe, but his accent is Dutch, and I suppose one could say that
his animus is Great Grey Music: Ancient to the Future. It would
take several pages just to list the source materials that went into
their 90-minute set, and much of the list would be guesswork,
since Breuker specializes in fragmented phrases that sound like
familiar tunes but often become something else.

Random notes: The opening piece begins with a montage of
marches (including "Columbia, the Gem of the Ocean"), each
shaped by the punctilious percussion figures of Rob Verdurmen,
turns into a folk melody reminiscent of "Love, Oh Careless Love,"
makes room for a Breuker saxophone solo that is all split-tones
yet right on the chord changes, and finally becomes a montage
of swing and beer-garden themes, with—this amazes me still—
the orchestra maneuvering from one rhythm to the next without missing a beat. Another piece switches gears between a sultry
tango and a brisk march, then, after a Harry Jamesian trumpet
solo (by Boy Raaymakers or Andreas Altenfelder), builds variations on the keynote phrase of "Take the A Train"; during a
swing drum solo, Breuker plays a game with a phrase that falls
somewhere between Monk's "The Theme" and a-shave-and-a-
haircut—he pretends to try and catch the band offguard by playing the first few notes before they can stop whatever they're doing
(talking, strolling about) and finish it.

About midway through a number, Breuker walked offstage and
returned with his hair greased back and wearing a red and black
dinner jacket. As he sang in a '50s lounge style, the other winds
disappeared and returned in tux jackets with narrow lapels, and
accompanied him with spastic dance moves and Dixieland obbligati, plus occasional King Curtis licks and Albert Ayler multiphonics. At the end of his song, Breuker stepped into the audience to clasp hands and kiss cheeks. It was a five-minute lesson
in the connectedness of several generations of American musical
styles.

There was much undercutting of the familiar; the pianist, Henk
De Jonge, obviously trained in the classics, started a solo that

sounded like the cadenza of the fifth Brandenburg Concerto as interpreted by Cecil Taylor. A gallimaufry of bugle calls and tailgate trombone gave way to a bumptious routine in which Breuker soloed and soloed around a tonic chord but could not find the note of resolution. They harmonized "Sentimental Journey" in split-tones and imitated glockenspiels by playing "Oh You Beautiful Doll" on bottles. They explored a Spanish montuno, accompanied by the pianist's accordion and paid homage to Rahsaan Roland Kirk as the saxophonists (Breuker, Andre Goudbeek, and Maarten Van Norden) either mouthed two instruments simultaneously or helped out with the fingering.

Does this sound like vaudeville? In a sense, it was. But the experience was so lively and mutable that you never had time to question motivations. Rather, you kept making discoveries about the superficiality of stylistic differences as Breuker's pandemic influences folded in on each other. And the constant pleasure of instrumental mastery—ranging from Rudy Wiedoft-style triple tonguing (in unison!) to Ayler-like overtones (in unison!!)—kept one's jaw hanging in expectation. It is, finally, that sense of sitting on the edge of your chair that is lost on records. Significantly, Breuker's records, which must find wider distribution here (*Live in Berlin, Summer Music,* and *The European Scene* are good introductions), settle for smaller canvases. The same is true of most recent Art Ensemble records, though *Urban Bushman,* recorded live, comes closest to conveying the experience of a concert performance. You have to imagine the blue flag or the slickbacked hair, but that's no great accomplishment. What's hard is to conjure the circus atmosphere stimulated by a music in which the primary effect is surprise. Eclecticism is a poor substitute for genius, but when it's proffered with the volatile originality of the AEC and Breuker, distinguishing between the two becomes a pedant's game.

(November 1983)

Chilled Classics
and the Real Thing

What if it doesn't get any better? What if we've simply run out
of geniuses? What if all we've got to look forward to in these final hours before Reagan hits the bunkers is more hash and re-
hash, cut and paste, review and revise? Neoclassical post-modernist eclecticism, or whatever's been going on for the last 10 years,
has its moments, no doubt about it. But we're long over due for
the leatherstocking genius—poet, dramatist, musician, whatever—who can lead us out of the morass, force us to abandon
the scissors and glue, the special effects. Of course, we'll nail him
or her to the wall for doing it, but in later years, rocking in our
post-nuclear hovel, we'll weepily rejoice that we too had our Joyce,
our Bird, our Welles. In the meantime, fusion spreads like ra-
diation. You might as well pull the covers back over your head
as read any further.

Most of the fusion we suffer is horizontal: a little jazz, a little
rock, some of this and that—all of it contemporary—blended in
a Cuisinart and heaved at the *Billboard* charts. But now there's a
surge in vertical fusion, of which Linda Ronstadt's *What's New*
(marvel at the deep irony of the title) is the most commercially
successful example. In this genre contemporary performers don
Mommy and Daddy's clothes for a reactionary game of musical
chairs. You like Frank Sinatra? *Be* Frank Sinatra. I'm not talking
about the Elvis-impersonating sort of thing, which is too unso-
phisticated for New York (unless it's a man doing Judy Garland),

but a more subtly political movement that, having crowed at the demise of the '60s, seeks to replace it with our worst nightmare: the '50s. The cheerleaders for this movement (including such as Sid Zion, Rex Reed, Jonathan Schwartz, and the entire staff of WNEW) are in a peculiar position. Their motives were once at least half-pure; outraged by a greedy commercialism that strangled the lifeblood out of American music and obliterated choice from the airwaves, they stumped for vindication of their youthful vanities. So now they're stuck with promoting such answered prayers as the new Linda Ronstadt album, which in 1957 would have been dismissed as simply inept.

The cannibalism of old middle-of-the-road pop styles is unusual. We've long had young folkies trying to imitate original folkies; white bluesmen trying to be black bluesmen; and jazz repertory attempts at recapturing the spirit of another generation's spontaneous invention. Some were good, some not. But pop performers, driven by business considerations, were rarely encouraged to look back. Every major icon—Jolson, Crosby, Sinatra, Presley—represented a new juggernaut; you either got behind it or were crushed. Other than Tiny Tim, what pop performer made a living, however shortlived, by reviving the very pop excesses that intervening generations had put to rest? A couple of years ago, Carly Simon recorded an album of torch songs with orchestral arrangements that can best be described as ersatz corn. Ronstadt has gone all the way—her corn is the real thing, straight from the fields.

On the cover of *What's New* (Asylum) she is decked out in pink tulle (the last time I saw that gown was on a 1961 Shirelles album called *Tonight's the Night*). Inside she moos nine first-rate songs from the Golden Age accompanied by some of the most moribund writing Nelson Riddle has ever commited to disc. Her craving for good songs and a mature and monied audience is excusable, but the political overtones are chilling. Ronstadt conveniently summed them up for Stephen Holden in the *New York Times* a few weeks ago: "People seem grateful for this album in a way I've never experienced before. Older people finally feel in-

cluded and validated in some way. I think their feelings were hurt
in the 60's when our generation rebelled. The older generation
tried to supply us with the secure things they hadn't had, and we
grew up into the most horrible little ingrates. The whole generation of people who went through World War II was just swept
aside and made to feel completely helpless. I'd be delighted to
think that this record, in its own little way, has helped to build a
bridge back." These words—to be thoroughly savored they ought
to be read aloud in the voice Jean Hagan affected in *Singin' in
the Rain*—may be wasted on ingrates, but they suit a year in which
mushmouthed journalists beat their breasts for not having served
in Viet Nam, and Bob Dylan makes Philip Roth's "Eli the Fa-
natic" read like an exercise in naturalism. Who can avoid guilt?
My parents fed and clothed me and sent me to college; the least
I could have done was keep Perry Como's picture under my pil-
low. But no, I repaid them by spending long nights at the Village Vanguard. Luckly, Linda gives us all a chance to repent. And
repent is what you will do as soon as you hear her sob "how" at
the opening of "What's New," her vibrato madly oscillating, or
moan—with Patti Page sincerity—"adieu" in the same song.

Ronstadt made a jazz album a couple of years ago with such
notables as Tommy Flanagan and Al Cohn, which much to her
credit she kept out of release, though a tape is in circulation. She
may feel safer with Nelson Riddle's oceanic strings, but even here
she can't hide her superficial understanding of the lyrics, her solemn recitation of melody, her mannered heart-throbs. She doesn't
seem to know that the line "could you coo" in "I've Got a Crush
on You" is supposed to be coy, not desperate; or that "What'll I
Do" is dead meat without at least a soupçon of syncopation; or
that Billie Holiday's appogiatura on "Lover Man" loses something when imitated with a rural twang. (Only the great and neglected Kay Starr could bring that off.) Her accents are so predictable that as soon as she starts "(I Don't Stand a) Ghost of a
Chance," you know she's going to make the word "stand" light
up like a Christmas tree. It's worth recalling here that when Sinatra recorded these songs he was only a couple of years older

than Ronstadt, but managed to sound as though he'd lived their bittersweet epiphanies. What is most galling about Ronstadt is her emotional negligence; she sings as though she respected these grand old songs because they are grand and old. But even if she could make them work for her, why the concept—why Nelson Riddle? The best of the arrangements he wrote for Sinatra were distinguished by telling juxtapositions of strings and brass, of massed instruments and darting soloists. He brought little of that robustness and wit to Ronstadt's sessions. Maybe he recognized the project for what it is—a former sinner playing grown-up. The result is corny, presumptuous, and perfunctory. (Are you listening Sammy Cahn? "You're corny, presumptuous, and perfunctory/you make these songs sound like bunk t' me." No charge.)*

It's hard to believe that *What's New* answers the protocol of Sid Zion and others who mean to crush the rock and roll conspiracy. Ronstadt fans too young to have sinned in the '60s have argued with me about this record, and then clammed up when I played versions of these songs by people who know how to sing them. But what's WNEW's excuse, other than hasty propoganda? A music biz person told me it's unfair to compare Linda with Sarah, Ella, Billie, Frank, Nat, Peggy, Rosemary, Dinah (Washington, not Shore), and other "swept aside" parental types, as though special points should be accorded her for being under forty. I'm content to compare her with Carmen Lundy, who, after six years in New York boîtes has yet to make a record, and who, when she does, will very likely be loaded down with the very accoutrements of horizontal fusion that Ronstadt was able to jettison.

But gosh, kids, there are some copacetic platters out there, too— '50s art by '50s artists. If you want to apologize to Mom and Dad for being a cultural ingrate, you might give a spin to the long unavailable *Sarah Vaughan Sings the George Gershwin Songbook* (Emarcy 814 1871). This was the second and lesser of two two-record albums she made with Hal Mooney in 1956 and 1957; in

---

*Sammy Cahn wrote back, "I will accept corny and presumptuous, but perfunctory NEVER! . . . I speak of the pure against the impure rhyme. I would have written—'You're corny, presumptuous and perfunct t'me . . .' "

fact, her stunning reading of "But Not for Me" originally appeared on the previous release, *Great Songs from Hit Shows*. Mooney was by no means as clever an orchestrator as Nelson Riddle could be, but then even in the dark ages of 1957, Vaughan fans bought these records not because of the lumbering strings but in spite of them. The tempos are uniformly slower than the material demands, the claustrophobic strings occasionally hamper the singer's creativity, and some of the performances sound as though she first encountered the songs in the studio—especially the verses, which, in any case, are of variable quality. Having said all that, I must also point out that every track has something to admire, and the best of them are sublime. Vaughan is neither Sinatra's nor Holiday's equal at reading lyrics but that's because her purposes are almost exclusively musical. The pleasure she affords is always the pleasure of the virtuoso who quickens and retards, bends and stretches phrases and beat. When she sings of "losing at backgammon" on "Isn't It a Pity" or sighs "alas and lackaday" on "But Not for Me," I'm not convinced that she's ever played the former or thought the latter. Yet there are other instances where she unleashes all her coquetry to get right to the point of a lyric, as when she winks at "my rep-u-ta-tion" on "Aren't You Kinda Glad We Did," or becomes "a lit-tle lit-tle girl" on "Looking for a Boy," or makes a fog of her voice on "Foggy Day," or switches between coyness and patrician certitude on "I Won't Say I Will." Her operatic chops negate the charm of "He Loves and She Loves," but distill every glorious interval of "My Man's Gone Now." In his characteristically eloquent notes, my good friend J. R. Taylor compares this *Songbook* with the five-volume Gershwin project Ella Fitzgerald (and Nelson Riddle) embarked on a year or so later. I think a more relevant comparison is with Vaughan's *Gershwin Live!* (Columbia FM 37277) in 1982, when Michael Tilson Thomas's theatrical symphonic arrangements boosted her energy to highs only hinted at in '57—especially her long-perfected tempo-changing romp through "Fascinatin' Rhythm" and her inspired "The Man I Love." The aspect of Vaughan's genius that shines most clearly in the later recording is her humor, something Hal Mooney managed to put on hold. Polydor, which reissued the Vaughan, released the Fitzgerald Gershwin box (Verve 2615 063) earlier this year, and it remains a matchless feat of intelligent, articulate consistency; she never wrings a false emotion, and though she isn't a profound interpreter of lyrics either, she never subverts their meaning. For the *Songbooks*, Fitzgerald opted for definitive and respectful readings, shorn of any kind of self-conscious artiness. For Ella at her expressive best, however, her finest Gershwin interpretations are the eight wonderfully sensual performances she recorded in 1950 with pianist Ellis Larkins as her sole accompaniment: *Ella Sings Gershwin*, recently reissued (MCA 215), is one of the great records of that decade, and proof that she never needed all that fancy-dan arranging. Polydor has also just issued *The Ella Fitzgerald Set* (Verve 815 1471) as part of its Jazz at the Philharmonic Series, and although the sound is dire, these previously unissued concert performances from 1949 to 1954 are worthy additions to her admittedly sprawling discography. Hank Jones headed her trio in those years, but he was never much featured on her studio recordings, as he is here. All of the songs (including versions of "Later" and "Basin St. Blues" recorded shortly before the studio ones) are good except "Hernando's Hideaway," which she manages to salvage with irony.

Another savory vocal reissue, by a relatively little-known singer supplies the best basis for comparison with the Ronstadt fiasco. Jane Harvey, who worked briefly with Benny Goodman's band, isn't really a jazz singer; the jazz influences (notably Holiday) in her work are transformed by Broadway bravura, sometimes resulting in histrionics. She has authority and pays constant attention to the words, even when they aren't worthy of her care—which makes a dumb song like "I'll Never Go There Anymore" dumber than it need be. More to the point, she's always up for a good lyric, such as "It Never Entered My Mind" or "Here's That Rainy Day" or "My Ship," all of which she recorded for a 1964 Audiofidelity album called *I've Been There*, now available as *It Never Entered My Mind* from Discovery (DS 888). Ray Ellis, who arranged Billie Holiday's last gold-lamé strings album, did this one with results no less nondescript, though at least he doesn't get in Harvey's way. Like Ronstadt, she stretches vowels and bites certain consonants. Yet compare their versions of "Guess I'll Hang My Tears Out To Dry," and from the first measures you hear the difference between a singer who is discovering her material and one who is in full possession of it. If Harvey is still singing this well, she ought to get back to the studios. Or is she unwilling to wear pink tulle?*

(December 1983)

The Limits of Global Unity

The German pianist Alexander von Schlippenbach, who used to appear on records as Alex Schlippenbach, brought his Globe Unity Orchestra to New York for the first time on December 16. The Public Theater, which presented the evening at the Astor Place Theater, had put out a press release with all the right buzz words: "The compositions are demanding and the fluidity with which they are performed, weaving in and out of sophisticated free improvisations, requires an unusual degree of skill and sensitivity . . . eclecticism . . . everything from 12-tone structure to Jelly Roll Morton." This sounds like the mixture as before; yet the mixture presented by the GUO turned out to be one from just before before. No compositions, no serialism, no Morton. Beginning 30-some minutes late (a jazz tradition unto itself), Schlippenbach announced that we would hear "two sets of totally improvised

---

*She won't need to. Harvey is singing exceptionally well, as a subsequent night-club appearance demonstrated, and will soon record.

music." Which seemed okay to me. The cast of twelve included some of the most daring free improvisors of the past two decades, including Evan Parker, George Lewis, Gunter Christman, Bob Stewart, and a musician I'd been eager to see for many years, the innovative trombonist Albert Mangelsdorff. By the time the first set was over, however, I was thoroughly enervated. A little Jelly Roll would not have been unwelcome.

Schlippenbach founded the Globe Unity in 1966, a time when universal love, religious ecstasy, political awareness, and free jazz supposedly went hand in hand: a black fist clasped to a white one, a psalm to a chant, a split-tone to an overtone. Coltrane's 1965 *Ascension* was a turning point—11 musicians united only by sincerity and a triad, playing two takes of a work that alternated frenzied ensembles (crescendos and diminuendos) with frenzied solos. Lacking the politeness, wit, and charm of Coleman's earlier *Free Jazz*, it was more a manifesto than an experiment, more cri de coeur than ars gratia artis. The GUO was Europe's first major response to the American New Wave and proved the most enduring band of its kind, excepting Sun Ra's Solar Arkestra. It was soon followed by the Jazz Composers Orchestra, the Instant Composers' Pool, and the Willem Breuker Kollektief, not to mention such smaller units as the Art Ensemble of Chicago, the Creative Construction Company, and the Revolutionary Ensemble. As '60s' rhetoric was quelled and buried, the forces of composition and improvisation were uneasily mated in a transitional phase that finally found formalists coming into their own (again) in recent years. Schlippenbach, however, held to the purity of free improvisation; although some of the GUO's compositions were dauntingly rigorous, the rigors were often less concerned with scratchings on a score than with huge choreographed happenings, such as Peter Kowald's notorious *Jahrmarkt/Local Fair*, in which various groups of musicians (including 25 accordionists) were situated in a town square at distances that made it impossible for one band to hear the others playing the same piece. Still, the reputation of the GUO subsisted largely on its ability to assemble many of the world's best and, needless to say, most committed free players for its performances.

My response to the GUO's American debut, which could not have been more different than the punctilliously conceived performance by Willem Breuker at the Public Theater in October, is somewhat ambivalent. You don't hear much free jazz these days, and the GUO goes at it with brio. There were moments of sheer caterwauling that I found as bright and irreverent as *Ascension* and a good deal more shapely. But for the most part I found myself waiting impatiently for the solos, especially those that were accompanied sparingly or not at all. These exhibitions of virtuosity, though not always animated by musical impulses, entailed a celebration of self that is perhaps not possible even for so minuscule a microcosm of the Globe as this. Ellington, a master of metaphor even when his musical powers were at half-mast, introduced the first of his Sacred Concerts with a celebration of expertise called "In the Beginning God." Reasoning that each of us prays with a unique voice, he developed the piece as a kind of revue in which a few of his virtuosi would go the limit with precisely those powers that made them unique—e.g., Paul Gonsalves's energy, Louis Bellson's speed, and Cat Anderson's high notes. The best solos at the GUO concert suggested a similar delight in instrumental trickery.

Toshinori Kondo, holding a straight mute backwards at the bell of a trumpet, did everything he could with his instrument but make it sing in its traditional voice; he made kissing and guttural sounds, while drummer Paul Lovens scratched the fat end of his stick against an upturned cymbal lying on his snare. George Lewis demonstrated his remarkable tonguing technique throughout the range of the trombone, turning what might have been a mere etude into something more by dynamically varying his lexicon of strange brassy sounds. Schlippenbach began a piano solo by invoking Cecil Taylor's woolly percussiveness, but quickly opted for dense parallel phrases in his very short and disconcertingly fickle interlude. Trombonist Gunter Christmann played tuned air occasionally interrupted by concrete notes; he wheezed and snorted, eventually suggesting a slapstick tussle with his intransigent instrument. Kenny Wheeler, on the other hand, seemed out of place in precisely the same way Freddie Hubbard was out of place on *Free Jazz* and *Ascension:* he tried valiantly to overcome his habit of playing harmonically dictated melody, but he couldn't quite do away with his need for the coherent arpeggio.

Since Albert Mangelsdorff soloed no longer than anyone else, the celebration I expected to write of him will have to wait for another occasion. His fleeting eighth-note passages were colored by a fascinating and judicious use of harmonics that widened and tightened his intonation, so that single pitches were set in contrary motion to the two- and three-note chords that he uses for rhythmic as well as harmonic accent. The ensemble caved in around him all too quickly. I'd like to hear a whole evening of just Manglesdorff, or perhaps him and a few others soloing at length, one at a time. The solos by Bob Stewart on tuba, Gerd Dudek, Ernst-Ludwig Petrowsky, and Evan Parker on reeds, and Cecil Taylor alumnus Alan Silva on bass were less distinctive. Recalling his mesmerizing 1978 album, *At the Finger Palace,* I found Parker especially disappointing; he was barely audible over the ensemble that shadowed his every step.

I left after the first set, remembering something that a first-generation American jazz avant-gardist once told me. We were at a European festival listening to an ensemble from East Berlin screeching its heart and lungs out, and he said, "Let's get something to eat. This stuff is great to play but not to listen to." I disagreed then and still do, simply because there are too many exceptions to make generalizations about free jazz any safer than those made about any other school in the music's history. It's usually individuals rather than movements that make a musical style enduring. Yet I find that I'm increasingly suspicious of ensembles that make phrases like "totally improvised" a badge of honor, and not because few people without an emotional (that is, nostalgic) or political (that is, sentimental) investment in this old New Wave can respond to it. The compositional end of the jazz equation has the upper hand in the 1980s, and it seems arrogant and even lazy for an ensemble not to strive for textures more accomplished than the primitive call-and-response blasts mustered by the GUO. The avant garde served several purposes in the '60s, one of which was thumbing its nose at the tired formulas of the past. But new formulas are being tested, and until free ensembles can do something more organic and convincing with their freedom—something that may not be possible for Westerners, yoked to individualism as they are—the thumb is on the other hand. At this juncture, it's the composer who is in ascension.

(January 1984)

Carmen on Holiday

Of all the candidates for the pantheon of jazz vocalists, Carmen McRae is perhaps the most puzzling. She didn't begin recording as a single until she was 32 (in 1954), attained an unexpected crescendo of inspiration in the early '60s, recorded dreamy pop as well as jazz to survive the rock age, and proved strangely uneven in her subsequent concert and club appearances. Her private demeanor seems so at odds with her professional persona that sometimes her offstage gruffness and no-nonsense bile intrudes on the gowned and cheery image she presents in the spotlight, as if her blues were too personal to channel into mere music. The enigma is heightened by her voice and style, which are absolutely original, and her physical presence, which defies time. In the 20 years I've been going to see her, she has broadened her girth and cropped her hair, but the expansive plains and handsomely chiseled features of her great stone face, so perfectly matched to her implacable intonation, are unchanging. She has become an axiom in American singing, and when she works as well as she did these past couple of weeks at the Blue Note, coiffed with a white gardenia ("we're trying to be as authentic as possible") to celebrate Billie Holiday, she is as good as anything American singing can offer.

I know little of McRae's relationship with Holiday, except that her first champion was the gifted songwriter Irene Kitchings, whose work was immortalized by Holiday, and that McRae has described herself as Billie's protégé. Yet if Holiday influenced her style, it was on a level too subtle for my ears to appreciate—I hear more Holiday in Sinatra than I do in McRae, who, even in her earliest work, suggested more affinity with the harmonic and rhythmic leanings of her contemporary, Sarah Vaughan. But the connection must be a powerful one because Holiday's music transforms McRae, lightening her demeanor and brightening her attack. In 1961, she recorded a recently reissued tribute called *Lover Man* (Columbia PC 30072) that is, cut for cut and measure for measure, one of the best vocal jazz albums ever made. As if to underscore the differences between Holiday and herself, she chose as her chief accompanist Eddie Lockjaw Davis, a far cry stylistically from Lester Young, and never once drew on Holiday's mannerisms—her "Strange Fruit" is entirely persuasive on her own terms, as was her 1958 reading of the hymn closely associated with Ethel Waters ("His Eye Is on the Sparrow"). The general feeling of the date is encapsulated in the spontaneous laughter Davis's playing elicits from her at one point.

At the Blue Note, she was chaperoned through several selections per set by the no less individual Zoot Sims, who accompanied her vocals with clouds of tenor sax and complemented them with pungent and sensuous solos. Some of her most memorable moments, though, were accompanied only by the Marshall Otway trio, such as a crafty reading of "Fine and Mellow" that replaced Holiday's wan sexuality with the kind of witty and theatrical purposefulness that makes each chorus a discrete adventure.

It began as a slow blues, sketched in growls and large intervals, with every phrase mined for meaning; it grew feverish with implied stop-time in the second chorus and funny-risqué in an interpolated chorus of orgasmic moans; the penultimate verse swelled with threats ("you're gonna drive me away") and the climax ("love is like a faucet") roared with cagey abandon. This kind of performance has closer parallels to the blues divas of the '20s than to the more sophisticated chanteuses of the '30s. The most moving sequence found McRae alone at the piano (she's an expert self-accompanist with Monkian touch), providing herself with precisely the right legato groove on "She's Funny that Way."

The sets combined familiar Holiday anthems ("Lover Man," "God Bless the Child," "Miss Brown to You") with delightful trifles that no one sings anymore, like "I'm Gonna Lock My Heart" and "Painting the Town Red." For his solo portion, Sims played, exquisitely, "That Ole Devil Called Love"; his mischievous set-closer was a chorus of Charlie Parker's "Billie's Bounce." Throughout they found ways to clear the mothballs from songs that are so old they're new, as when McRae made the line "Sit down" in "Good Morning Heartache" a blistering command, or when she freely improvised phrases, finding unlikely chords and casually blueing sweet cadences with her acidic brand of alchemy. The concept behind this engagement was too natural to require much comment, except to say that any kind of concept can be a boon for a performer as road-weary as McRae sometimes seems. It assured her and the audience of refreshing material, united her with a peer, and resulted in mutual—or four-way, if you reckon the ghosts of Holiday and Lester Young—inspiration. Which reminds me: isn't it about time Carmen McRae dusted off some of those songs that Dave and Iola Brubeck wrote for her?

(January 1984)

Thelonious Monk

1. In Walked Monk

When Nathan Zuckerman fishes for approbation in Philip Roth's
The Ghost Writer, the great Lonoff tells him he has "the most
compelling voice I've encountered in years, certainly for some-
body starting out. I don't mean style. I mean voice: something
that begins at around the back of the knees and reaches well above
the head." Voices like that are rare in any art, but when one turns
up in the jazz world it often has an unusually comprehensive and
immediate effect. I'm referring to the kind of musician with a
voice so startling—a grasp so sure—that the whole music seems
to stop in its tracks to confront the interloper, and emerges enhanced and fortified. This was certainly the case with Armstrong, Young, Parker, and Coleman. But not with Thelonious
Monk, who conducted his first record session at thirty, organized
his first working band at forty, and dropped from sight at about
fifty-five. Although a small coterie of musicians (notably Coleman Hawkins, Mary Lou Williams, Dizzy Gillespie, Charlie Parker, and Bud Powell) esteemed him from the beginning, he la-
bored in solitude for much of his most creative period. His records
were ignored, his compositions pilfered, his instrumental technique patronized, his personal style ridiculed. Yet no voice in
American music was more autonomous and secure than Monk's,
and no voice in jazz relied more exclusively on jazz itself for its
grammar and vision.

The controversy about Monk must be difficult for younger listeners to comprehend. One can readily appreciate why Schoen-

berg and his disciples or the jazz avant garde of the '60s caused dissension. Those musics were conceived as attacks and practically demanded rejoinders. Monk's music is more accurately compared to Stravinsky's early ballets, which, though new and daring for the time, proved accessible to the general public long before intransigent critics saw the light. Monk isn't merely accessible; he's almost gregarious in his desire to entertain, as long as the listener is willing to be entertained on Monk's terms. By this, I don't mean to suggest that Monk's music is lightheaded or lighthearted, though on occasion it can be both, but that everything he did was designed to heighten the listener's response to melody, rhythm, and harmony. His tools were traditional, his craftsmanship impeccable. Monk relished swing and the blues and the freedom to do with them as he pleased (his motto was "Jazz is freedom"); he pursued his muse with dauntless concentration, impressive faith, and an almost childlike glee. This, after all, was the musician who more than anyone else transformed the minor second from mistake to resource.

Immersing oneself in Monk's art, as a spate of reissues has encouraged me to do these last couple of months, is both an exhilarating and dispiriting experience—the former because his music is eternally fresh, the latter because so much else seems tame and trite by comparison. I thought I knew his Blue Note recordings pretty well, but rummaging through the treasure box that is *The Complete Blue Note Recordings of Thelonious Monk* (Mosaic MR4 101), I find that even the most familiar pieces unveil new mysteries and reveal new charms. One obvious reason is that this four-record box, comprising the six sessions he conducted for the label between 1947 and 1952, plus a middling 1957 session under the leadership of Sonny Rollins, includes no less than fourteen previously unreleased performances. Eleven are alternate takes, but don't for a moment think that they are merely flawed warm-ups with slightly different embellishments or changes in tempi. In almost every instance, they afford us the chance to hold familiar gems to the light and discover new refractions of Monk's genius; his work on some of the alternates—including "Nice Work

If You Can Get It" and "Skippy"—is actually superior to that on the master versions. The remaining discoveries (all from 1952) are a mildly amusing reading of an obscure Fred Ahlert melody ("I'll Follow You"), and two takes of a previously unknown Monk original, "Sixteen," that reharmonizes "Ja-Da" much in the way "In Walked Bud" reharmonizes "Blue Skies." Although Monk never officially recorded the tune, he recycled a key lick from his tumbling, all-in-one-breath first-take solo five months later for his improvisation on "Little Rootie Tootie." Some years later, Sonny Rollins employed similar changes for "Doxy," and one can't help but wonder if they were a lesson from the master.

The Blue Note years capture Monk in the throes of youthful assertion, training musicians of varying abilities in the exigencies of a music unlike but indebted to the hopped-up modernism of the age. They remind us, as indeed all of Monk's work does, that he was the quintessential New York jazzman. A proudly chauvinistic resident of West 63rd Street—where a circle is now named in his honor—for most of his life (his family moved there from North Carolina when he was six), Monk lived and breathed the sounds of the city as surely as Louis Armstrong was nurtured by New Orleans. It's there in everything he wrote and played—the clangor and ambition; the nostalgia and irreverence; the influences of the church, big bands, Tin Pan Alley, Harlem stride, modernism. He embraced it all. Yet despite a teenaged sojourn at Julliard, he knew less of the European tradition than most of his contemporaries, particularly Parker and Gillespie; Quincy Jones once credited this combination of self-absorption and willful ignorance with Monk's ability to avoid "contrived" experiments. Monk's modernism may once have seemed difficult to comprehend and remains extremely difficult to play, but it was never self-conscious. Michael Cuscuna, co-partner with Charlie Lourie in the Mosaic venture, wisely devotes much of his copious notes to musicological comments by such as Gunther Schuller, Ran Blake, Steve Lacy, and Martin Williams. Listening through their ears, we can perhaps better enjoy the harmonic and rhythmic innovations that inform these performances, but our appreciation of complex Monkian neologisms in no way vitiates our ability to listen ingenuously, too. Monk delights the brain, but he also animates the heart and viscera.

His first masterpiece, appropriately called "Thelonious," was recorded at the close of his first session, and was greeted by *Billboard* as "a controversial jazz disking worked out on a one note riff." Though only a prelude to the more accomplished work to come, it merits close inspection. I don't know a better example of the way a musician can draw extensively on the jazz past and come up with something indigenous and wonderful. A first listening tells us nothing if not that the composition and execution are pure Monk, and something new in jazz in 1947. Yet the materials continuously summon ghosts from the past. For starters, there is the rhythmic/melodic concept that governs the entire piece—a hammering, repeated theme that appears to be confined to one note, though it is really built on three. The antecedent I'm reminded of is the first of Louis Armstrong's two choruses on "Muggles" (1928). Armstrong constructed the entire episode by ping-ponging two notes, A and C, and then climactically springing up an octave to high C. Monk works just as exclusively with F and B-flat, increasing tension with B-flat octaves, only he sustains this motif for the entire performance. Monk announces his rhythmic intentions with an introduction by piano and drums. The theme is voiced on piano while the winds (in their sole contribution to the piece) play descending arpeggios— not functionally unlike the vamp for reeds at the beginning of Ellington's "East St. Louis Toodle-oo" (1927). Ellington is more explicitly suggested in the theme's unusual structure: AABA with a 10-bar release, plus a two-bar interlude between choruses. The unchanging interlude may also remind us of the kind of blues fillips Jimmy Yancey often employed as transitions between choruses (cf. the 1939 "How Long"). The eight bars of B-flats that end the first improvised chorus recall not only Armstrong, but the king of the one-note ride, Lester Young, especially since the sequence begins a measure ahead of time (a favorite Lestorian ploy). The second chorus, however, opens with stride piano out

of James P. Johnson (albeit with Monkian minor seconds), and
concludes with an au courant rhythmic lick that contemporaries
called "Salt Peanuts" (after Gillespie's record) but that older fans
may have remembered from Armstrong's "I'm a Ding Dong
Daddy." And the final chorus climaxes with a series of triplets à
la Count Basie. So here, in three minutes, we can reasonably in-
fer echoes of Armstrong, Ellington, Yancey, Young, Johnson,
Gillespie, and Basie in a performance that any fool knows is 100
percent Monk. I don't suggest that Monk was much interested in
sprinkling his music with homages or clues; the lesson here is that
Monk found in jazz all he needed to elaborate his own devious
fantasies. By contrast, a good many deliberate glorifications of the
jazz tradition sound fabricated and coy.

Monkian revelations proliferate in these recordings. How did
he think of so many odd notions that sound so unalterably right
in performance—such as the single measure of boogie woogie bass
in the bridge of his gorgeous ballad, "Ruby, My Dear," or the
introduction to "In Walked Bud" that is nothing more than a
cascading arpeggio that caroms into the oddly accented theme
with algebraic precision (Art Blakey's press rolls in this piece have
the same effect), or the two measures of whole-tone phrases right
before the first improvised turnback on "Off Minor." Blakey, of
course, requires more than parenthetical mention as one of Monk's
finest collaborators. You can almost hear him hearing the pianist, so deftly and empathically does he shift dynamics, bearing
down when appropriate, floating the rhythm with unfaltering
exactness. The other major voice here belongs to Milt Jackson,
whose unperturbed grace inspired Monk to some of his most
outlandish conceits, such as the erupting sevenths on "Misterioso" that might have been turned into a new tune, in the manner of "Evidence." There are memorable turns by other players
as well, but it's Monk who consistently steals the show, whether
he's doubling the bass line behind the trumpet solo on "Subur-
ban Eyes" or closing an eight-bar solo on "All the Things You
Are" with blues licks or clipping chords (raising all his fingers but
one) and pounding minor seconds on "Introspection" or playing

havoc with 4/4 by displacing the melody accents of "Criss Cross" or making his sole comment on the cool school with the melodious "Let's Cool One" or voicing ripe alto sax on only the third and 11th bars of "Round Midnight" or orchestrating tritones on "Skippy" or playing with waltz meter on "Carolina Moon." This is music that pleases first time out, but I wonder if it ever gives up all its secrets. Perhaps the biggest surprise this box will have for veteran Monk enthusiasts is the alternate to "Well You Needn't." Apparently, he hadn't absolutely determined the way the piece should be played when he arrived at the studio; after he recorded the master, he tried a version with a slight change in the thematic accents—the result is practically a new piece.

The Mosaic production is exemplary in all important aspects, but I have two quibbles. First, there is much talk in the notes of still unreleased takes, some of them described in detail, which means they exist. I'm willing to believe Cuscuna when he calls them tedious (though it's hard to believe they are entirely dispensable), but I wish he'd use more caution in calling his collections Complete; eight years ago (when he collated *The Complete Genius* for Blue Note), Complete didn't allow for the 14 new performances in this set, and who knows what it will mean a few years hence. Second, there is a splendid discography that solves many puzzles (including the seemingly deliberate errors on Columbia's 1966 *Misterioso*), but pointlessly ignores live recordings that weren't originally intended for commercial release on the grounds that they aren't "legitimate." By what logic are discarded takes from the Blue Note vaults legitimate, while the 1941 Jerry Newman tapes from Minton's, which have either been widely available for 37 years or issued responsibly by Xanadu in the '70s, aren't? Record producers should be moral, upstanding citizens and the scourge of bootleggers, but discographers should just be scholarly. There are also a few typos, of which "In Walked Dud" is the most egregious. This limited edition (7500 copies worldwide) was created for Mosaic Records of Santa Monica, California.

2. *Rhythm-a-ning*

Michael Cuscuna points out in his notes to *The Complete Blue Note Recordings of Thelonious Monk* that the label capitalized on Monk's rumored eccentricities for promotional purposes. In addition to brandishing phrases like "the High Priest of Bebop," it issued a press release that referred to him as "the genius behind the whole movement [modern jazz] . . . an unusual and mysterious character . . . a strange person whose pianistics continue to baffle all who hear him." Monk's oddest behavioral trait, by all reports, was his reticence: he didn't talk a lot, and saw no need to promote himself through the usual channels. Although his few interviews show him to have been articulate and candid, he usually chose to let the music speak for itself. Very weird. Granted, Monk did nothing to discourage his growing reputation for being odd. He became famous and finally notorious for his hats, his bamboo-frame sunglasses, his dancing on stage, and his faith in Charlie Rouse and in a small body of compositions that he played nightly. By 1969, Columbia could get away with (and win a prize for) displaying him amid armaments, Nazi paraphernalia, and a slogan of the French resistance on the album *Underground*. His detractors attacked him first because he was too far out, and later because he wasn't far out enough. Monk, of course, kept his own counsel.

Still, the phrase from Blue Note's press release that had the widest currency was "genius." In 1951, the label issued his 78s as LPs entitled *Genius of Modern Music,* and when they were collected anew in 1976, the title was *The Complete Genius.* The only other American performer I can think of who was publicized so hyperbolically was Ray Charles. But in Charles's case there was a large record-buying public pulling the bandwagon. Blue Note's enthusiasm was generally regarded as hype of a peculiarly desperate sort. It was as if you had to be a genius yourself to join the club and understand his angular music. This misconception might have been quickly righted if Monk had been on view. But the same year that greeted his first album also found him con-

victed on a trumped-up drug charge. LaGuardia's medieval cabaret laws were never exploited more flagrantly than in the early
'50s, and Monk lost his cabaret card for six years; from the age
of thirty-four until he was forty, he couldn't work in any room
in New York that sold alcohol.

So Monk continued to work in a kind of solitude, except that
he was surrounded by many of the best young musicians in the
country. Genius shrivels up if it isn't shared, and Monk responded to his misfortune with an astonishing increase in energy—not only as composer and pianist but as teacher. Monk's
role as a teacher goes back to the early 1940s, when he proved a
constant source of ideas for Parker, Gillespie, Powell, and, other
more immediately accessible modernists. In the '50s, he had an
equally great impact on several of the musicians who would
dominate the music during the following decade, including Sonny
Rollins, who credits his command of thematic improvisation to
Monk, and John Coltrane, who said he learned how to play chords
on the saxophone from him. There are numerous stories of young
players rehearsing with him, and being forced to play above what
they deemed their own capacities. "But this is impossible," the
novice protests. "You a musician? You got a union card? Then
play it," Monk insists, and somehow it gets played. Though not
always. At the *Brilliant Corners* session in 1956, they had to splice
together a master version of the title tune, so daunting were the
tempo changes and intervallic leaps. Even when Monk had no
audience of his own, then, his genius was seeping into the mainstream. In a sense, his disciples prepared the way for him. By
the time he began to sustain his own following (after making one
crucial compromise with the audience: a couple of sometimes
pallid albums of standards), he was still regarded as eccentric, but
no one doubted his competence.

If Monk's first acceptance came as a teacher, his second came
as a composer. A familiar refrain of the 1950s was the line about
how he wrote wonderful tunes, but wasn't much of a pianist. By
then Monk's writing was impossible to ignore. "Hackensack" and
"Epistrophy" were bop classics, " 'Round Midnight" was a hit,

"Straight No Chaser" and "Blue Monk" were fast becoming post-bop standards. Strangely enough, he never recorded (and hardly ever played) his most famous melody after " 'Round Midnight," "52nd Street Theme," yet this piece was as close as Swing Street ever came to an anthem. Monk has been called the greatest jazz composer after Ellington, yet his output was relatively small. By my count, there are 70 pieces, including the posthumously discovered lead sheet for "A Merrier Christmas" (debuted by Sphere last November). Other unpublished tunes may come to light, but it's doubtful they'll add greatly to Monk's reputation. In this number are a couple of contested items, like "Eronel" (the late Sadik Hakim claimed partial credit) and "Rhythm-a-ning" (which combines a lick from Ellington's "Ducky Wucky" with an episode from Mary Lou Williams's "Walkin' and Swingin' "), but not items that Monk is believed to have written but received no credit for (like "Dizzy Atmosphere").

It's a modest number, though much larger than that of Varèse or Webern, and with no more fat. " 'Round Midnight" is the only Monk ballad that has won wide acceptance from singers as well as instrumentalists, but it's only one of several beautiful compositions, and by no means the best; of the others, "Reflections," "Ruby My Dear," and "Ask Me Now" might profitably be fitted with lyrics, while "Crepuscule with Nellie" and "Comin' on the Hudson" are more exclusively instrumental. No tally of Monk's writing is complete without mention of the many standards he adapted and transformed into original works for the piano. His various recordings of "April in Paris," "All Alone," and "Just One Way To Say I Love You" are ultimately as indigenous as many of his blues and riff compositions. His 1957 recording of "I Should Care" is a no less original and startling invention than some of the configurations he built on familiar changes, like "Evidence" ("Just You, Just Me") or "Bright Mississippi" ("Sweet Georgia Brown"), and two classical recitalists have performed a transcription of it. Nor can Monk's work as a composer be separated from the way he organized his groups, not merely as regards the orchestrations, but also the improvised piano accompaniments and architectonic designs for the rhythm section.

It's often assumed that Monk's greatest flowering as a composer took place during the 1940s, but I would argue that the 1950s were just as fruitful and even more ambitious. He introduced 23 originals at the Blue Note sessions (including the posthumously discovered "Sixteen"), but between the final months of 1952, when he first recorded for Prestige, and 1961, when he concluded his sojourn with Riverside, he introduced 33 pieces. These include "Little Rootie Tootie," "Trinkle Tinkle," "Reflections," "Bemsha Swing," "Monk's Dream," "Friday the 13th," "Let's Call This," "Think of One," "Wee See," "Nutty," "Work," "Gallop's Gallop," "Brilliant Corners," "Crepuscule with Nellie," "Comin' on the Hudson," "Jackie-ing," and "Light Blue"—a selection that would itself constitute one of the most impressive bodies of melodies and springboards for improvisation in American music. This same period also accounts for many of his most ingenious blues, ranging from the exceedingly personal tour de force "Functional" to the irresistible "Blue Monk." In the early '60s, Monk's output as a composer fell off sharply—some 13 pieces in more than a decade, the best of them blues. But his ability to pump energy into his quartets remained, and Charlie Rouse, notwithstanding his fondness for his own lexicon of licks, became an increasingly incisive interpreter; not even Coltrane's tenor blended as evenly with Monk's piano. Monk himself often played more ebulliently, and at long last he achieved widespread recognition in the third realm of his genius, as a piano player. Paul Bacon's 1948 observation that the technique of Horowitz might not be up to Monk's needs as a pianist finally became a commonplace.

Several of Monk's classic albums for Prestige and Riverside have recently been issued in their original covers, and in some cases they are preferable to the twofers. You can now hear the 1957 *Monk's Music* (Riverside OJC-084) as Monk intended, with the wind arrangement of the hymn "Abide with Me" as the opener and the lovely hymnlike "Crepuscule with Nellie" as the closer. The latter, incidentally, was never used by Monk as a blowing piece; in all his recorded versions, he played it alone on piano, and arranged the final half-chorus for the ensemble. Coltrane, who isn't mentioned on a cover that boasts Hawkins, Blakey, and Gigi Gryce, plays with respectful emotional fervor—that is, he's emotional on Monk's terms. Coleman Hawkins, robust and curious, makes for stimulating contrast, especially as he swallows whole the changes to the release of "Epistrophy." Monk's solo here is only one chorus, and it's a miracle of compression and mathematical rectitude. For the first eight bars, he paraphrases the tune, accenting raised fifths and minor seconds; the next eight alternate chromatic runs with repeated sevenths; the release consists of a single phrase prodded, tailored, and lengthened (it's like a miniature version of "Straight No Chaser"); the amazing last-eight reduce the theme to clusters, the last two of which arrive right where you least expect them (on the downbeat of the penultimate measure).

Of the three Prestige reissues, the 1952–54 *Thelonious Monk* (OJC-010) is a thoroughly delightful sampler of his piano-playing virtuosity and vitality—he brazenly recreates the sentimental "These Foolish Things" in his own dissonant, wildly swinging image; displaces all the accents on "Trinkle Tinkle," which has a surprisingly melodic release; demonstrates his ability to treat the keyboard as tuned drums on "Bemsha Swing" and "Bye-Ya"; and ruminates over one of his most lyrical creations, "Reflections" (for my taste, the most songful version of this affecting melody is by Steve Lacy). *Thelonious Monk with Sonny Rollins* (OJC-059) and *Monk* (OJC-016) are boisterous sessions from the same period, and the former, highlighted by quartet versions of "Friday the 13th" and two sunny standards, is an essential record of the Monk-Rollins collaboration; the latter has two quintets (one with French horn) playing an all-Monk program, but is less successful.

During the '60s, Monk recorded for Columbia, and, although the early sessions were excellent, some of the later ones, especially a big band date arranged by Oliver Nelson for which Monk was importuned to play two pathetic pieces by producer Teo Macero, should never have seen the light of day. Any doubts that the company employed more than its share of knuckleheads was removed when it released three twofers after Monk's death that were better than some of the music issued while he was alive. These are typical souvenirs of Monk's quartet in concert, and are as much tributes to the unfairly maligned Rouse as to the leader. The current offering, *Tokyo Concerts* (C2 38510), is the least of the three. But don't miss *Live at the It Club* (C2 38030), with its rare performance of "Gallop's Gallop," and *Live at the Jazz Workshop* (C2 38269), which has a stunning Monk solo on "Well You Needn't": he begins the second chorus with telescoped references to three unlikely folk themes, a spiritual ("Happy Am I with My Religion"), a cavalry song ("The Girl I Left Behind Me"), and the West Indian piece Charlie Parker called "Sly Mongoose." There is no hint here (in 1964) that Monk was running out of steam and would, within a decade, feed the wildest speculations of all by simply disappearing from the scene. The only thing odd about this music is its genius.

(January 1984)

Frank Sinatra

1. An Appreciation

American music has made its mark in the 20th century with such fabulous abundance that it's hardly ever wise to single out one artist at the expense of his or her colleagues. Who is our greatest orchestrator or song writer or improvisor or blues shouter or instrumentalist or rock icon or bandleader? No matter whom you name, a persuasive argument can be made for someone else. Yet among singers of popular songs, a field more populous than most with bona fide stars, one remarkable artist clearly looms above the rest. For nearly half a century, Frank Sinatra* has been a vital and stubbornly individual force in the development of American singing.

Sinatra likes to refer to himself as a saloon singer, although his natural habitats are the concert stage and the recording studio. He speaks generously and thoughtfully about the singers—especially Billie Holiday, Bing Crosby, and Mabel Mercer—who influenced him and the tradition he sustains. But it's impossible to categorize him. A conscientious, knowing craftsman, he is a school unto himself. He sounds like no one who preceded him, and no one else sounds like him. S. J. Perelman's description of rock stars who "hatch one evening and perish the next with the mortality of mayflies" could just as well be applied to most of Sinatra's imitators. Yet Sinatra endures with a peculiarly dangerous energy, untrammeled by nostalgia or cheap sentiment. Undoubtedly, there are people who attend his concerts in expectation of a jog down memory lane, but from the moment he strides on stage, they know they're in for something deeper.

At sixty-eight, Sinatra remains the consummate performer. His elegance and charm are dazzling, not least because they mask the possibility of unwarranted explosion. For all his experience and professionalism, he is always himself—which means that his performances tend to reflect his moods. On an off night, he can be peremptory and rude. But on good nights (and in recent years they have been the rule), he is simply mesmerizing. Duke Ellington wrote of him, "Every song he sings is understandable and, most of all, believable, which is the ultimate in theater." Sinatra is never a greater actor then when he maps out a favorite song, combining the economy of Gielgud and the charisma of, well, Sinatra. When he wants to emphasize a lyric, a flick of the wrist or a focusing of the eyes is enough to do the trick.

*A slightly different version of this piece appeared in *Stereo Review* when Sinatra received that publication's 1984 Mabel Mercer Award.

Perhaps Sinatra's commitment to performing is the key to his greatness. We tend to think of him, justifiably, as a modernist, as someone who replaced cool crooning with adult emoting. But we're learning with increasing clarity and regret that he also embodies the end of something. In many respects, Sinatra represents the culmination of a performing style that harkens back to vaudeville, with its implicit social contract between the audience and the entertainer. Modern jazz, rock, and post-rock pop have accustomed us to singers who contemplate the middle distance, their navels, and each other. They might ignore us or pummel us, but only on rare occasions do they openly and continuously sing to us. Sinatra has no peers in creating the illusion that he is looking into the eyes of every person in the room.

Like any great interpreter, he also gives the illusion of creating the material he sings. People often assume that many of his songs were written for him, and indeed some were. It's interesting to recall that those songs—many of them fashioned by Sammy Cahn and Jimmy Van Heusen, including "Come Fly with Me," "Come Dance with Me," "My Kind of Town," and "Ring-a-Ding-Ding"— are neglected by other singers in a kind of unstated homage. Yet the widespread assumption of ownership extends to much of his repertoire, from "It Happened in Monterey," a forlorn 1930 waltz before Sinatra taught it to swing, to "My Way," adopted from a French song by Paul Anka for himself. Paradoxically, the Sinatra imprimatur guarantees a song long life while discouraging other singers from tampering with it.

"My success," Sinatra has said, "has been . . . specialized because no one in the audience can sing my way. I'd love to hear a good imitator—a good mimic of Sinatra. But where is there one?" There have been dozens of bad imitators who sling trench coats over their shoulders and attempt his vocal mannerisms, but no one has ever captured his elusive tonal quality. Recently, comedian Joe Piscopo satirized Sinatra by parodying his style in the service of current rock hits. The routine is malicious and hilarious, but you only have to return to the real thing to realize that Piscopo doesn't lay a glove on him. Sinatra was dubbed "The

Voice" early in his career, but although the voice has changed, it remains difficult to characterize and impossible to reproduce. Henry Pleasants once described it as a "typical Italian light baritone with a two-octave range from G to G, declining, as it darkened in later years, to F to F." The uses to which Sinatra put his instrument are more easily discussed.

Sinatra clearly knew from the beginning what he wanted his voice to do, and he embarked on an obsessive regimen of training. This is how he described it in a 1964 interview with David Lewin: "I wanted a certain type of voice phrasing without taking breath at the end of a line or phrase. I studied the violin playing of Heifetz to see how he moved his bow over the fiddle and back again without seeming to pause. I applied it to singing. When I joined Tommy Dorsey I watched how he took his breath when he played. He never seemed to open his mouth to draw breath at all. I learned to control my breath by swimming the length of an Olympic pool under water. I increased my lung power by pacing myself on a running track every day . . ." Etc. The result was peerless legato control that enabled him to dramatize songs—the melodies and the words—with maximum expressive impact.

Standard popular songs are frequently parsed in four-bar phrases, but few singers can glide over them at medium tempos without grabbing an extra breath or leaning on vibrato. Sinatra's phrasing is so natural that it never calls attention to the singer's virtuosity. If you want to test how imaginative and seamless it is, sing along with him, trying to anticipate his accents and caesuras. Consider, for example, his 1956 recording of "Anything Goes," paying special attention to the way he attacks the release (he sings its first six bars on one gulp of air), and the twist he gives subsequent phrases by applying vibrato to the word "propose" and withdrawing it on "goes." When he sings the release a second time, he breaks it up differently to increase the tension. Or consider the implacable smoothness with which he navigates Nelson Riddle's swinging arrangement of "I've Got You Under My Skin," or the sweetly caressed yet firmly enunciated vowels in such ballads as "Willow Weep for Me" and "She's Funny That Way," or his impeccably modulated, Dorsey-like exposition in the 1961 version of "Getting Sentimental Over You."

These songs, all first-rate, draw our attention to another aspect of Sinatra's talent—an uncommon sagacity (though one, to be sure, that has failed him from time to time) in choosing the right songs. Sinatra was able to mature into the most assured and commanding interpreter of Tin Pan Alley's quality songs in part because he can tell a diamond from cut glass. This ability shouldn't be so rare, and among jazz singers it isn't, but stack up Sinatra's recording career against even a stylist as gifted as Nat Cole, and you begin to appreciate the pressures on a pop performer to record novelties and trash. Sinatra *has* succumbed to those pressures—first in the early 1950s, at the nadir of his career, when Columbia records, under the malefic hand of Mitch Miller, attempted to fit him into the same mold as Patti Page and Guy Mitchell, and then in the late 1960s, when he appeared to be pandering to a still younger audience.

Significantly, he's rarely allowed trashy material to infect his concert appearances, and his current programs are, for the most part, a solid line-up of the best of Porter, Berlin, Rodgers, Gershwin, and the other melodists who shared in the songwriting renaissance of the 1930s. Perhaps the central irony in Sinatra's career is that he was nurtured and apprenticed on the rhythms and melodies of the Swing Era, yet attained his greatest maturity as an artist during the same years that witnessed the rise of rock and roll. And it should not be forgotten that his initial fame with the bobbysoxers as an almost effeminately tender ballad singer and his subsequent incarnation as the super-hip, super-confident swinger of the affluent Eisenhower years was separated by a period of nonstop humiliations. The matured Sinatra was the product of a renewed sense of identity and an impressive act of will.

The general outline of Sinatra's odyssey is too well known to require much retelling. Francis Albert Sinatra was born in 1915 in one of New Jersey's toughest neighborhoods, Hoboken. He quit school at sixteen and immediately started hustling for work as a singer. His first break came in 1935, when his vocal quartet, the Hoboken Four, won first prize on *The Major Bowes Amateur Hour* radio show. He soon returned to working as a single, but it wasn't until 1939 that Harry James, Benny Goodman's featured trumpeter, heard him on the radio and signed him to the band he was organizing. Within months, Tommy Dorsey convinced Sinatra to leave James and join his own far more established band. During the next three years, Sinatra recorded prolifically, and his contributions to such Dorsey classics as "I'll Never Smile Again" and "Star Dust" made his voice an indelible part of the era.

In 1943, he went out on his own, and his success was phenomenal—swooning teenagers, a movie contract, cover stories everywhere, one record hit after another, and an Oscar for his short film about religious and racial intolerance ("The House I Live In"). Things started to go awry in 1947, when several journalists accused him of having ties with organized crime and/or Communism. During the next couple of years, Sinatra's personal life fell apart: his widely publicized divorce was followed by a brief and stormy marriage to Ava Gardner. His press agent died, his record sales fell off, and his attempts to rejuvenate his career through radio and TV series fell flat.

It all turned around again in 1953, when he won a best supporting actor Oscar for *From Here to Eternity,* and signed a recording contract with Capitol. At thirty-eight, he was now about to crest one of the more fabled of all show-business comebacks. Almost immediately, Sinatra's recordings revealed a probing undercurrent, a darkness around the edges of his voice, a resolute desire to sing the best songs in lavish but functional arrangements. His key collaborator was Nelson Riddle, an orchestrator with an uncanny knack for combining disparate elements in fluid and quietly provocative arrangements. Employing wind, string, and exotic percussion instruments, a buoyant rhythm section, and top-notch jazz soloists (notably the great Count Basie trumpeter Harry Edison), Riddle helped Sinatra to reclaim standards from the past 30 years, many of them long neglected. Most important of all, he seems to have arrived at precisely the right rhythmic gait for Sinatra—a broad, optimistic bounce that fell somewhere between the keening motion of jazz and the foursquare gallop of big-band pop.

The performances were brisk and to the point—with Sinatra usually singing no more than a chorus and a half—and the albums were uncommonly generous: *In the Wee Small Hours* contained 16 selections, and *Songs for Swinging Lovers,* which along with *Only the Lonely* (a ballad collection) is widely regarded as Sinatra's and Riddle's masterpiece, contained fifteen. Here was a new Sinatra; the skinny kid in need of coddling was gone, replaced by a man of authority and sensitivity. Not insignificantly, his resurgence as the personification of an adult singer happened at the very time Elvis Presley was helping to usher in the age of rock.

Although Sinatra welcomed Presley home from the army on a 1960 television "spectacular," their respective audiences remained at loggerheads. It wasn't until 1965 that Sinatra returned to the Top Ten for the first time in a decade, with "It Was a Very Good Year," and it wasn't until the late 1970s that a relatively new breed of journalist, the rock critic, began to make a serious reassessment of his art. In retrospect, it seems safe to say that the split in sensibilities that divided Sinatra's audience from Presley's in the '50s was less decisive than most people assumed at the time. Sinatra was working loosely within an idiom that predated the war, but he embodied a rather provocative stance toughened by a worldly sexuality that, unlike Presley's, was shorn of sentimentality and nurtured on the acceptance of loss and defeat.

In 1961, Sinatra started his own record label, Reprise, for which he still records, and after completing a number of albums that continued the approach patented at Capitol, as well as collaborations with Count Basie and Duke Ellington, he embarked on a cycle of autumnal, autobiographical songs, culminating in "My Way." At the age of fifty-five, in 1971, he announced his retirement. Happily, he changed his mind two years later, though a few rough and unsteady recording and television projects briefly suggested that his talent was no longer up to his ambition.

By the '80s, however, Sinatra scored a tremendous hit with "New York, New York," probably the most intelligent non-rock recording to hit the charts since Louis Armstrong's 1964 comeback with "Hello Dolly," and a couple of uneven but largely impressive new albums, including the three-volume *Trilogy*. Once again there was a new Sinatra, with a loamier voice, a hard-earned and expressive tremor in the low notes, and a stoic determination to use aesthetically the trappings of age—sibilance, wavering, harshness.

Sinatra cannot be said to have mellowed such in recent years. He's been embroiled in more controversies than ever with the press and politicians, usually concerning his alleged Mafia connections and his attempts to suppress unauthorized biographies. He has more than his share of enemies, many of them well earned. Sinatra is a difficult man, capable of legendary generosity and notorious pettiness and egomania. Those who dismiss his talent, however, are apparently immune to the innate decency and pride of craft that allow him to bring the contradictory elements in his personality to bear on achingly personal and persistently renewed ballads, that enable him to lift a concert hall by its roots and swing it as though all time but his had come to a halt. Frank Sinatra remains unique, the master explicator of the complexity and power of American popular songs, the entertainer as shaman; he is the founder of his tradition and its principal heir.

2. For Collectors

All cultivated people are collectors to some extent. Stores can pack only so much culture on their shelves, most of which is dictated by mass demand, so if you've developed a taste for the novels of Ludwig Lewisohn or the music of Jelly Roll Morton you are likely to find yourself reading catalogues and haunting musty cellars. However, there are two basic species of collector: the B collector—sensible people like you and me who know what we want and how to get it; and the A collector—fanatical people with checklists and a preternatural instinct for barter. B's are trustworthy, literate, and friendly; A's are shifty, solemn, and cynical. When B's were learning to read, A's were buying commemorative stamps. There's no denying that B's owe much to A's, who are endowed with the patience to compile bibliographies and discographies, who type catalogues and stock musty cellars. Of course, A's also create artifical price lists, monopolize art, and hawk bestsellers bound in hand-tooled leather.

Collectors of both types are the targets of the Original Master Recordings series created by Mobile Fidelity Sound Lab, an audiophile company whose current offering is a 16-volume, $350-boxed extravaganza called *Sinatra*. Culled entirely from the recordings Frank Sinatra made for Capitol between 1953 and 1962, it is irresistible on some counts, and resistible on others. The plus column leads off with the music, about which I will presently say little, since you already know that much of it is prodigious. Here is the premiere interpreter of Tin Pan Alley's wizards at the peak of his career, accompanied by classy arrangers (Nelson Riddle for the most part, but also Billy May, Gordon Jenkins, and Heinie Beau) and, from time to time, such obbligato specialists as Harry Edison and Buddy Collette. The diverse material includes some of Sinatra's jazziest sessions (the pivotal and rare *Swing Easy/Songs for Young Lovers* and the underrated *Swingin' Session*); ballad marathons (the incomparably programmed *In the Wee Small Hours* and the more eloquently sung *Only the Lonely*); and Ur-Sinatra masterpieces *(Songs for Swingin' Lovers, Come Fly with Me, A Swinging' Affair, Come Dance with Me,* and *Nice and Easy)*. Every album was mastered at half-speed from the master tapes, and pressed on virgin vinyl—you've never heard quieter surfaces.

Mobile Fidelity wasn't concerned with completeness, which is just as well, though to read the press releases and the reviews you'd think just a handful of rather negligible items were omitted. Precisely because the company is run by A's, the decision was made to go with originally released LPs (collectors' items) rather than the best individual sides, so anyone who purchases the handsome silver box (which measures six-and-a-half inches wide, incidentally, requiring the shelf space of some 40 albums) will be

surprised to find many of Sinatra's most famous Capitols missing. Of the 309 sides he recorded for the label, 207 are in the
box. Absent items include such hits as "Young at Heart," "The
Gal That Got Away," "Love and Marriage," "The Tender Trap,"
"Bewitched," "Time After Time," "The Lady Is a Tramp," and
the longtime Sinatra theme song, "Put Your Dreams Away," not
to mention such highly interesting but virtually unknown (except
in England) gems as "Memories of You," "The One I Love," and
"Where or When." Instead of superior compilations like *This Is
Sinatra,* you get a mediocre one like *Sings of Love and Things,* not
to mention the notoriously unlovely *Come Swing with Me,* which
Sinatra slumbered through while Billy May arranged as though
he had just discovered stereo (the orchestra is his shuttlecock).

The box is big and sturdy and somewhat makeshift. It was
designed to hold 18 records, not 16. Each disc has a rice-paper
sleeve that fits into a wraparound cardboard folder which in turn
fits, much as thread fits through the eye of a needle, into a cardboard sleeve that fits into the box. The wraparound pieces should
have been sleeves, especially since they replicate the original album jacket. On the back of each wraparound is some very useful
discographical material (which could have been printed in a separate insert), and a disclaimer from Mobile Fidelity about possible errors. The listings are generally accurate (an impressive feat),
although when I looked up the vibes soloist on *Come Swing with
Me,* I was dismayed to find no vibist listed. Incredibly, the selections are not individually dated.

I'm carping because I think that for $350 we B's have a right
to expect perfection. To compensate, though, Mobile Fidelity is
trying to reach the A struggling for recognition in the heart of
every B. They've printed a limited edition of 25,000 sets, each
numbered and accompanied by a "signed certificate of authenticity." That's right, friends, *Sinatra* is an investment. I quote from
a press release concerning Mobile Fidelity's last bonanza: "According to one collector, 'If interest in *The Beatles/The Collection*
remains steady, prices could reach over $2,500.00 by Christ-
mas.'" Makes you long for Santa, although if you actually play

the records you risk deflating their value: the favorite letter of every A is m (for mint). Maybe I'm feeling peevish because the reason *Sinatra* is such a welcome event is not the virgin vinyl or the numbered box, but simply because the philistines at Capitol have either suppressed, edited, or disfigured (through electronic rechanneling) so much of this music. Still, this B wants to remind you that *Songs for Swingin' Lovers* is as inspired an example of American popular music as you will ever hear.

(February 1984/November 1983)

Harmolodic Hoedown

1. Ornette's Coloring Book

Twenty-six winters ago, two jazz musicians of nearly the same age—one a proven and popular innovator, the other viewed suspiciously by most of the few people who'd heard him—issued recordings that were to have a dramatic and immediate impact on all jazz and, a decade or so down the road, on much pop. Miles Davis's *Milestones* toyed with song and blues form to the modest but significant extent of substituting scales (modality) for chords (chromaticism), an idea long in the air and one that was brought to fruition the following year on Davis's monumental *Kind of Blue*. In effect, he had built a six-lane highway out of bebop's apparent harmonic cul de sac, and the traffic behind him was bumper to bumper. Ornette Coleman's *Something Else!* was something else—a nervously executed assault on form, swing, and tempered pitch that found its full voice a year later in the aggressively titled *Tomorrow Is the Question!* and *The Shape of Jazz to Come.*

This was another kind of highway, also six lanes, but the traffic was sparse for a while. With Davis, you were riding on concrete: four beats to a measure, familiar road markings, an underpinning of piano chords. With Coleman, there were no bar lines, no stop signs, no piano. Davis, in a characteristically generous mood, declared Coleman unlistenable.

Yet Coleman's influence was undeniable, and, surprisingly, the first troops who followed him into the never-never land of what he called free jazz included established contemporaries, some of whom had earlier associations with Davis. Before long, John Coltrane, Sonny Rollins, John Lewis, Eric Dolphy, Albert Ayler, and Archie Shepp had made Coleman-styled recordings, usually employing Coleman's disciples (Don Cherry acted as his ambassador at large) and compositions. The free jazz movement soon inspired Davis himself, who made his peace by elaborating his own notions of interplay, flexible form, and expressionism, and combining them with the solid rhythmic foundation and extravagant but tempered colors of rock. Then something utterly unexpected happened. In the summer of 1977, Coleman released the mesmeric *Dancing in Your Head,* his first record in five years, and a reconciliation of jazz, rock, and African musics that provided a further parallelism with Davis. They have this is common: each man successfully advanced *two* profoundly different sonorous images (in Aaron Copland's phrase), thereby setting into motion two schools of disciples, two frequently warring audiences, and two lexicons of critical jargon. As a means of forestalling critical shyness and the post-Milesian implications of the term fusion, Coleman even gave us a word—part label, part philosophy, part smokescreen—with magical properties: harmolodic. Ta da!

It is Coleman's fate and genius to be an eternal thorn, and *Dancing in Your Head* predictably aroused the ire of the mouldy figs ("listening to it closely is torture," one opined). But the carping proved irrelevant in the face of the new coalition it created. For the first time in years (perhaps since Davis's *Bitches Brew* and Tony Williams's *Emergency*), an uncompromisingly expansive, dissonant jazz improvisation caused critics on the left in jazz and rock to harmonize (in harmolodic fashion) their huzzahs. What's more, this mutual interest has extended to Coleman's new family of disciples, which cannot be said of most of the fusion that proceeded down Davis's interstate. Bipartisan enthusiasm of this sort needn't mean much aesthetically, and, as demonstrated by record sales of the Colemanites, it means almost nothing commercially. Critics are often most adamant about music they consider beyond the ken of a mass audience, and when that music offers the illusion of wide appeal, they will wallow in hyperbole in the hope of effecting a self-fulfilling prophecy. (Not since Coltrane's last recordings have I seen such overwrought writing from usually sober citizens: e.g., "the kind of music Coltrane and Hendrix would've made in a New Orleans whorehouse if Chick Webb were their drummer" or "a groove as syncopated as the Meters', as hot as James Brown's Fabulous Flames', and as trenchant as the MGs'." All that's missing is, "and able to leap tall buildings at a single bound.") Nor is much of a case made by comparing the excitement generated by harmolodics among a coterie and the now widespread disaffection with Davis's modalized fusion.

Still, facts are facts, and it's a fact that the harmolodic contingent is answering needs that span the great divide. When a Protestant rock critic who sees jazz as the Catholic Church delivers a beatitude to Blood Ulmer, and several of his colleagues (including the Dean, who considers Ulmer's *Odyssey* the best record of 1983) join him in making Ulmer the only jazzman to score high on the Pazz & Jop Poll,* you have to wonder why—why Ulmer, why not Davis or Cecil Taylor or the World Saxophone Quartet or David Murray or Arthur Blythe or Henry Threadgill or George Russell or Muhal Richard Abrams or Steve Lacy or Wynton Marsalis or Count Basie? At the same time, you have to ask yourself why jazz critics for whom Jimi Hendrix is Sominex, Herbie Hancock a whore, and George Clinton clever and danceable but, well, nothing to *listen* to—why are they developing a metaphysic that

*The Pazz and Jop Poll is a feature of *The Village Voice,* compiled by the Dean, Robert Christgau, with the aid of numerous pop critics; the Protestant rock critic is Tom Carson, also of the *Voice.*

will lay claim to this same Ulmer? I'm reminded of the way Ray Charles strode through the late '50s, with jazz in one pocket and pop in the other, gearing up to invade Nashville—especially since *Odyssey* has more than a dram of country. But there's this difference: real people, in the lingo of TV, liked Charles as much as the critics did. Real people often find harmolodic music to be torture. This music doesn't convey to them as it does to critics echoes of Coltrane, Hendrix, Dixieland, Muddy Waters, James Brown, Wes Montgomery, Bartòk, the Master Musicians of Jojouka, and the Sex Pistols.

It's probably true that some of the pop enthusiasm for Ulmer, Ronald Shannon Jackson, and Jamaaladeen Tacuma is the result of snowballing word-of-mouth matched by the availability (thanks to affiliations, albeit brief ones, with major record labels) of their work. Maybe if every voter in the P&J Poll had a copy of WSQ's *Revue*, it too would have scored. Maybe not. But it's undoubtedly true that the most accessible handles for dealing with Ulmer from a pop vantage point are the same ingredients that made rock agreeable to many jazz musicians in the *Bitches Brew* period: coloration and rhythm. Add to this the crowning factor that harmolodic music *sounds* new: no matter what you're accustomed to listening to, *Dancing in Your Head* and its progeny came as a splash of ice water. The familiar elements—funky bass lines, four-four, Ulmer's bluesed-out voice—are all but subsumed in the novelty of context, so that regardless of how many ghosts one may hear in the shadows, this music emerges as not only free of cliché but indisputably of our time. Responses in the jazz community are perhaps more difficult to comprehend. Rock coloration and rhythm are Rubicons for many of the most devout of Coleman's original boosters; they'd like to see a reunion of the early quartet, which—two decades later—sounds as warm and comforting as *Kind of Blue*. Those of us who are enthralled by Coleman's harmolodic brood recognize, I think, that the new Coleman is the old Coleman in disguise. The freshness of context has stimulated the recycling of such verities as collective improvisation, counterpoint, song structures, and swing rhythms. Which brings us back to the key word, Coleman's open sesame: harmolodic. It's a contraction for harmony, movement, and melody. But what does that mean? Apparently, whatever comes into the head of its spokesman at the time he is asked. Jackson once told me that he couldn't define harmolodics, and that Coleman never used the word at rehearsals. He knew, however, that it was the antithesis of simply playing free, that it had something to do with "everyone playing in different keys and yet being equal." Coleman explained it to *N.Y. Rocker* thusly: "Harmony describes a certain position in an ongoing melody. Movement is how you get to that position. And melody, at its simplest, is just a single interval, a movement from one note to the next. That single interval can suggest or *be* the harmony, it's part of the melodic line, and it shows you the direction of the movement." This sounds like a partial recipe for Bach's *The Art of the Fugue,* but its primary significance for jazz is that melody dictates harmony instead of vice versa. In place of a sequence of chords pinned to a cyclical chorus structure, you have the unencumbered movement of melody; if Coleman is the lead voice, the other musicians modulate along with him, so that the resultant harmonies are virtually fortuitous. But, you ask, how does that differ from what Coleman was doing 25 years ago, when bassist Charlie Haden was doggedly pursuing Coleman's acoustic streams of consciousness and trumpeter Don Cherry was harmonizing as best he could? It doesn't. Indeed, some of the controversy about this music puts me in mind of Lester Bowie's old Q and A (on "Jazz Death?"): "Is jazz, as we know it, dead? "Well, I guess it all depends on what you know."

Is harmolodics new? Blood Ulmer, in an instructive interview with Chip Stern, said, "With harmolodic music I hope to find a balance between the body and the mind," and "In harmolodic music, you are playing individually together. The lines are related less through chords than by melody and rhythm," and "The way I play allows you to use all the chromatic notes, but not in half steps; so the listener will hear key sounds, but this lets the player play all 12 notes," and "The main thing is for everybody to work independently, modulating together to give the illusion of harmony." All of which could be said of such Coleman classics as *This Is Our Music, Free Jazz, Ornette!*, and *Ornette on Tenor*, which were made when Ulmer was playing in doo-wop bands. Jamaaladeen Tacuma, who at twenty-six (Ulmer is forty-two) represents the latest generation of Colemanites, told Greg Tate, "Through playing harmolodically, I've developed the ability to make my patterns move in sequential order when I'm improvising . . . what I try to get going is a succession of notes that move in a compositional direction. And not many bass players have figured out how to do that." To which Tate replied, "Nor many musicians, period." One wonders in what direction they think the notes of Jimmy Blanton or Lester Young or practically every great improvisor in jazz history are moving if not in a compositional one. So far, harmolodics comes across as a liberating teaching tool (Tacuma), a grammar for new jazz (Ulmer), an incentive for compositional direction (Jackson), and a personal code of musical ethics (Coleman), which is a lot to say of any word. Yet it doesn't suggest much about why harmolodic music *sounds* new. I suspect that the answer, like the purloined letter, is simply too obvious to see—coloration and rhythm.

Harmony, melody, and rhythm open so many mathematical and philosophical trapdoors that they're more fun to talk about than coloration. But as Dizzy Gillespie discovered a long time ago when he added Chano Pozo to his rhythm section and all but created the genre of Latin jazz, it can make an explosive difference. Bach sounds different played on harpsichord, piano, and synthesizer, and such differences are radicalized if the colors are allowed to suggest new rhythms as well. Coleman didn't change his basic playing style for *Dancing in Your Head*. He changed the tableau. Yet in embracing the colors of electric string instruments (guitar and bass), he found it useful to adopt other elements associated with them, particularly countable time. Possibly because of his experience with the Jojouka Musicians (documented briefly on the same album), he didn't return to a strict four, but to a near-primitive chanting rhythm that was contiguous with the rhythmic pulse always apparent in his work (for a bald example, hear the 1961 "T. & T."). The electric colors also kindled his unique notions about transposition. In the notes to his mighty and sadly undervalued symphony *Skies of America* (1972), he explained how the musicians in the orchestra, although playing fully notated scores, could improvise range at will, and added, "The movements are written free of key and use the total collective blending of the transposed and non-transposed instruments using the same intervals." Coleman discovered that by notating the melody ("the same intervals"), while encouraging the "blending" of instruments that aren't transposed to the same key, he came up with a fresh harmonic approach that had both the density of clusters and the spaciousness of multiple keys. *Dancing in Your Head* was the first small-band result, a wildly energetic and sustained blues roar that, despite the careful musicianship of all involved, created the illusion of music so elemental that anyone could join in. With *Of Human Feelings* (1979, released 1982), Coleman drew on his rhythm and blues days and, without compromising his own quartertone pitch, his affection for gusty lamentations, and those jarring keys, revived classic structures ("Jump Street" is a blues with a bridge) and countable time.

Coleman, however, is always more radical than the best of his followers. When Charlie Haden, Don Cherry, and Dewey Redman aren't paying homage to Coleman in Old and New Dreams or likeminded bands, they are as much at home with the tempered modalities of Keith Jarrett, Third World folksongs, or African chants. The harmolodic apostles are similarly gifted with the eclectic impulse. More importantly, they've found ways to adapt Coleman's lessons to their own needs. Or maybe it's more accurate to say that Coleman's tutelege showed them the way to make those needs functional in the modern world, so that Ronald Shannon Jackson can have a dynamic swing band, Blood Ulmer a broodingly expressive rhythm and blues band, and Jamaaladeen Tacuma a swank funk band, none of which sound remotely like other bands in their preferred genres or a whole lot like each other, and all of which have that harmolodic sheen. Coleman is doomed forever to be himself, a maverick in life as in music, walking on the edge of traditions much as his pitch is on the edge of the tempered scale. So it's no surprise that he holds a position in the jazz of the '80s analogous to the one he held in the '60s. The avant garde he helped create attacked from three directions—jazz itself (Coltrane), the academy (Cecil Taylor), and rhythm and blues (Coleman). In the present neoclassical period, the best young musicians are aligned in similar groupings, working to stretch modernism backwards and forwards. David Murray and Arthur Blythe are among those working within the jazz tradition; Anthony Davis and James Newton are among those in touch with the academy; and manning the rhythm and blues front are the graduates of Ornette Coleman's harmolodia.

2. *Speaking in Thumbs*

The only movie ever directed by the great cinematographer James Wong Howe, *Go, Man, Go,* is a fictitious but amusing account of the Harlem Globetrotters with a good metaphor for the often exigent nature of jazz know-how. When manager Dane Clark hears of a possible recruit for his new team, he visits the young man's home and finds him effortlessly pitching a basketball through a hoop mounted in his bedroom. The athlete explains that he had to teach himself to do without a backboard so as not to disturb his parents with the noise of his practicing. Jazz is filled with similar make-do stories, not all of them credible, like Armstrong inventing scat because the sheet music fell on the floor during a recording, Hines developing ironclad octaves so as to be heard over an orchestra, Basie spurring head arrangements to compensate for a dearth of written material, and Wes Montgomery learning to play with his thumb so as not to wake his baby. Perhaps Ornette Coleman discovered the abrasive appeal of nontransposed instruments playing together because he had never mastered the principles of transposition. In any case, it should come as no surprise that a musician who effortlessly pitched his notes in the cracks, as it were, of the tempered scale (with unerring intervallic consistency) might find the clashing of keys a brave prospect.

One difference between his Prime Time recordings *(Dancing in Your Head, Body Meta, Of Human Feelings)*—and, to a lesser extent, his early chamber music—and the massive *Skies of America* is the reduction in muddiness, since each instrument's harmonic turf is defined with relative clarity. The harmonic clash has a unique bracing quality, as each instrument attacks a given piece in a separate but equal manner. Small wonder that Coleman often begins his concerts with a round-robin of unaccompanied solos that puts the differing stylistic inclinations on the table. But despite the interlock of bass and drums, the enunciated rhythms, and the formal structures, Coleman's playing remains as gravity-free as ever. His phrasing, no less now than 25 years ago, resolutely defies traditional cadences. The new band may give you more to nod your head to, but when you concentrate on Coleman's alto you are flying in mid-air and your only hope of landing safely is to hold tight to the melodies he spins.

In one way or another, all of Coleman's harmolodic beneficiaries have moved in the direction of grounding the music, and this is why Ulmer, Jackson, and Tacuma (like Cherry, Haden, and Redman) are "easier" to listen to, even though none of them has a solo voice nearly as compelling as Coleman's. Indeed, solo voice in Ulmer and Jackson has been all but replaced by compositional interaction, and nowhere is that interaction more winning than on Ulmer's sixth and most arresting album, *Odyssey* (Columbia BFC 38900). This is one of those rare works that at first seems to have sprung from the head of Zeus, though subsequent listenings tend to point up ways in which it relates to the earlier music. Ulmer, who was born in South Carolina and spent long periods playing a variety of religious and secular musics in Pittsburgh, Ohio, and Detroit before arriving in New York, joined with Coleman in 1972. I first heard him at Coleman's 1975 Five Spot engagement, when his splayed and roiling chords gave the band an electrifying undercurrent but suggested little in the way of a new conception.

Nor did his first record *Tales of Captain Black* (as James Blood), which was dominated by Coleman's alto, and reflected his further influence in the rankling keys. Still, one could already hear the incipient rhythms of a Southeastern gambol in contrast to Ornette's Southwestern blues hollar.

Are You Glad To Be in America, recorded little more than a year later (January 1980), represented a startling advance, integrating a raucous wind section that would be ripened on his first Columbia album, *Free Lancing*, an acidic funk bottom that would be hardened for Columbia's *Black Rock*, and the contrapuntal melodies that would be refined on his third and apparently last Columbia album, *Odyssey*. But before he moved to the big time he recorded *No Wave* in Germany, an unabashed jazz quartet that is dismissed by some of his admirers (and, I'm told, by Ulmer himself), though I can't imagine why. True, it suggests the unwieldiness of a jam and Amin Ali's bass is at times annoyingly busy, but considering the calibre of jammers (Ronald Shannon Jackson at his menacing best, David Murray roaring with uninhibited glee, and Ulmer playing his only extended solos on record) and the charm of the brief themes, it's a worthy anomaly. Beginning with *Free Lancing*, Ulmer would concentrate on short, scrupulously constructed pieces and a coloration that withers the boundaries between jazz and rock.

The most significant color change on *Odyssey* is the substitution of violin for bass and/or saxophone. As played by Charles Burnham, it has an elegaic quality that softens and unites the trio (Warren Benbow is the very attentive drummer). He makes the climax of "Love Dance" a reel and suggests the tang of a hoedown on "Little Red House." They whoop it up with a devilishness that reminds me of Walter Huston's satanic grin as he fiddled for the square-dancers in *All That Money Can Buy*, chanting "faster, faster." But there's more here than country ruminations; on "Little Red House," mad fiddling competes with rock tonalities, blues grunting, and parade drumming redolent of a Sousa march. The fiddler is mournful after the stop-time transition on "Church," and rueful stating the splendid secondary theme of

"Are You Glad To Be in America." His double-stops are a high-light of "Please Tell Her," which not only recalls but just about replicates an old-time fiddle band in the instrumental interlude. Ulmer is no less various in his uses of a guitar style that, like Wes Montgomery's, is built on speedy thumb-work, but, unlike Montgomery's, eschews fluid phrasing in favor of splattered notes and plucked chords. The flat-picking implications of his style, teasingly evident in his solo on the high-stepping "Open House" (on *Black Rock*), comes into flower in an unexpectedly jaunty solo on the fast shuffle "Swing and Things." Then there are those surprising zithery chords at the end of "Odyssey," a mood piece set in part against a legato two-beat, and the shrapnel-like notes, a kind of speaking in thumbs, on the mercurial "Love Dance." Ulmer never uses the guitar merely to extemporize melodic fig-ures; dynamics and color are of equal consequence. Not capable of (or, let's be generous, interested in) sustained improvisations of Colemanesque stature, he has contrived an ensemble music in which the guitar has orchestral responsibilities. When the trio is cooking, it's difficult to know who's carrying the bass line or the time or the lead. Also, Ulmer is not wed to Coleman's harmo-lodic views on unison keys, and there are pieces here of quite orthodox harmony, notably the delightful "Election." Part heral-dic march, part Scottish jig, the melodic content is merely a five-note theme that sounds like an elliptical take on "Pop Goes the Weasel," but it's enough to fashion a coherent piece of music that progresses sensibly from solemn proclamation to lightstepping exeunt. The contrast between the consonance of "Election" and the key-split in the neighboring "Odyssey" points up the optional uses of harmolodics.

Odyssey is ripe with rhythmic change-ups, though perhaps less so than *Black Rock*, with its bald homage to Coleman, its ersatz bop, and soul gestures. But in all of Ulmer's rock there is a fun-damental trust in the propriety of four-four. His rhythms have momentum, dash, style, and in this respect they are firmly in the tradition of jazz. Rhythm is the most personal and least discuss-able aspect of jazz; the mathematical laws of music are of no help

in defining "momentum" or "swing." Since swing cannot be notated, it has to be learned in practice. Even the difference between Swing Era swing, bebop swing, and the various other kinds
of swing defy codification, so that normative standards of swing
are impossible to lock down. For me, Dave Brubeck's piano solos
usually don't swing, and the fact that I've heard him swing at all
convinces me I'm right; but the person sitting next to me in a
concert hall, tapping his foot in rhythmic empathy, would obviously disagree. American jazz musicians in Europe have, for half
a century, acclaimed the bassists and pianists, while despairing at
the inadequacy of the drummers, who fail to understand where
they've gone wrong, since quite often they are virtuosos. What
they lack are those indefinables—not only dash and momentum,
but rhythmic elegance, a graceful way of advancing time that
suggests ironic distance from the time itself. These qualities—cu-
mulatively known as swing—are unique hallmarks of jazz rhythm,
ties that bind Baby Dodds and Tony Williams. And they distinguish the music of the Colemanites from like-minded bands that
lean more to the Euro-rock side of the jazz-rock synthesis. To
pick one example, a band I admire but am not moved by, the
Golden Palominos seem to me rhythmically static; Anton Fier's
drumming, accomplished and clever as it is, marks patterns
around the beat instead of advancing it. The rhythms endemic
to the exponents of harmolodics embody their ties to jazz, and
are exemplified by Ronald Shannon Jackson's Decoding Society.

Jackson plays drums as though he weren't just moving time,
but furniture. His energy level is tremendous, and though close
listening reveals a montage of complex fractions in his rhythmic
figures, he never fails to swing. So irresistible is his pulse that
Jackson can make the singular claim of having powered Coleman *(Dancing in Your Head)*, Ulmer *(No Wave)*, and Cecil Taylor,
who was driven by Jackson's backbeat to forgo his energy-is-as-
energy-does patterns for an occasional stomp (cf. *3 Phasis*). Jackson, a 44-year-old native of Coleman's home town, Forth Worth,
created an outlet for his harmolodic spunk that approximates the
forward march of a swing band. He voices the electric and acoustic

instruments in his band in the high register, but his rhythm takes its cue from the authoritative barrelhouse beat he sustains on the bass drum. As a composer, Jackson has extended the notion of clashing keys into clashing melodies. For example, "Theme for a Prince" (on the 1980 *Eye on You*), his attractive homage to Coleman, features guitarist Bern Nix and saxophonist Byard Lancaster playing different melodies simultaneously while saxophonist Charles Brackeen improvises between them, drawing on whatever he wants to form his solo. On *Nasty*, he crafted short riff tunes that underscore his propensity for raucous swing, and an ambitious (and almost inaudible, due to a bad mix) piece called "When We Return," in which the theme is stated first on drums and then passed to the other musicians. His exuberance crested on the highly polished *Mandance*, which employs a second line beat on the title piece, as well as unexpected remnants of Southern expressionism, such as the vocalized writing and parade drumming on "Alice in the Congo" (a kind of harmolodic answer to King Oliver's mutes), and the unison banjo and bass on "Iola."

But Jackson, like Ulmer, has been moving to a centrist position, sanding the edges of his music, and clarifying the rhythms. He just hasn't come up with as convincing an answer yet. Of his two recently released albums, *Street Priest* (Moers 01096), recorded in 1981, is more discordant and witty and street-wise than 1983's studio-wise *Barbecue Dog* (Antilles 1015), which, though replete with interesting moments and expertly mixed, is too slick for its own good. One difference is the replacement of a second sax with Henry Scott's high-note trumpet, which puts the wrong kind of gloss on the ensemble; to be blunt, some passages are more reminiscent of Maynard Ferguson than of *Eye on You*. Yet the album has what may be Jackson's first consensus underground hit in "Gossip"—the selection that everyone seems to respond to, and with good reason. Jackson is so spirited that he manages to make a familiar ploy like bashing the fourth beats seem momentous; the ensemble is efficiently deployed—an ominous bass line (so much of Jackson's music has a menacing qual-

ity) and a second-tier melody for the winds, while Vernon Reid's
guitar rises up the scale and the trumpet, voiced Louis-like an
octave higher, proffers a glistening top. On "Harlem Opera," a
mournful composite of African and Eastern melodies, Jackson is
quite brilliant, avoiding four in the initial episode and then bearing down in the machine-gun style of the heroic Chick Webb for
part two; Scott's brass sound is appealing here, but the ensemble
is cluttered and the exotic sounds seem gimmicky. Perhaps the
title "When Cherry Trees Bloom in Winter You Can Smell Last
Summer" should be taken programmatically, since the themes for
winds and brass are in contrasting tempos—the effect is less contrapuntal than converse (like winter and summer). Still, here and
in the jocular funk of the title piece, the addition of conventional
big band trumpet whelping suggests a Kenton lab band. On the
other hand, "Mystery at Dawn," a dirge ballad ("Lonely Woman"
with an Oriental accent) stated by a reflective, kotolike banjo,
makes for icily compelling night music, and the Ornettish "Say
What You Will" is exultant free jazz, with Reid crackling over
Jackson's firestorm.

     If Coleman, Ulmer, and Jackson demonstrate the range of
rhythms congruous with this thing called harmolodic, Jamaaladeen Tacuma's maiden voyage, *Show Stopper* (Gramavision 8301),
is more self-consciously fashionable on two counts: it's oriented
toward crystalline funk, and it's eclectic to a fault. Conceptually,
the album is reminiscent of the debut of another bass wizard, Jaco
Pastorius. They try to do everything first time out, but they don't
do everything equally well. On the plus side, we have "Rhythm
Box," an intriguing amalgamation of Colemanesque melody and
rock and roll feeling; "Show Stopper," gentrified hard bop with
blistering work from Julius Hemphill; and "From the Land of
Sand," in which Tacuma manages to make his bass sound like
Ulmer's guitar. On the debit side, there's "The Bird of Para-
dise," movie music of the most maudlin sort for string quartet
and voice; "Sunk in the Funk," which is almost too pristine to be
funky; and "From Me to You," a ballad which threatens to melt
in your fingers. Still, an instrumentalist as gifted as Tacuma may
achieve greater depth as a leader. Closer study with Coleman, who

reinvented the slush-free ballad, may even rinse away some of his sentimentality. Coleman studies, incidentally, proceed apace, well beyond the circle of disciples. A good current example is violinist Billy Bang's *Untitled Gift* (Anima 3BG9), which, with Don Cherry and two Coleman originals, cheerfully navigates the byways of pre-harmolodic free jazz.

There's been lots of talk about harmolodic commercialism; sales figures, though, not to mention the conclusive evidence of the music itself, which is as challenging as anything on the contemporary menu, testify to the non-commercial zone Coleman and his acolytes patrol. The idea that records as obsessively personal as *Odyssey* and *Barbecue Dog* were intended to revive the thoroughly flogged dead horse of fusion is, at best, winningly naive. You won't be seeing Ulmer on MTV or Jackson selling Pepsi; you are lucky to find their records. That their music is *about* commercial currents, however, seems to me beyond question, and it may be that the chief lesson of Coleman's harmolodics is this: you can't cut yourself off from the musical world around you, but you needn't surrender to it either. In the seven years since *Dancing in Your Head* was released, Jackson has created an ingenious small band in which swing finds a purely contemporary context; Ulmer has managed to blend 30 years of musical wanderings into a whole that is compelling above all for its seamless coherence; and Tacuma is poised to go off every which way. The phrases jazz-rock and fusion can't begin to encompass such victories. But harmolodic, a word every bit as meaningful and meaningless as bebop, will do fine for a handle, until a handle is no longer necessary.*

(March 1984)

*Some of the records mentioned above are difficult to find. I've provided catalogue numbers for the recent releases, but it may be helpful to know the label affiliations of the others as well. All the Miles Davis albums, *Skies of America*, *Free Lancing*, and *Black Rock* are on Columbia. All the early Ornette Coleman albums are on Atlantic, except *Something Else!* and *Tomorrow Is the Question*, which are on Contemporary. *Emergency* was reissued as *Once in a Lifetime* on Verve; *Revue* is on Black Saint and *3 Phasis* is on New World. Three labels that are either defunct or in trouble are Horizon *(Dancing in Your Head)*, Artists House *(Body Meta, Tales of Captain Black, Are You Glad To Be in America)*, and Antilles *(Of Human Feelings, Mandance)*. *No Wave* and *Nasty* are on Moers Music, and *Eye on You* is on About Time. Several titles are available from NMDS, 500 Broadway, NYC 10012.

Not for Dancers Only

Duke Ellington played with his audiences, flirting with their expectations and assumptions, and responding—ingenuously, it sometimes seemed—to the stimuli they offered. Night after night, the band bus, trailing Harry Carney's Imperial with Ellington riding shotgun, pulled into American cities and towns of every size to offer a music that had to please dancers and listeners as well as the musicians in the band and, above all, Ellington himself. Except under special circumstances—the debut of a new suite, a command performance, a virgin audience (which would have to be found in pretty exotic places by the '50s)—the distinction between routine and inspired sets was determined more by the chemistry of bandmembers and customers than by the status of the occasion. A tuxedo didn't necessarily get you a better show than a pair of overalls. Enthusiasm did.

I had the chance to learn this firsthand in the late '60s, when, in the space of a month, I saw the Ellington band in the small farming community of Oscaloosa, Iowa, and at Lincoln Center. The Iowa concert-dance—chairs were removed from the auditorium after the first set, enabling us to tell the concert music from the dance music—was sponsored by the local 4-H Club, and if ever there was an audience made to be charmed by the maestro's references to the prettiest "Satin Doll" in the house, this was it. He answered requests for that song three times. The musicians strolled on stage with the usual air of boredom, but as Ellington began calling unusual titles ("Warm Valley" for one) and demanding encores of his best and/or most recalcitrant soloists, and as the audience became increasingly rapturous, the band loosened up and a routine gig became an electrifying event. By the onset of the dance half, the musicians had socialized with half the room, and were raring to have a good time. This despite the fact that the only black not on stage was a college student who was importuned by a cop for dancing with a white woman. Ellington watched the incident from the piano, grimaced and shook his head, and kept playing. The tempos got brighter, the solos zestier, the ensembles sharper.

The concert at Philharmonic Hall was billed as the band's only New York performance of the season, and I attended it with the naive assumption that for such an affair there would be some new music or at least a smashing performance. There were, in fact, two exquisite moments related to new or recent music—Cootie Williams's "The Shepherd," from the Second Sacred Concert, and Harold Ashby's as yet untitled feature ("Chinoiserie") from what became *The Afro-Eurasian Eclipse*. For the rest, it was a desultory evening—two short, strangely patronizing sets, with Paul Gonsalves playing "In a Sentimental Mood" while wandering through the aisles, and two overwrought singers shouting "One More Time" more relentlessly than they had in Iowa, where it didn't seem quite so offensive. In *Music Is My Mistress*, Ellingon singled out Iowa as the "state where forever friends drive a hundred miles in the snow to hear us"; still, one imagines even now that his heart would beat faster for those who arrived by subway.

The tone of an Ellington one-nighter was invariably defined to some extent by the mood of the band. Like Fletcher Henderson before him, Duke was no disciplinarian. Henderson once told a well-meaning friend, who advised him to fire unruly musicians who arrived late or looked disheveled on the stand, that, yes, there were discipline problems, but, "When they're all up there together playing the way they can, I have the best damn band in the world. So I guess I'll just have to keep them." Ellington put up with much worse, and is said never to have fired anyone except Charles Mingus (for reasons hilariously detailed in Mingus's *Beneath the Underdog*). Ellington's willingness to countenance alcoholism and drug addiction in his musicians was only an extreme instance of his tolerance. He managed to sustain the loyalties of more than a dozen of the most creative performers in American musical history largely by practicing laissez-faire. When you attended the band's dances, you did not see a spit-and-polish ensemble attentively waiting on the bandstand, while an announcer introduced the leader, who then strode on stage, acknowledged the applause, and counted off the opening selection. On the contrary, Ellington was usually one of the first on stage. The rhythm section was probably up there, and maybe half the band. Ellington would "vamp till ready," stacking riffs at the keyboard, while the latecomers casually took their places. Then the vamp would become a familiar intro, the pianist would cue the orchestra with an "Ahhhhhhhhhhh," and suddenly the A train was shuttling down the tracks. What's that—Cootie was the last one out, barely made it in time for his "A Train" solo? Since he just put in his dentures, punishment will be an encore: "Thank you, ladies and gentleman. Cootie Williams wants you to know that he too loves you madly. And now Cootie Williams returns for . . ." And somehow Ellington managed to keep these volatile personalities satisfied and, more to the point, inspired—for years, decades, and in one instance nearly half a century.

In the 10 years since his death, dozens of Ellington records have been released for the first time—my conservative estimate is about 50 hours of new music. Most of these have been bootleg productions, culled from private tapes, though some of the most interesting resulted from the numerous hours of studio time that Ellington bought to document works which would not otherwise have been recorded. Apparently he did not discourage private taping; without it, we would have no account of *Black, Brown & Beige* or *Deep South Suite*. If you thumb through the 16 volumes of the Ellington discography by Massagli-Pusateri-Volonte, you'll find that hundreds of hours of documented music remain unissued.

To those only marginally familiar with Ellington's music, this won't seem especially surprising or interesting. How many versions does anyone need of "Take the A Train" or "Mood Indigo"? Yet what makes this posthumous legacy remarkable is how varied, distinguished, and frequently unique the performances are. It's one thing for a soloist to improvise differently on a tune every night, and quite another for an orchestra leader to tinker unceasingly with proven arrangements. Sitting at the piano, conducting not the instruments but the specific personalities hired to make those instruments come alive, Ellington found numberless ways to freshen his music and his musicians. So the more new Ellington we get, the more surprises we get. Moreover, it's a mistake to view the performance tapes, radio broadcasts and transcriptions, and alternate takes as simply addenda to the body of commercially sanctioned recordings. Precisely for the same reasons that Iowa might coax a better performance than Lincoln Center, grateful dancers might earn a better accounting of a piece than a studio engineer. Pieces too heady to earn a place in the regular book—a "Daybreak Express" or "Braggin' in Brass"—exist only in impeccable and isolated studio performances. But more popular or jam-oriented pieces, not to mention the new works—Ellington's well never dried, never even showed signs of drying—that occupied his attention for a month or a year or five years, were toyed with constantly. And because some of the best alterations were fortuitous, only a handful could be retained and refined for subsequent records. Two recently released albums exemplify Ellington's gift for the serendipitous, and underscore once again the amazing constancy of his greatest creation—his band.

Duke Ellington and His Orchestra—1952 (Folkways FJ 2968) and *All-Star Road Band* (Doctor Jazz W2X39137) are good focal points for the major Ellington story of the 1950s—his triumphant return to form after a financially and critically bleak period. The Folkways selections were culled by Peter O'Brien from four or five nights in Washington and Oregon in the spring of 1952; the Doctor Jazz album was taken entirely from a dance in Carroltown, Pennsylvania, in the summer of 1957. Although 10 members of the 15-piece orchestra are the same for both dates, a couple of the substitutions greatly affected Ellington's music and spirit.

The earlier record was made at a time when Johnny Hodges, the band's most widely admired soloist from the time he signed up in 1928, took a four-year leave; drummer Sonny Greer (recruited 1926) and trombonists Lawrence Brown (recruited 1932) and Tyree Glenn (recruited 1946) had left the same year. Ellington was delighted to get Louis Bellson, the most assured and precision-oriented of the band's drummers, for a year; the irreplaceable Brown wouldn't rejoin until 1960, but in the meantime Ellington found two excellent trombonists, Quentin Jackson, one of the cagiest of all wah-wah specialists, and the virtuoso Britt Woodman. He also had the beginnings of a new kind of trumpet section, with the introduction of Cat Anderson's high notes, Clark Terry's bebop whimsy, and Willie Cook's straight-arrow lyricism. Perhaps the most significant new induction was tenor saxophonist Paul Gonsalves, formerly with Basie, and shortly to prove himself a marathon crowd pleaser. Still, Hodges's absence was deeply felt. Willie Smith, the star altoist with Jimmie Lunceford and Harry James, was an intelligent replacement, but though he was a respectable soloist he failed to give the reed section its former sheen. Besides, with so many changes it would take a while before Ellington sufficiently grasped the "poker-playing habits" of the new men to get the most out of them. The studio records from this period are extremely uneven—the leisurely, sensuous concert expansions of *Masterpieces by Ellington,* counterbalanced by awkward attempts at reconciliation with the hit parade. The live performances, privately taped, are another story.

The 1952 Northwestern tour took place near and on Ellington's birthday, always an occasion for intense celebration, and the maestro was in great spirits. (Note to the discographically minded: the dates given are often at odds with those in Massagli, though the general time frame is right.) Time and again on these Folkways selections, we find him tinkering with the orchestra and luxuriating at the piano. On "Take the A Train," he interpolates a bit of Fats Waller and a lot of Betty Roche's vocal rendition of the song in what amounts to a three-chorus vamp before Ray Nance and the band come on board. His comping—contrapuntal chords, parries, and thrusts—all but steals Willie Smith's thunder on "Tea for Two," and he introduces a blistering "Ornithology" ("How High the Moon") with bitonal glee. You expect Gonsalves to run off with "Cottontail," but not on the heels of two piano choruses that combine angular chromatic figures with a jaunty stride melody that Ellington later recorded as "Janet."

Jimmy Hamilton is in superb form, turning what might have been throwaway readings of "Time on My Hands" (Wendell Marshall's loping bass does the work of the band) and "Deep Purple" into memorable vignettes, and proving that he was Artie Shaw's rival for the loveliest clarinet sound in big band music. Ellington caught Hamilton's style in "The Tattooed Bride," which is heard here in a truncated version (the second theme only). Every version I've heard of "Sophisticated Lady" from this period is different; the one on hand favors Ellington's accompaniment since Harry Carney's bass clarinet is badly miked, as well as solos by Hamilton and Smith. The ensemble gets to shine too, of course, digging in behind Roche's vocal on "Sunny Side of the Street" as though she were Hodges, and brushing the sky on Mary Lou Williams's "Trumpet No End." Two performances are especially outstanding. "Ornithology" is bebop salmagundi—the aforementioned piano intro, three-way trumpet exchanges, whirling Hamilton, tireless Gonsalves, punishing Bellson, and climactic tuttis. "It Don't Mean a Thing" is heard in what amounts to a workshop performance for the rare 1953 recording on Pickwick: Ray Nance is late getting to the mike, so Ellington regales himself at the piano for two choruses; after the vocal, the band sidles loosely, restively into the arrangement, and then suddenly kicks off a fierce, boppish chorus that precedes exchanges between Nance and Cook, and later between Gonsalves and Hamilton. Never has a better case been made for the virtues of huggermugger leadership.

By 1957, Ellington's fortunes had changed considerably. Hodges had returned to provide the band with the perfect reed section; the trumpets were enhanced by the return of Harold Baker; and the rhythm section was given a new kick by Sam Woodyard, who had little of Bellson's finesse but knew where the beat was and pursued it energetically. At the 1956 Newport Jazz Festival, Ellington had given his single most commercially significant performance. The highlight came when the orchestra eagerly attacked one of his most ingenious configurations on the blues, "Dimineuendo and Crescendo in Blue," and Gonsalves rampaged through a 27-chorus "interlude." The audience went mad, and a reporter from *Time* used the event to marshall a cover story on Ellington. His star never faltered again. During the next few months, he performed with the New Haven Symphony and at Stratford, where he was commissioned to write his masterful Shakespearean suite; he composed, recorded, and then debuted on the *U.S. Steel Hour* his oratorio, *A Drum Is a Woman;* he toured the Midwest, returned to New York to play Birdland and record *Such Sweet Thunder,* and went on the road again. Which is where we pick up on him—in Carroltown, a farming town in the Alleghenies.

The two things about *All Star Road Band* that make its release an occasion for rejoicing are the conviviality of the evening and the engineering. Jack Towers, whose name appears on so many audiophile jazz recordings of recent years, mastered both the Carroltown and Folkways recordings. But because the 1952 material gave him less to work with (comparison with earlier releases testifies to his improvements) and because Folkways uses inferior pressings, the sound is only adequate. The sound on the 1957 dance comes as close to capturing the true sonorities of the Ellington band, and the interplay between Ellington and the band and the audience, as any record available. It documents a typical or better than typical Ellington one-nighter for dancers as definitively as *The Great Paris Concert* (1963; released 1973) captures a more formal presentation. The first time I saw the Ellington band live, I was mesmerized by the reed section—by the realization that at the same time you heard perfect unison phrasing, you also heard each distinct voice. When RCA (in the days of Dynagroove) issued Ellington's masterpieces of the mid-'60s, *Far East Suite, The Popular Duke Ellington,* and *And His Mother Called Him Bill,* the sumptuousness of the orchestra was almost captured. In audio terms, the Carroltown dance comes surprisingly close to those later recordings.

The music isn't bad either. From the first splattered arpeggios of "Take the A Train" and its immediate reprise, in which Ray Nance sings variations on the Roche vocal, you know that everyone is glad to be in the Alleghenies. By the end of the night, when Ellington has led the troops through a brilliantly executed "Diminuendo and Crescendo in Blue" (26 choruses by Gonsalves) and announced the imminent closing of the bar, the band is clearly exhausted, but still mellow. I think this album should improve Sam Woodyard's reputation; he keeps everyone sharp—relentlessly stomping the beat on the bass drum, rumbling over the toms, and pressing the cymbals for an extra shimmer. He boosts Clark Terry's already stratospheric spirits in their trades on "Perdido," and fans Hodges's fires on "Jeep's Blues." The entire band gives a handsome account of Othello's march in "Such Sweet Thunder." Some 25 years ago, the English critic Burnett James wrote of this piece, "Duke Ellington catches the nature of Othello with delicate imagination. The swinging theme for saxophones is eloquent of the unclouded trust and honesty of the man; the plunger-muted brass evoke the deep, elemental strain in him . . . Then comes Ray Nance's sweet-talking trumpet with the tale to win a noble bride." This performance is spliced, not unappealingly, into Carney's noble "Frustration." A special delight is a "Mood Indigo" that anticipates the version Ellington was to record three months later for *Ellington Indigos*. Here the theme is voiced by two trombones and bass clarinet, and the soloist is Willie Cook. For the recording, the ensemble and Cook were replaced by Shorty Baker, who borrowed phrases Cook played in Carroltown. Another workshop performance is "Bassment," a second cousin to "Happy Go Lucky Local" that Ellington eventually recorded in a nonet version for *The Cosmic Scene*. The second half of the album is more familiar and irresistible—the "Dimunuendo," yet another new take on "Sophisticated Lady," a Shorty Baker "Stardust," and four numbers by the patient and wily Hodges.

A colleague tells me that if he were asked to recommend one

Ellington album, *All Star Road Band* would be it—reasonable choice, considering the engineering, the spirit, and the repertoire. But the irony of choosing a tape from an obscure dance in a Pennsylvania farming community is as much an indictment of the shameful laxity among record labels that control Ellington's best studio work as it is a testament to the circuitous ways of jazz. I note that French RCA has finally reissued the long unavailable *And His Mother Called Him Bill,* one of the most sublimely conceived and executed long-playing records ever made, although it remains a mere collector's item in America. Under the circumstances, it's difficult to feel pious about independents who violate already questionable copyrights in releasing music that its lawful owners (not the musicians-composers, but the record labels) continue to suppress. One can only feel grateful when a collectors' club collates and remasters, as the Merit Record Society is presently doing, 48 albums from the 1945–46 broadcasts Ellington made for the Treasury department.

That Ellington's music is very much alive is never more evident than during his birthday month. At the ASCAP Meet the Composer concerts a couple of weeks ago, Mercer Ellington made the case eloquently with performances of "Harlem Air Shaft" and "Cottontail," which, despite his unnecessary revisions, made most of the other composers seem timorous and ersatz by comparison. Performances of Ellington's music have been scheduled throughout April. The most ambitious Ellington repertory presentation in a long while took place on Sunday at the Duke Ellington Society's 25th Anniversary concert. Mercer Ellington, an accomplished conductor, led his orchestra through a daunting batch of Ellingtonia, ranging from the 1926 "Birmingham Breakdown" to excerpts from *Queenie Pie,* the opera Ellington was writing shortly before his death. The presentation was extremely uneven, sodden with endless stage announcements, and cheapened, in part, by Mercer's disastrous decision to modernize the rhythms of such pre-swing landmarks as "East St. Louis Toodle-oo" and "Birmingham Breakdown." When he retained the original rhythms, tempos, and sonorities (including banjo) on "Hot and Bothered" (Anita Moore did a fine Baby Cox), "Old Man Blues," and "Rockin' in Rhythm," the musicians and the music were regenerated. This band cannot stand much comparison with Ellington Senior's—of the major soloists, only trombonist Art Baron and bassist J. J. Wiggins were consistently on target; trumpeter Barry Lee Hall, who also did many of the transcriptions, has the bite of Cootie Williams, but not the accuracy. The highlights (in addition to the world premiere of Mercer's *Music Is My Mistress*, a tripartite dedication with a couple of catchy Ducal themes) were nervous but acceptable readings of the ingenious railroad-verité orchestration "Daybreak Express" (though Mercer resorted to artificial effects eschewed by Duke) and especially the superbly crafted *Tone Parallel to Harlem*, a cross between a rhapsody and a concerto for orchestra. Other than obvious flubs, the chief problem was inauthenticity. Yes, I know a living repertoire must breathe anew with each interpreter. But since these performances were as shadows to the originals, I continue to believe that unless you play them Duke's way, you're playing them wrong. All the more reason for Columbia, RCA, MCA, Polygram, and EMI to recognize, organize, and present sensibly the Ellington catalogue for what it is, quintessential American music.

(April 1984)

The Definitive Bill Harris

Everything about Woody Herman's First Herd was astonishing, but the trombone solos of Bill Harris were especially so. His first tour of duty with Herman, 1944–46, established him for a short while as the most innovative new trombonist in a decade. Although his style suggested several influences (the brassy exuberance of J. C. Higginbotham, the eccentricity of Dickie Wells, the sly wit of Vic Dickenson, the romanticism of Jack Jenny), the result was an idiosyncratic blend of whimsy and conviction, bathos and satire, tradition and modernism. In a Harris solo, the melody was the subtext; the real story was conveyed through intonation. He would wobble nervously for one phrase, attack the next with rapid-fire staccato blasts, and float the third with shy glissandi. Alternately stony and lyrical, he was always thinking, always finding ways to make his absolute control of lip vibrato and slide effects complement each other. Harris's riffs were simple, but he was a master of sequencing and of motivic development. His sequences even more than his expressionism make him seem especially modern today.

Born in Philadelphia in 1916, Harris was a latecomer who didn't take up trombone until he was twenty-two. He'd played other instruments before, but his approach to the slide was so indigenous that it's difficult to imagine what he might have sounded like on trumpet or tenor. A slow reader, he passed through several bands, including Benny Goodman's for a year, before he found his niche with Herman. Harris's best features with the First Herd were Ralph Burns's "Bijou" and his own "Everywhere," models of economy, emotional control, dynamics, and intonational variety. Yet even his more episodic appearances were memorable—undermining the rites of marriage on "Put That Ring on My Finger," leaping into "Your Father's Mustache" as though about to declaim "Vesti la giubba," mixing barrelhouse slurs and fast tonguing on "Apple Honey," sustaining bold vibratoless whole notes before paraphrasing the melody of "Let It Snow!" or following surging Serge Chaloff with maidenly decorum on his own 1946 octet, "Woodchopper's Holiday."

Harris's preeminence, notwithstanding a dozen jazz poll victories, was short-lived. J. J. Johnson was just around the corner, and most trombonists promptly followed his punctilious lead. Yet touring with Jazz at the Philharmonic (from today's vantage point, it's Harris's jocular anticlimax rather than Flip Phillips's honking that seems the real highlight of "Perdido"), Harris continued to offer a useful alternative, and his burry tone, terminal vibrato, and sloshing slide work were picked up in varying degrees by Kai Winding, Eddie Bert, Jimmy Knepper, and Roswell Rudd, whose first album, *Everywhere*, was in part a homage to Harris. He also influenced the sound of section trombones, as Shorty Rogers demonstrated in his Herman arrangement of "Back Talk" when the massed brasses imitate Harris's style while backing up his solo. Still, Harris made few records under his own name, and most of his last 15 years were spent in relative obscurity; his death in 1973 was little noted even in the jazz press.

Now, suddenly, we have a Bill Harris windfall: the two albums he made in 1957 have been reissued, as well as four volumes from his years with JATP. Of the latter, the most interesting in terms of Harris's work is *The Challenges 1954* (Verve 815 154 1): 10 choruses on a "Jazz Concert Blues" that illustrate his ability to sequence limited material, a characteristically winsome ballad, and a positively ebullient building of riffs on "The Challenges." The 1957 material is more substantial on every level. If '45 was the year that put Harris on the map, '57 was the year he perfected his art—in addition to making two albums in eight days, he was the featured soloist on three fine sessions arranged by Billy Ver Planck for Savoy and World Wide (one was reissued a few years ago on Savoy's *The Trombone Album*). On paper, *Bill Harris and Friends* (Fantasy 3263) would seem to be the more imposing of the two: Harris shares the front line with Ben Webster, who is in top form; the rhythm section is led by ex-Hermanite Jimmy Rowles (already flirting with Monk, cf. "Crazy Rhythm"); and the standard songs are first rate. But the session was maybe too free-wheeling. Harris and Webster interlace successfully only on "I Surrender Dear," though their consecutive solos on "In a Mellow Tone" encourage you to dream about what Ellington might have done with Harris, and their parody of "Just One More Chance" is funny because they acknowledge similar tendencies to gild the gild.

No, it's the justly retitled *The Bill Harris Memorial Album* (Xanadu 191), in which five ex-Hermanites—including a pleasingly restrained Terry Gibbs—play First and Second Herd material, that is definitive. The lachrymose tendencies once apparent in Harris's work are gone, replaced by a profound and entirely personal commitment to melody. The highlights are various and constant: Harris's two symmetrical choruses on "Blue Flame" that begin as a low drone, and employ chromaticism, sequencing, and variable vibrato in ways that anticipate Rudd or Craig Harris; his purring, elliptical shadowplay on "Early Autumn"; his jetting, extroverted solos on "Apple Honey" and "Lemon Drop"; his superbly controlled phantom tones and slide work on his masterful theme "Everywhere." This is one of those desert island records that encapsulate the talents of a presumably marginal performer and force you to wonder how marginal he was.

(April 1984)

The Return of New Orleans

The New Orleans Jazz and Heritage Festival, which gets under way this week, can't help but impress visitors with the variety of music still thriving in that most heterogeneous of American cities. The festival's periodicity, however, also underscores the myopic bumbling of those city fathers who allowed a lavish tourist racket to slip through their fingers. Too racist or stupid or both to recognize the rainbow before their eyes, they missed the chance to capitalize on their most celebrated resource. So while Nashville gentrified its Opry, turning a two-lane town into an institutionalized mecca, the country's most exotic and naturally musical port made do with a little sweatbox called Preservation Hall, a tawdry nightclub scene content to make heroes out of the likes of Al Hirt and Pete Fountain, and the annual bacchanal of Mardi Gras. It's a thrill, no mistake, to see the statue they've erected of Louis Armstrong—especially if you recall the humiliation Armstrong endured there long after he'd achieved international renown. Yet, you wonder, if New Orleans music had had the right complexion, would its mythic cradle now boast a jazz concert hall, a repertory company, a museum, awards, TV specials, and a localized recording industry? Would historic landmarks have been duly proclaimed and preserved? Could a jazz homeland have succeeded in establishing the music's birthright and continued good health? The mind reels.

New Orleans figures in jazz history twice. Between 1890 and 1925, it produced the first great jazz improvisor (Bolden), teacher (Tio), band (Oliver's Creole Jazz Band), soloists (Bechet, Armstrong), composer (Morton), recording unit (Original Dixieland Jazz Band), bassists (Braud, Foster, Brown), drummers (Dodds, Singleton), and much more. By the time Henry Red Allen, the last of the city's trumpet kings, arrived in New York, jazz had attained a worldwide footing, but New Orleans had become a preserve for folklorists out to document its allegedly untrammeled roots. During its second stage as a newsworthy jazz center, in the '40s, New Orleans came to represent a holy land for revivalists, sentimental fans disenfranchised by those twin enemies of nostalgic purity—commercialism on the right and modernism on the left. They bought Bunk Johnson teeth and canonized George Lewis. Though soon to be enmeshed in a vital rhythm and blues movement, the city seemed to have little to offer jazz's future. Enter Al Hirt.

Then came the '80s, and suddenly jazz has a dose of New Orleans fever again. When Art Blakey showcased Wynton and Branford Marsalis, their backgrounds were of passing interest. But when he replaced them with two more New Orleanians, Terence Blanchard and Donald Harrison, and when rumor promised lots more where they came from, notably a flutist named

Kent Jordan, the city began to loom once again in the imagination. Especially since each of these musicians was schooled in classical as well as jazz music—just like the Creoles of Color who set the standards for jazz musicianship at the turn of the century. Only this wave seems to have been generated by one educator in particular, Ellis Marsalis, formerly a pianist with Al Hirt, who managed to combine the roles of exemplary improvisor (i.e., Bolden) and lettered teacher (i.e., Tio) at the New Orleans Center for the Creative Arts, where he taught all five wunderkinder. He wasn't alone: the great clarinetist Alvin Batiste of Baton Rouge and the saxophonist Edward Jordan (Kent's father) of Southern University in New Orleans were also formidable influences. You've read plenty about Marsalis's son Wynton, who recently copped awards for his recordings of both jazz and trumpet concertos. Four new records by other members of this button-down generation fill in the larger picture.

Ironically, only the most mature production of the lot, Ellis Marsalis's *Syndrome* (Elm JS4834), is independently distributed (by New Music Distribution Service). Although the notes have Marsalis referring to jazz as a lingo of motifs—"short musical statements that previous musicians have made, little gems, little nuggets, which have been played on recordings"—there is little of the academician in his playing. His melodic gift is impressive, at times sumptuous, and his long and dulcet phrases are quite unmarred by the vanities to which lyrical piano improvisation has become subject in recent years. He builds tension with bobbing figures that encompass most of the keyboard, and when he is in full throttle, as on "The Garden" or "Tell Me," his two hands animate each other with measured flamboyance. "The Fourth Autumn," entirely composed, suggests in part an aggressive extension of the two-chord meditation Bill Evans recorded as "Peace Piece," though Marsalis has a more various piece in mind. On four of the nine selections, his trio (bassist Bill Huntington, drummer James Black) is augmented by Kent Jordan, whose flute and piccolo solos are longer on energy than nuance. The quartet attacks Coltrane's "Moment's Notice" in midflight—variations first, then the theme.

Jordan is an impressive technician, but his feelings about jazz are, well, ambivalent, judging from his debut as a leader. *No Question About It* (Columbia FC39325) is mayonnaise, produced by and in the image of Stanley Clarke, who, for all *his* prodigious technique has yet to create a memorable album in the decade he's been filling cut-out bins. But he's got that California touch, plus an arrangement of "Theme from 'Terms of Endearment,' " and so Jordan is sacrificed—a Christian in the lions' den—to the inglorious dream that has already made fertilizer of such once staunch flutists as Hubert Laws, Art Webb, and Dave Valentine. There is no fun in this kind of trash—it's too coolly calculated. Improvisation is treated like plague, even on the two-minute sop to jazz (an Alvin Batiste variation on "Giant Steps"); mindless vamps proliferate. On the tune called "California," background voices chant, "Cal-i-for-nia fan-ta-sy." "But do I have a hit?" the Christian inquired, head bowed before *Billboard*. "Chomp, chomp, chomp," said the lion.

New York Second Line (Concord Jazz 3002), by trumpeter Terence Blanchard and altoist Donald Harrison, is another story—a bit green, but witty and daring. Working with an attentive rhythm section (Mulgrew Miller, Lonnie Plaxico, Marvin Smith), they derive evident pleasure from toying with song form, and make the most of solos that rarely exceed two choruses. The head on "Duck Steps" is AABA, except that the last A is only two bars. The solos, however, are 48 bars—that is, two 24-bar choruses, the first ending with a release built on a shift in modulation that leads into the second, which goes out on a different cadence. Blanchard, who likes to lean back on the beat, resolves his solo with a nifty high-note flourish. "New York Second Line" is a strange concatenation of riffs tied to a New Orleans beat, echoing "Blue Monk" in the first chorus and "A String of Pearls" in the last. Harrison's first phrase here is straight from the heart of Johnny Hodges, though the thin intonation that dominates the rest of his light and airy solo identifies him as a child of his time. Much as saxophonists in the 1940s took up tenor to avoid sounding like Charlie Parker, Harrison's smart choice of alto disguises his debt to Coltrane and Shorter. Blanchard's solo on the same piece opens with a Milesian motif that he develops after making a reference to "Laura." He gets a pretty, reflective sound on the trumpet, and paces himself well. "Doctor Drums" and "Subterfuge" show off an affinity for complex rhythms; the latter is welded to a fast vamp in six, with built-in time changes, including rubato transitions, and an extended release. Despite such obstacles, or because of them, a cheerful disposition is sustained throughout.

Better still is Branford Marsalis's *Scenes in the City* (Columbia FC38951), a singularly classy production, with effective cover art by Henrietta Condak and Duane Michals (a montage of Branfords, wearing the same suit and different colored ties), superb engineering by Tim Geelan, and informative notes by the ever stylish and sensible A. B. Spellman. The music is intense, almost stony, and remarkably authoritative. Marsalis's prime influences, Wayne and Trane, are everywhere apparent, but after several listenings I find my attention fixing increasingly on the probity and persuance of his own ideas. Besides, how can you resist a musician who recreates Charles Mingus's eccentric and obscure "Scenes of the City," taking full advantage of superior recording techniques while keeping true to its '50s milieu (the litany of bop giants, the reference to Eisenhower)? In the past decade, repertory companies have tackled everything from Morton to Coltrane, but this has to be the first time anyone's attempted to resurrect a slice of poetry-and-jazz. Wendell Pierce is a persuasive narrator, and the band puts its heart in the familiar Mingus melodies; still, I wish they'd explored those melodies in more depth—what promises to be a splendid Robin Eubanks trombone solo is no more than a teasing fragment. Though inspired by Sonny Rollins trio recordings, an impromptu blues called "No Backstage Pass" is more reminiscent of the blistering attack Shorter used on some of his Blue Notes (i.e., *The All-Seeing Eye*), and Marsalis's beadroll of glinty, knotty phrases is meticulous and arresting. He plays tenor and soprano on "Solstice," a reworking of Coltrane's "Equinox" that lets him explore the brittle low register. He's especially relaxed on "No Sidestepping," a 20-bar theme that works for him like a concise "So What." Kenny Kirkland and Mulgrew Miller are the efficient pianists; Ron Carter tackles most of the bass responsibilities, but don't miss Charnett Moffett's high-range chase figures on the slightly crazed "Waiting for Train."

Considering the pervasive influence of Miles Davis's quintets on these musicians, I'm not sure there's anything indigenously Southern about this flurry of New Orleans talent—except perhaps for the uncommonly skillful musicianship that precedes their quest for originality. Judging from their liner comments, they aren't especially concerned with being original, and they are quick to catalogue the particular lessons of particular masters. They approach jazz with refreshing detachment, as though it were a music to be mastered and not a spontaneous revelation of soul. How novel. Their youthfulness (they are between the ages of twenty-two and twenty-five) is less novel, perhaps, but it too is something of a throwback to an earlier time. Since 1960, many key jazz innovators—Coleman, Coltrane, Dolphy, Rivers, Abrams, Threadgill, Hemphill, Ulmer, Jackson—first attracted attention in their thirties and forties. Ellis Marsalis hasn't unleashed an assemblage of geniuses, but rather a cadre of impeccably schooled musicians. Following them as they rise to the challenges that their abilities and backgrounds dictate will be one of the chief pleasures of jazz listening in the '80s.

(May 1984)

Euphoria

Euphoria, in music as in life, is a candle lit at both ends. It can light the way to the kind of aggravated sense of pleasure we call rapture, or blind you with delusions of ecstasy. Beware the Kreutzer Sonata, Tolstoy warned. In jazz, euphoria seems to prosper in the absence of stark introspection—achieving a more substantial foothold in the polyphony of New Orleans, the chanting exuberance of big bands, or the confluent hollering of new music than in the feverish inventions of a lone soloist. Generalizations are dangerous, though, as any number of honking tenor saxophonists will argue. Still, I mean to define euphoria as a very specific kind of excitement, with the accent on sublimity rather than frenzy, well-being rather than zeal. Jelly Roll Morton remains the premier composer of jazz euphoria, in helium-inflated ensemble passages (i.e., "Dead Man Blues") or such quietly effective melodies as the trios to "The Pearls" and "Frog-i-More." In a famous passage in his "Smoke House Blues," he fills what should have been a piano break with the moan, "Oh, Mr. Jelly!" as though no notes could convey his feeling. Louis Armstrong, the nonpareil king of improvised rapture, proves—in performances as diverse as "When You're Smiling" and "Blue Turning Gray Over You" (1955 version)—that euphoria supersedes such earthly matters as tempo and drive.

I bring up the matter in relation to Sonny Rollins, because for several years he's been moving in the direction of a music that suggests the fires of blessed inspiration with none of the penalties. His intonation has grown, quite literally; it's fatter, grittier, more colorful, and less sour than ever before. His phrasing, regardless of tempo, has become increasingly bold—antic, exhilarated, fustian—yet it's never been emblazoned with more melody. The most rhythmically inventive musician of his generation, he seems to have realized that the Ur-calypso he's been exploring for nearly 30 years has become his mandate, a key to his current vision. The result is a fervent positivism that, far from being easily won—consider all the misfires of the past decade—celebrates its victory over the night in every measure. God bless the child that's got his own. *Sunny Days Starry Nights*, indeed.

Rollins was never comfortable with the lavish disclosures of self, the musical glossolalia, the narcissism let loose in the wake of Coltrane. He had to make his own way through the excesses of freedom, fusion, and tradition, and with his new album he seems finally to have resolved a host of ambivalences. By strange coincidence, *Sunny Days Starry Nights* (Milestone 9122) was released almost simultaneously with the rarest of his early records, the 1957 *Tour de Force* (Prestige OJC-095). The differences spell the nature of Rollins's maturity, but the similarities prove that his basic interests have remained the same. *Tour de Force,* his major statement between the more widely known records *Saxophone Colossus* and *Way Out West,* was an experiment: it combined two sentimental ballads sung by Earl Coleman with two furiously discursive improvisations—"B. Quick" based on "Cherokee" and "B. Swift" based on "Lover" (which he was to record in orthodox waltz meter three months later under Max Roach's name)—that took the standard song form to extreme limits. The album's masterpiece is the blues "Ee-Ah," in which every lively phrase is mindfully anchored by an insistent, three-note motif.

The new album also has sentimental ballads, a freely conceived assault on a pop song, motific solos, and unbridled fury. Yet it's a better, stronger, wiser work on every level but one: the new rhythm section (Mark Soskin, Russel Blake, Tommy Campbell) is no match for the old (Kenny Drew, George Morrow, Max Roach). While Soskin is restrained and tasteful, Campbell clutters the time without varying it, a drawback for a record as decidedly upbeat as this one. Still, as important as the ripeness of the ensemble is to the success of the project, Rollins's might overshadows every infelicity. Calypsos, broadly speaking, predominate; he had made the form, the rhythm, his own—there are no banana boat songs here. "Mava Mava" is superb Rollins, replete with offpitch tones that terminate on pitch, and register-hopping call-and-response. "Tell Me You Love Me" is a sweet melody made into unabashed dance music; this is the euphoric Rollins, embellishing the eight-bar phrases (and four-bar exchanges with the drums) with a low and lusty honk, a growl, and a couple of squeaks reminiscent of Roy Eldridge, yet never forsaking the almost-cloying tune. The most windblown and haphazard of these pieces is "Kilauea."

The other three selections are closer to the ground, although

"I'm Old Fashioned" is as irreverant a tour de force treatment of a standard as "B. Swift." It begins with a characteristic Rollins riff, then charges deep into the chords where the melody has yet to be born. By the second chorus, Soskin hints at Jerome Kern's tune, but Rollins skitters around it, nodding occasionally as at an old acquaintance, and loses himself in gritty variations until Clifton Anderson's trombone joins in; the polyphony that follows intoxicates Rollins, and the fadeout suggests the feeling-no-pain heedlessness of that Morton break in "Smoke House Blues." "Wynton," a ballad that may remind you of Henry Mancini's "Charade" (they share a five-note phrase), makes amusing use of celeste in the theme, and allows Anderson and Blake to solo; they are filler—only the leader seems to know exactly where he's going. More enchanting is his reading of Nöel Coward's unlikely anthem from 1929, "I'll See You Again." Rollins has long been known for the pleasure he gets from sentimental melodies (he resurrected Frederich Hollander a couple of albums back), and he makes the most of Coward's schnozzled nostalgia through overdubbing; in effect, he gets to be the singer and the accompanist. *Sunny Days Starry Nights* may not be as ecstatic an experience as seeing Sonny Rollins in concert, but it's a perfectly delectable performance by a guiding light who's seen the light.

(June 1984)

Orchestral Jazz

The era when charismatic jazz orchestras crisscrossed the land, fueled by maverick soloists and audacious arrangements, is fast receding into a myth as nostalgic and unreliable as that of the

Wild West. Young listeners often associate big bands with a period music suitable for accompanying tuxedoed vocalists and
ringing in the New Year. The sheer power of a dozen brasses
and reeds riffing in conjunction with a swinging rhythm section
is harder to appreciate in an age of electronic overkill; when a
big band (for example, Maynard Ferguson's) achieves financial
success today, it is likely to gloss over the nuances of orchestral
writing with electronic lacquer. Recently, a friend asked me to program a swing tape for her 30th birthday party. Much to my cha-
grin, people jammed the dance floor when her paid disc jockey
cued the thumping bass of disco, but drifted over to the bar when
he grudgingly played Count Basie's "Jumpin' at the Woodside"
or Benny Goodman's "Let's Dance." I was reminded of that pro-
phetic moment in 1956, when Alan Freed fired Basie from the
"Camel Dance Party" because kids couldn't dance to him.

Dance styles and rhythms change, and lamentations are worse
than useless; they can never recreate the musical excitement of
a bygone era and may lead to the petrified images and sounds
of ghost bands, which deserve all the abuse they get. Something
more than passing fashions is at stake, however: the very notion
of a jazz orchestra, a unique and peculiarly American institution
that balances composition and improvisation more evenly than is
possible in a chamber-sized jazz group, has been foundering since
the demise of the Swing Era. Last winter, Woody Herman, who
at seventy-one is the youngest of the Swing Era pioneers and the
last still committed to the road, taped a TV ad for dentures to
help finance his orchestra for another year. Between sets one night
at New York's Rainbow Room, he told me, "Duke was right—
having a big band is an avocation. It's no business." Herman was
one of dozens of big band veterans who attended Count Basie's
funeral service in May. When Basie's guitarist of 47 years, Freddie Green, told the congregation that he didn't know what to do
now that Basie was gone, you might have thought he was speaking for jazz itself—as though the great man's passing symbolized
a withering away of the music's grandest aspirations. In some ways,
it does.

In the 52-page booklet that accompanies *Big Band Jazz: From the Beginnings to the Fifties,** a six-record anthology produced for the Smithsonian Collection of Recordings, the editors and annotators Gunther Schuller and Martin Williams write: "Perhaps future generations will perform and listen to the best swing band instrumentals rather the way we now listen to the best European baroque music and the best American ragtime: that is, as danceoriented music rather than music to dance to. Perhaps the instrumental classics of the swing idiom will be played and listened to in the same way that we now attend Rameau, Vivaldi, and Joplin." Actually, there have always been a few such performers and listeners. The pioneers of big band music set their sights on concert halls at least as far back as 1924, when Paul Whiteman commissioned Gershwin's *Rhapsody in Blue*. But most people fail to distinguish between music composed for a big band and danceband music, and this failure helps keep modern jazz orchestras on the ropes.

The Smithsonian anthology is a flawed but solid attempt—easily the most ambitious to date—to place big bands in a broader perspective. Schuller and Williams are out to bedzazzle the listener, without disparaging the impulse to dance or indulging in panegyrics to lost youth. In documenting the diversity of big band music over a period of 30 years, they make a case for the integrity of the large ensemble that should enlighten even those who regard orchestral jazz as nothing more than an improbable luxury of the Depression. Since the selection was made with several audiences in mind—from ballroom veterans to serious listeners to novices—the 80 performances by 31 bands include major hits, historical touchstones, and obscure gems. Fletcher Henderson, Earl Hines, Chick Webb, Jimmie Lunceford, Benny Goodman, Tommy Dorsey, Count Basie, Duke Ellington, and Woody Herman are generously represented, as expected. Paul Whiteman and Glenn Miller, peripheral figures in jazz but not in the history of big bands, are persuasively included, as are such unrenowned

*Available on records or cassettes from Smithsonian Recordings, P.O. Box 10230, Des Moines, Iowa 60336.

experimenters as John Nesbitt and Boyd Raeburn, and a handful of territory bands that never achieved national recognition. Enthusiasts will take exception to certain choices, but not to the quality of the music, which is generally high. In order to keep the project manageable, the anthologists imposed severe restrictions on themselves, some of them questionable. For example, they eschew "vehicles for star instrumentalists," thereby excluding an important style of big band writing— the concerto, of which Duke Ellington was the foremost creator, and Louis Armstrong and Roy Eldridge among the most glorious performers. A more eccentric decision was to confine the Ellington selections to the years 1938-46; his impact on the evolution of the genre in the 1920s is ignored, along with his more ambitious achievements of later years. Most distressing of all is the "arbitrary cutoff date" of 1950.

Over a period of 30 years, big band music evolved from rag-influenced orchestrations with multiple themes, two- and four-measure breaks, and simple call-and-response antiphony, to a virtuoso concert music of broad colors, outlandishly complicated melodic phrases, and exotic rhythms. Although it's logical to compare the role of big bands in jazz with that of the symphony orchestra in European music, the analogy is limited because symphony conductors and musicians are merely interpreters of a written score. A better analogy might be found in film, specifically in the responsibilities of the director (the bandleader), the scenarist (the arranger), and the actors (the soloists). Most big band classics are products of collaborative tension, even though the final effect—as in a movie—is determined by a dominant personality. Records by Duke Ellington and Count Basie reflect chiefly the personalities of the leaders, those by Jimmie Lunceford and Claude Thornhill the arrangers, and those by Louis Armstrong and Gene Krupa the soloists. Basie once observed that it was dangerous to let a band rely on its soloists, because when you lost your stars you were out of business; he switched from a scrappy band filled with stylish soloists in the 1930s ("One O'Clock Jump") to a precision-oriented arranger's band in the 1950s ("Shiny

Stockings"). Yet as different as those orchestras were, the foundation for each remained Basie's piano, his rhythmic style, and his insistence on simplicity and economy. Benny Goodman, by contrast, based his band on arrangements that had been conceived for the orchestras of the pioneering Fletcher Henderson (who ended up on Goodman's payroll when his own band folded) and Chick Webb; and Tommy Dorsey made Jimmie Lunceford's sound his own by hiring Lunceford's arranger Sy Oliver.

Despite the absence of "star vehicles," this collection luxuriates in the give-and-take of ferociously talented individualists committed to a music dependent on teamwork. Perhaps the most striking of several surprises are two arrangements for McKinney's Cotton Pickers by John Nesbitt, a trumpeter and arranger who has been completely neglected since his early death in 1935, because he was overshadowed by his associate Don Redman, a gifted composer ("Cherry," "Gee Baby, Ain't I Good to You") and instrumentalist (all the reeds). Redman, as Fletcher Henderson's arranger and aide-de-camp, and as the brains behind the Cotton Pickers and the Chocolate Dandies, is justly recognized as a premier architect of big band jazz. Yet "Put It There" and especially "Stop Kidding," a roller coaster excursion into multiple rhythms and mutable forms that would have scared dancers to death, prove that Nesbitt was a formidable innovator, too. Other unexpected highlights include Jesse Stone and his Blue Serenaders' 1927 "Starvation Blues," with its wonderfully undulating last chorus; Glenn Miller's self-consciously experimental 1937 arrangement of "I Got Rhythm," with sudden silences and fancy counterpoint; and a rare alternate take of Henderson's 1924 "Copenhagen" that finds second-raters Charlie Green and Buster Bailey improvising their pants off, and Louis Armstrong, whose blues chorus made this number an instant classic, playing exactly the same solo as on the master take.

The more familiar performances kindle new insights—not least because the Smithsonian employed Jack Towers, the engineer, to scrupulously remaster the original recordings, adjusting pitch where necessary and beefing up the sound. (A miraculous job of cosmetic splicing has removed the sax squeak from Chick Webb's "Stomping at the Savoy.") On the first two discs alone are Henderson's "Down South Camp Meetin'," building via an ingenious interlude to a heady climax; Bennie Moten's "Toby," based on "Sweet Sue," with Basie striding à la Fats Waller, Ben Webster tearing through the chord changes, and a final chorus in which the band splits into sizzling sectional counterpoint; Earl Hines's "Madhouse," an exuberant Jimmy Mundy arrangement in which Quinn Wilson shows how valid the tuba could be in a rhythm section, and Hines's "Grand Terrace Shuffle," in which arranger Budd Johnson sets up his own steamy saxophone solo with keening orchestral riffs; four Chick Webb numbers with clever details (the rise-and-shine beginning of Pete Clark's alto solo in "That Naughty Waltz"), flashy virtuosity (Chauncey Haughton's whirling clarinet in "Harlem Congo"), and Webb's impetuous rhythms (everywhere); Sy Oliver's alchemical juxtaposition of instruments in unusual combinations on Jimmie Lunceford's "Organ Grinder Swing"; and Benny Goodman's "Sometimes I'm Happy," with a chorus of saxophone variations written by Henderson (among other things, Goodman's was a fine repertory orchestra). Masterpieces by Basie, Ellington, Shaw, Herman, Gillespie, and Thornhill follow.

It's impossible not to take issue with some inclusions and omissions. The only musically unsatisfying selection is Lunceford's simpering "Mood Indigo," which seems especially jarring since Ellington's sublime version is missing. Andy Kirk's "Big Jim Blues" is a savvy choice for demonstrating his band's adventuresome approach to song form, but arranger Mary Lou Williams would have been better served by other Kirk recordings. Then there is the puzzling absence of such leaders as Red Norvo, Harlan Leonard, Gene Krupa (who is unfairly castigated in the notes), and Lucky Millinder, and such arrangers as Eddie Sauter, Deane Kincaide, George Handy, and Shorty Rogers. The princely arranger Billy Strayhorn is represented by "Take the A Train," but not by any piece with the dreamy impressionism that was his trademark. Because of the ban on "star vehicles," Louis Armstrong appears in an undistinguished Joe Garland jump riff ("Leap Frog") instead of in the bravura arrangements written to show off his genius. The Latin influence on Dizzy Gillespie's band is entirely ignored. Yet there are two pieces each by Charlie Barnet and Harry James (one each would do), four by Tommy Dorsey, and five arrangements by Sy Oliver. These are quibbles. The larger problem is that "arbitrary cutoff date," which I suspect will simply enforce the prejudice this collection should be putting to rest once and for all—the idea that big band music is purely a phenomenon of the Swing Era.

The Smithsonian has released two equally ambitious precedents for *Big Band Jazz—The Smithsonian Collection of Classic Jazz,* which proffers the word "classic" to justify its cutoff date (which, in fact, is rather late: 1966), and *The Smithsonian Collection of Country Music,* which goes right up to 1975, proving to country dilettantes like me that Nashville did not lose its soul with the deaths of Hank Williams and Lefty Frizzell. The big bands set should have followed the latter plan. Either through tougher editing or the addition of another disc, some recognition of the orchestral styles of the past 30 years should have been included to prove the enduring value of the big band tradition. Although Bill Holman and Frank Foster are each represented with an appropriate arrangement (the only exceptions to the 1950 cutoff date), no mention is made of such orchestrators as George Russell, Johnny Richards, Ernie Wilkins, Neal Hefti, Charles Mingus, Al Cohn, Manny Albam, Quincy Jones, Sun Ra, Bill Potts, Oliver Nelson, Thad Jones, Bob Brookmeyer, Sam Rivers, Carla Bley, Muhal Richard Abrams, Chico O'Farrill, Anthony Braxton, Toshiko Akiyoshi, or the later styles of Gil Evans, for starters. As the closest thing we have to a ministry of culture, the Smithsonian needs to be especially wary of giving the impression that this kind of collection is a museum piece, an artifact from our past ready to be filed away. Introductory comments under the heading, "What Did the Music Mean?," give precisely that impression. This survey would have done greater service to big band music had it shown how the idiom has survived despite the loss of popular support and the lack of subsidization.

An orchestra that plays concert jazz has only a minimally better chance than a symphony of surviving the marketplace. But symphonies are subsidized in the public and private sectors while big bands are still expected, 35 years after the collapse of the Swing Era, to compete as pop. Imagine the classical European idiom reduced in our time to the scale of chamber groups, and you get an idea of what's really at stake. With the loss of Count Basie, the number of full-time jazz orchestras that buy arrangements and apprentice jazz soloists has been diminished dramatically. Indeed, big band music has been in large measure shunted to university campuses and student orchestras. Yet the desire, and tenacity, to work in this form is constant, and new orchestras are always starting up. This past year we've seen the call-to-arms from bandleaders of every generation, from Artie Shaw, who is fronting a band for the first time since his retirement in 1954, to Illinois Jacquet, who traded in his quartet for a swing orchestra, to David Murray, who assembled some of New York's brightest young modernists for a big band that appears all too infrequently in local clubs. Most big bands have a short life span, but some persist. Gil Evans is working more than he ever has, George Russell is on tour, Mel Lewis and the Jazz Orchestra are celebrating 19 years of Monday nights at the Village Vanguard, and various European ensembles—including the Vienna Art Orchestra, Willem Breuker, and the Globe Unity Orchestra—are showing Americans how the newest techniques in their music can be elaborated in larger settings.

The idea of a stable big band music that keeps its eye on the future while celebrating its past is long overdue. Jazz orchestras can and should be maintained in the same houses and by the same boards of directors that conserve philharmonic orchestras; under those circumstances, they can offer the proven repertory and commission new works, which need not be written exclusively by jazz composers. Stravinsky wrote the *Ebony Concerto* for Woody

Herman because he was intrigued by jazz instrumentation, as opposed to jazz style. For economic reasons, a jazz orchestra is more likely than a symphony to take artistic chances on the new and unproven. But boards will be boards, and before that can happen, orchestral jazz will have to acquire a significant change in status. The Smithsonian Collection shows how rich the classic repertory is; a more comprehensive approach would have made a still stronger case for the enduring glories of big band music.

(June 1984)

Index

Abercrombie, John, 18
Abrams, Muhal Richard, 15, 24–25, 44, 61, 154, 237, 267, 276
Adams, George, 105
Adams, Pepper, 133-34
Adderley, Cannonball, 122, 133, 177, 192
Adler, Larry, 48
Ahlert, Fred, 216
Air, 25, 87
Akiyoshi, Toshiko, 276
Aklaff, Pheeroan, 186
Albam, Manny, 276
Albee, Edward, 96
Ali, Amin, 244
Ali, Rashied, 19
Al-Khabyyr, Nasyr Abdul, 182
Allen, Fred, 45
Allen, Henry Red, 51, 70, 89, 158, 263
Altenfelder, Andreas, 199
Altschul, Barry, 43
Ameen, Ramsey, 10–11
Ammons, Gene, 110, 115
Anderson, Cat, 209, 254
Anderson, Clifton, 270
Anderson, Fred, 44
Anderson, Ivie, 30
Anderson, Jay, 191
Anderson, Ray, 43-44
Anka, Paul, 193, 227
Arlen, Harold, 168
Armstrong, Louis, 6, 35, 46–47, 54, 70–72, 90–91, 95, 113, 116, 118–19, 149, 158, 161–62, 184–85, 214, 216–18, 232, 242, 248, 263, 268, 273–75
Arnheim, Gus, 112
Arodin, Sidney, 116
Art Ensemble of Chicago, the, 18, 164, 195–98, 200, 208
Ashby, Harold, 251
Atkinson, Lisle, 76
Ayler, Albert, 58, 97–99, 101, 156, 171, 173, 199–200, 236

Babs, Alice, 31
Bach, Johann Sebastian, 4, 126, 158, 239-40
Bacharach, Burt, 57
Bacon, Paul, 223
Bailey, Buster, 274
Bailey, Dave, 125
Bailey, Donald, 136
Baker, Dorothy, 80
Baker, Harold, 255, 257
Bang, Billy, 100, 249
Banks, Stanley, 138
Barbarin, Paul, 184
Barefield, Eddie, 182-83
Bargeron, Dave, 43
Barker, Thurman, 43
Barnet, Charlie, 276
Baron, Art, 259
Barron, Kenny, 105
Bartók, Bela, 8, 238
Basie, Count, 14, 65, 93, 112, 115, 143, 151, 179–82, 218, 230–31, 237, 242, 254, 271–75, 277
Batiste, Alvin, 120–22, 264–65

Beau, Heinie, 233
Bechet, Sidney, 68, 140, 171, 185, 263
Beckett, Fred, 40
Beethoven, Ludwig van, 39, 82, 126
Beiderbecke, Bix, 15, 92
Bellson, Louis, 26, 29, 209, 254–56
Benbow, Warren, 244
Benford, Tommy, 91
Bennett, Tony, 65–68
Bennink, Han, 170–71
Benson, George, 6, 166–67
Benton, Walter, 36
Berigan, Bunny, 89–90
Berlin, Irving, 30, 229
Berman, Sonny, 114
Berry, Chu, 48, 70
Berry, Chuck, 148
Bert, Eddie, 41, 261
Betsch, John, 186
Big Sky Mudflaps, the, 63–65
Bird (see Parker, Charlie)
Biscoe, Chris, 104
Bishop, Joe, 113
Black, James, 264
Blackwell, Ed, 10, 178
Blake, Eubie, 137
Blake, John, 62
Blake, Ran, 216
Blake, Russel, 269–70
Blake, William, 102–4
Blakey, Art, 132–34, 158–59, 194, 218, 224, 263
Blanchard, Terence, 263, 265
Bland, Bobby "Blue," 96
Blanton, Jimmy, 47, 49, 53, 240
Bley, Carla, 102, 188, 276
Blood, James (see Ulmer, James Blood)
Bluiett, Hamiet, 156, 174–75
Blythe, Arthur, 18–19, 25, 61, 85–88, 237, 242
Bogart, Humphrey, 114
Bolden, Buddy, 263–64
Bolling, Claude, 72

Bonds, Gary U. S., 69
Born, Georgie, 104
Bostic, Earl, 5
Boswell Sisters, the, 65
Bowie, Lester, 3, 15, 18, 97, 198, 239
Bowler, Phil, 160
Brackeen, Charles, 99–100, 247
Bradford, Bobby, 173, 177
Braud, Wellman, 263
Braxton, Anthony, 43–44, 276
Bream, Julian, 140
Brecker, Michael, 56, 58
Breuker, Willem, 43, 164, 195–96, 198–200, 208–9, 277
Bridgewater, Cecil, 38
Bridgewater, Dee Dee, 137
Brodey, Hugh, 182
Brookmeyer, Bob, 41, 276
Brooks, Roy, 136
Brown, Charles, 96
Brown, Clifford, 4, 35, 77, 133, 160
Brown, Garnett, 42
Brown, James, 134, 237–38
Brown, Lawrence, 39–40, 254
Brown, Oscar, 36
Brown, Ray, 25–26, 28–29, 52
Brown, Ruth, 65
Brown, Steve, 263
Brown, Trisha, 196
Brubeck, Dave, 85, 96, 213, 246
Brubeck, Iola, 213
Brunis, George, 39–40
Burnham, Charles, 244
Burns, Ralph, 114, 260
Burr, John, 66
Burrell, Kenny, 166–68
Burton, Gary, 57–58
Butterfield, Billy, 89
Byard, Jaki, 3–7, 24, 122–24
Byas, Don, 50, 69, 71–72, 94, 182
Byers, Billy, 29, 32–33

Cahn, Sammy, 204, 227
Cale, J. J., 64
Calloway, Cab, 162–63, 181

Campbell, Tommy, 167, 269
Cantor, Eddie, 147
Capone, Al, 112
Carey, Dick, 91
Carney, Harry, 180, 250, 255, 257
Carson, Tom, 237
Carter, Benny, 29, 48, 52, 72, 156
Carter, Betty, 47, 51, 98, 137–38,
    145, 162
Carter, John, 60, 96, 120–22
Carter, June, 34
Carter, Kent, 170–71
Carter, Ron, 6, 166, 266
Carvin, Michael, 179
Casimir, John, 184–85
Catlett, Sid, 48
Chaloff, Serge, 47, 50, 115, 260
Chambers, Paul, 10
Chaplin, Charlie, 4, 11
Charles, Ray, 20, 133, 220, 238
Cheatham, Doc, 70
Cherry, Don, 77, 192, 236, 239,
    241, 243, 249
Childs, Lucinda, 196
Chocolate Dandies, the, 40, 274
Chopin, Frederic, 58
Christgau, Robert, 237
Christian, Charlie, 140, 145
Christman, Gunter, 208–9
Cinelu, Mino, 154
Clarinet Summit, 119–22
Clark, Curtis, 176–77
Clark, Dane, 242
Clark, Dick, 147
Clark, Pete, 275
Clarke, Kenny, 23
Clarke, Stanley, 265
Clay, Omar, 37
Clayton, Buck, 51, 70, 89
Clayton, Jay, 25, 163
Cleveland, Jimmie, 41
Cline, Patsy, 64
Clinton, George, 133, 237
Clooney, Rosemary, 204
Coates, George, 196
Cohn, Al, 7, 47, 52, 89, 115, 119,
    156, 203, 276

Cole, Cozy, 49
Cole, Nat, 49–50, 204, 229
Cole, Richie, 108
Cole, Ronnie, 56
Coleman, Bill, 70
Coleman, Earl, 269
Coleman, Ornette, 56–58, 63, 77,
    79, 95–99, 101, 134, 159, 184,
    191, 208, 235–49, 267
Coles, Johnny, 50
Collette, Buddy, 233
Collins, Shad, 70
Coltrane, John, 19, 46, 51, 73, 79,
    86, 89, 95, 97, 102–3, 105, 107,
    121, 123, 127, 134, 177, 192,
    208, 221, 223–24, 236–38, 242,
    264–68
Como, Perry, 203
Compost, 17
Condak, Henrietta, 266
Condon, Eddie, 89
Cook, Willie, 254–55, 257
Cooper, Al, 13
Cooper, Buster, 42
Cooper, Jerome, 24
Copland, Aaron, 126, 236
Corea, Chick, 131
Coward, Nöel, 4, 270
Cowell, Henry, 4, 8
Cox, Anthony, 194
Cox, Baby, 259
Creative Construction Company,
    the, 208
Crosby, Bing, 113, 162, 202, 226
Crouch, Stanley, 173
Curtis, King, 199
Cuscuna, Michael, 216, 219–20
Cyrille, Andrew, 75–78, 87

Dailey, Albert, 131
Dameron, Tadd, 46, 134
Dameronia, 169
Dance, Stanley, 179
Daniel, Ted, 76–77, 173
Dara, Olu, 176, 186
Dauner, Wolfgang, 42
Davern, Kenny, 90–91

Davis, Anthony, 44, 59–62, 157, 176, 242
Davis, Dr. Art, 178
Davis, Eddie "Lockjaw," 110, 212
Davis, Les, 94
Davis, Miles, 6, 17, 23, 25–26, 44, 73, 77–85, 95, 97, 130, 133–34, 142, 152–56, 159, 176, 181, 187, 189, 192–93, 235–37, 249, 267
Davis, Richard, 6
Davis, Wild Bill, 182
Dawson, Alan, 6, 52
Decoding Society, the (see Jackson, Ronald Shannon)
DeJohnette, Jack, 17–19, 56, 58, 124, 172, 178
DeJonge, Henk, 199
Dennis, Willie, 41
Desmond, Paul, 51
DeSouza, Raul, 43
Dial, Garry, 190–91
Dickenson, Vic, 40–41, 44, 89, 260
Diddley, Bo, 96
Dietz, Howard, 45
DiGeronimo, Nick, 77
Dikker, Loek, 43
Dixie Hummingbirds, the, 151–52
Dodds, Baby, 94, 246, 263
Dodds, Johnny, 171, 185
Dolphy, Eric, 6–7, 18–19, 36, 95, 134, 156, 171, 236, 267
Dominoes, the, 149, 152
Donovan, 124
Dorsey, Jimmy, 72
Dorsey, Tommy, 39–40, 89–90, 228–30, 272, 274, 276
Dowd, Tom, 184, 187
Dresser, Mark, 173
Drew, Kenny, 269
Drummond, Ray, 135, 160
Dudek, Gerd, 210
Dudziak, Urszula, 163
Dylan, Bob, 203

Eckstine, Billy, 190
Edison, Harry, 70, 230, 233
Edwards, Teddy, 50

Eisenhower, Dwight D., 229, 266
Eldridge, Roy, 15, 47–49, 68–72, 105, 110, 192, 269, 273
Eliot, T. S., 102
Ellington, Duke, 4, 8, 16–17, 24–25, 29–35, 39, 49, 53, 60–61, 65, 82, 84, 114–15, 119–21, 124, 127, 129–30, 137, 140, 160, 170–71, 177, 179, 185, 209, 217–18, 222, 226, 231, 250–59, 261, 271–73, 275
Ellington, Mercer, 120, 258–59
Ellis, Ray, 206
Emerson, Ken, 149
Ertegun, Ahmet, 184
Ervin, Booker, 6–7, 123
Erwin, Pee Wee, 88–92
Etting, Ruth, 46
Eubanks, Robin, 266
Evans, Bill (piano), 4, 17, 53, 67, 264
Evans, Bill (saxophone), 81, 153
Evans, Gil, 80, 85, 88, 155, 168, 170, 192–93, 276–77
Ewart, Douglas, 44
Experimental Band, the, 24
Eyton, Frank, 47

Faddis, Jon, 192–94
Farlow, Tal, 143
Farmer, Art, 135
Farrell, Joe, 7, 133
Feather, Leonard, 154
Ferguson, Maynard, 247, 271
Fier, Anton, 246
Fitzgerald, Ella, 29–30, 32, 113, 125–26, 162, 204–6
Flack, Roberta, 138
Flanagan, Tommy, 52, 125–28, 170, 203
Fontana, Carl, 41, 193
Ford, Ricky, 110, 135
Foster, Al, 80–81, 127, 154
Foster, Alex, 18
Foster, Frank, 33, 136, 276
Foster, Pops, 263
Fountain, Pete, 263

Four Brothers, the, 156
Fournier, Vernel, 136
France, Percy, 93
Francis, Panama, 12–15, 181
Franklin, Aretha, 137–38, 195
Frazier, George, 182
Freed, Alan, 271
Freeman, Bud, 91
Freeman, Chico, 19, 24–25
Friedman, David, 165, 188
Frizzell, Lefty, 276
Frost, Robert, 54
Fulkerson, Jim, 43
Fuller, Buckminster, 195
Fuller, Curtis, 41, 135

Gaillard, Slim, 162, 165
Gale, Eddie, 10
Gardner, Ava, 230
Garland, Hank, 65
Garland, Joe, 276
Garland, Judy, 201
Garner, Erroll, 4, 51, 87, 96, 118, 126–27, 167
Garrison, Arv, 65
Gaslini, Giorgio, 42
Geelan, Tim, 266
Geller, Greg, 146
Gershwin, George, 82, 92, 162, 205–6, 229, 272
Gerun, Tom, 112, 116
Getz, Stan, 115, 119, 128–32, 156
Gibbs, Melvin, 99–100
Gibbs, Terry, 262
Gibson, Dick, 88, 90
Gibson, Maddie, 88, 90
Gielgud, Sir John, 226
Gillespie, Dizzy, 4, 6, 13, 21–23, 25, 70, 79, 97, 109–10, 120, 192–93, 214, 216, 218, 221, 240, 275–76
Giuffre, Jimmy, 115, 156
Glass, Philip, 196
Gleason, Jackie, 90
Glenn, Tyree, 40, 254
Globe Unity Orchestra, the, 207–11, 277

Golden Palominos, the, 246
Golson, Benny, 134–35, 194
Gomez, Eddie, 19, 42
Gonsalves, Paul, 110, 171, 173, 209, 251, 254–57
Goodman, Benny, 47–48, 53–55, 71, 88, 126, 142, 145, 206, 230, 260, 271–72, 274–75
Gordon, Dexter, 13–14, 52
Gospel Oak Primary School Choir, the, 103
Goudbeek, Andre, 200
Goulet, Robert, 21
Granz, Norman, 29, 32
Grappelli, Stephane, 140, 145
Graves, Milford, 76
Green, Charlie, 40, 274
Green, Freddie, 118, 271
Green, John, 25, 45–48
Greer, Sonny, 254
Grey, Al, 40
Grieg, Edvard, 62
Grimes, Henry, 10
Grimes, Tiny, 49
Grisman, David, 145
Gryce, Gigi, 224
Gumbs, Onaje Allan, 98

Hackett, Bobby, 70, 89–90, 92
Haden, Charlie, 42, 56–58, 239, 241, 243
Hadlock, Richard, 184
Hagan, Jean, 203
Haig, Al, 125
Hakim, Sadik, 222
Hall, Barry Lee, 259
Hamilton, Jimmy, 119–21, 255
Hampton, Lionel, 179, 181
Hampton, Slide, 41, 62, 134
Hancock, Herbie, 6, 96, 134, 159, 191, 237
Handy, George, 50, 275
Hanna, Jake, 118
Hanna, Roland, 125–26
Hannibal (see Peterson, Hannibal Marvin)
Harlem Boys Choir, the, 105

Harlem Globetrotters, the, 242
Harris, Barry, 51, 109, 125–26
Harris, Bill, 40–42, 44, 114, 169,
    259–62
Harris, Craig, 62, 157, 176–77,
    186, 262
Harrison, Donald, 263, 265
Harrison, Jimmy, 40
Hart, Lorenz, 32
Harvey, Jane, 206–7
Haughton, Chauncey, 275
Havens, Bob, 91
Hawkins, Coleman, 14, 22, 35–36,
    46–51, 69–70, 74, 93, 95, 126,
    173, 214, 224
Hawkins, Erskine, 14
Haydn, Franz Joseph, 158, 160
Haynes, Roy, 189–90
Heath, Albert, 135
Heath, Jimmy, 53, 133–34
Heath, Percy, 52
Hefti, Neal, 14, 114, 276
Heifetz, Jascha, 228
Helias, Mark, 43
Hemphill, Julius, 96–97, 156,
    174–75, 248, 267
Henderson, Fletcher, 40, 69, 251,
    272, 274–75
Hendrix, Jimi, 124, 237–38
Herman, Charlotte, 114, 117
Herman, Woody, 42, 111–19, 130,
    156, 164, 169, 259–62, 271–72,
    275, 277
Heyman, Edward, 45
Hicks, John, 19, 85, 87, 97, 135,
    178
Higginbotham, J. C., 40–41, 43–
    44, 89, 157, 260
Higgins, Billy, 125, 127
Hill, Calvin, 38
Hill, Teddy, 70
Hines, Earl, 5, 54, 72, 242, 272,
    275
Hinton, Milt, 92
Hirschfield, Jeff, 191
Hirt, Al, 263–64
Hite, Les, 47

Hodges, Johnny, 16, 22, 30, 129–
    30, 156, 254–55, 257, 265
Hoggard, Jay, 62, 157
Holden, Steven, 202
Holiday, Billie, 47, 49, 52, 54, 81,
    137, 142, 162, 191, 203–7, 212–
    13, 226
Hollander, Frederich, 270
Holley, Major, 56
Holloway, Red, 110
Holman, Bill, 119, 276
Holman, Libby, 45–46
Hopkins, Fred, 85, 87, 174, 186–
    87
Hopkins, Lightnin', 154
Horgan, David, 65
Horne, Lena, 34
Howe, James Wong, 242
Hubbard, Freddie, 134, 192, 210
Humes, Helen, 53, 65
Hummel, Johann, 160
Huneker, James, 8
Huntington, Bill, 264
Hupfield, Herman, 191
Huston, Walter, 244
Huxley, Aldous, 141
Hyman, Dick, 4, 90–91

Instant Composers' Pool, the, 171,
    208
Isley Brothers, the, 147

Jackson, Milt, 218
Jackson, Quentin, 40, 254
Jackson, Ronald Shannon, 10–11,
    95–101, 238–41, 243–44, 246–
    49, 267
Jacobs, Dick, 149–51
Jacquet, Illinois, 178–83, 277
James, Burnett, 257
James, Harry, 230, 254, 276
Jankeje, Jan, 140, 142, 144
Jarman, Joseph, 197–98
Jarreau, Al, 138
Jarrett, Keith, 56–58, 122, 241
Jazz Composers Orchestra, the, 42,
    208

Jazz Messengers, the (*see* Blakey, Art)
Jazztet, the (*see* Golson, Benny)
Jefferson, Eddie, 23, 49–50
Jenkins, Gordon, 233
Jenkins, Leroy, 24, 77
Jenny, Jack, 40, 260
Johnson, Bruce, 100
Johnson, Budd, 275
Johnson, Bunk, 184–86, 263
Johnson, Charlie, 40
Johnson, Gus, 13
Johnson, Howard (*alto*), 14
Johnson, Howard (*tuba, baritone*), 134, 188
Johnson, J. J., 32–33, 39, 41, 49, 74, 110, 260
Johnson, James P., 16, 218
Johnson, Keg, 40
Jolson, Al, 148–49, 151, 202
Jones, Claude, 40
Jones, Elvin, 42
Jones, Hank, 51, 125–26, 180, 193, 206
Jones, Isham, 88, 113
Jones, Jo, 13, 35
Jones, Quincy, 216, 276
Jones, Thad, 25, 126, 137, 192, 276
Joplin, Scott, 272
Jordan, Clifford, 38, 136
Jordan, Edward Kidd, 174, 264
Jordan, Kent, 264–65
Jordan, Louis, 65
Jordan, Sheila, 163, 188
Joyce, James, 201

Katz, Dick, 15
Keil, Charles, 194–95
Kelly, George, 14
Kenton, Stan, 248
Kern, Jerome, 30, 46, 270
Kincaide, Deane, 275
King, B. B., 94, 96, 140, 145, 154
Kirk, Andy, 275
Kirk, Rahsaan Roland, 7, 200
Kirkland, Kenny, 160, 266

Kitchings, Irene, 212
Kloss, Eric, 7, 122–24
Knepper, Jimmy, 41, 261
Kniel, Manfred, 165
Knox, Emile, 184
Koehler, Trevor, 187
Kollektief, the (*see* Breuker, Willem)
Kondo, Toshinori, 209
Konitz, Lee, 107
Kowald, Peter, 208
Krupa, Gene, 100, 273, 275

LaBarbara, Joe, 66
Lacy, Butch, 33
Lacy, Steve, 168–71, 216, 224, 237
Lagrene, Bireli, 139–46
Lagrene, Fiso, 144
Lagrene, Gaiti, 140, 142, 144
LaGuardia, Fiorello, 221
Lake, Oliver, 156, 174–75
Lancaster, Byard, 99–100, 247
Landers, Wes, 93
Lanza, Mario, 150
Larkins, Ellis, 206
Lateef, Yusef, 126
Laws, Hubert, 265
Lawson, Hugh, 125–26
Lea, Michael, 65
Lee, David, 20–21
Lee, Jeanne, 77
Lee, Peggy, 204
Leonard, Harlan, 275
Lewin, David, 228
Lewis, George (*clarinet*), 263
Lewis, George (*trombone*), 24–25, 43–44, 176, 208–9
Lewis, J. J., 138
Lewis, John, 126, 185, 236
Lewis, Mel, 126, 137, 192, 277
Lewis, Ted, 112
Lewis, Victor, 131
Lewisohn, Ludwig, 232
Ligeti, Gyorgy, 62
Lillie, Beatrice, 165
Lincoln, Abbey, 35–36
List, Garrett, 43

Little, Booker, 36, 38
Lloyd, Charles, 17
Lo, Beth, 65
Loeffler, Tschirglo, 140, 142–44
Lombardo, Guy, 149
Longo, Mike, 20
Lourie, Charlie, 216
Lovens, Paul, 209
Lowry, Peter, 183
Lunceford, Jimmie, 254, 272–75
Lundy, Carmen, 137–39, 204
Lyons, Jimmy, 9–11, 77

Macdonald, Dwight, 137
Macero, Teo, 80, 225
Maghostut, Malachi Favors, 198
Malik, Raphe, 10–11
Mancini, Henry, 270
Mangione, Chuck, 122
Manglesdorff, Albert, 39, 41–42, 208, 210
Manhattan Transfer, 137
Maono (see Cyrille, Andrew)
Marcuse, Herbert, 195
Marsalis, Branford, 134, 158–60, 263, 266
Marsalis, Ellis, 158, 264, 267
Marsalis, Wynton, 134, 142, 156, 158–61, 237, 263–64
Marshall, Wendell, 255
Martino, Pat, 124, 145
Massenberg, Sam, 13
Massey, Zane, 100
Master Musicians of Jojouka, the, 238, 240
May, Billy, 233–34
Mays, Lyle, 57
McBee, Cecil, 105
M'Boom Re: Percussion, 36–37
McCall, Steve, 85, 87
McEwen, Joe, 146
McFerrin, Bobby, 137, 163
McIntyre, Diane, 36
McKinney's Cotton Pickers, 274
McLaughlin, John, 82
McLuhan, Marshall, 195
McPhatter, Clyde, 150

McShann, Jay, 94
Mengelberg, Misha, 170–71
Mercer, Mabel, 226
Messiaen, Olivier, 8
Meters, the, 237
Metheny, Pat, 56–59
Meyer, Jeff, 190–91
MGs, the, 237
Michals, Duane, 266
Miller, Eddie, 91
Miller, Glenn, 116, 272, 274
Miller, Marcus, 81, 154
Miller, Mitch, 229
Miller, Mulgrew, 265–66
Millinder, Lucky, 14, 275
Mingus, Charles, 4, 6, 37, 62, 65, 98, 102, 124, 126, 133, 170–71, 176–77, 185, 192–93, 251, 266, 276
Minton, Phil, 102–4
Miracles, the, 172
Mitchell, George, 90
Mitchell, Guy, 229
Mitchell, Joni, 124
Mitchell, Roscoe, 25, 44, 198
MJT + 3, the, 24
Modern Jazz Quartet, the, 134, 175
Moffett, Charles, 97
Moffett, Charnett, 142, 267
Mole, Miff, 39
Moncur, Grachan, 42
Monk, Meredith, 163
Monk, Thelonious, 8, 23, 30–31, 37, 51, 60–61, 79, 82–83, 86, 89, 110, 126–27, 131, 133–35, 160, 168–70, 199, 214–25, 261
Montgomery, Wes, 141, 145, 238, 242, 245
Moody, James, 20–23, 50, 193
Mooney, Hal, 204–6
Moore, Anita, 259
Morgan, Helen, 46
Morris, Butch, 174, 176
Morrow, George, 269
Morton, Benny, 40, 43
Morton, Jelly Roll, 16–17, 62, 90–

91, 123, 184–85, 207–8, 232, 263, 266, 268, 270
Moses, Bob, 187–88
Moten, Bennie, 14, 275
Motian, Paul, 56
Moye, Don, 197
Mozart, Leopold, 160
Mozart, Wolfgang, 16, 126, 141
Mraz, George, 127, 131
Muchnic, Bill, 90
Mulligan, Gerry, 51, 89
Mundy, Jimmy, 181–82, 275
Murray, David, 18–19, 61, 120–21, 156, 171–78, 183, 188, 237, 242, 244, 277
Murray, Deidre, 187
Murray, Ming, 175
Murray, Sonny, 76
Murray Family Band, the, 172
Myers, Amina Claudine, 25, 87

Nance, Ray, 6, 254–55, 257
Nanton, Joe, 39–40
Napoleon, Phil, 90
National Jazz Ensemble, 12
Navarro, Fats, 46, 110, 181
Nelson, Oliver, 97, 224, 276
Nesbitt, John, 273–74
New Orleans Rhythm Kings, the, 39
New York Art Quartet, the, 41, 43
New York Jazz Repertory Company, the, 12
New York Saxophone Quartet, the, 174
Newman, Jerry, 219
Newman, Joe, 92
Newton, James, 59–63, 157, 242
Newton, Lauren, 163–65
Nichols, Herbie, 41, 168–70
Nichols, Red, 40
Nistico, Sal, 118
Nix, Bern, 100, 247
Noble, Ray, 88
Noone, Jimmie, 121, 185
Norden, Maarten Van, 200

Norvo, Red, 114, 275
Notations of Soul, the, 172

O'Brian, Floyd, 40
O'Brien, Peter, 253
Ochs, Phil, 63
O'Day, Anita, 162
Oddo, John, 118–19
O'Farrill, Chico, 276
Okra Orchestra, the, 87
Olatunji, 36
Old and New Dreams, 241
Oliver, King, 77, 90, 158, 171, 176, 185, 247, 263
Oliver, Sy, 274–75
Original Dixieland Jazz Band, the, 263
Ory, Kid, 39
Osby, Greg, 194
Osmonds, the, 23
Otway, Marshall, 212
Owens, Charles, 60

Page, Hot Lips, 70, 94
Page, Patti, 203, 229
Papp, Joseph, 174
Parker, Charlie, 6, 9–10, 13, 21–22, 26, 41, 44, 46, 49, 65, 93, 95–96, 107, 109, 118, 127, 133–34, 137, 149, 189, 201, 213–14, 216, 221, 225, 265
Parker, Evan, 208, 210
Parkins, Sam, 11
Parks, Gordon, 92
Parrish, Avery, 118
Pass, Joe, 26, 28, 145
Pastorius, Jaco, 248
Paul, Les, 49
Payne, Dexter, 65
Pemberton, Bill, 14
Pepper, Art, 106–8, 110
Pepper, Jim, 188
Pepper, Laurie, 106
Perelman, S. J., 226
Peterson, Hannibal Marvin, 88, 104–5, 124
Peterson, Oscar, 26–27, 110

Peterson, Pat, 105
Petrowsky, Ernst-Ludwig, 210
Pettiford, Oscar, 192
Phillips, Flip, 261
Pierce, Wendell, 266
Piscopo, Joe, 227
Pizzarelli, Bucky, 16, 92
Pizzarelli, John, 92
Plater, Bobby, 193
Plaxico, Lonnie, 265
Pleasants, Henry, 228
Pleasure, King, 180
Pope, Odean, 38
Porcino, Al, 193
Porter, Cole, 229
Potter, Tommy, 65
Potts, Bill, 276
Pousseur, Henri, 163
Powell, Bennie, 136
Powell, Bud, 4–5, 8, 38, 54, 110,
    125–26, 142, 214, 221
Powell, Ginny, 50
Powell, Maureen, 65
Powell, Steve, 65
Pozo, Chano, 240
Presley, Elvis, 148, 201–2, 231
Priester, Julian, 36, 43
Prime Time, 243
Procope, Russell, 120–21
Pugh, Jim, 43
Purcell, John, 157

Quebeck, Ike, 70

Raaymakers, Boy, 199
Rabbai, George, 118
Raeburn, Boyd, 5, 273
Rameau, Jean-Philippe, 272
Ravel, Maurice, 62
Reagan, Ronald, 201
Real New York Saxophone Quar-
    tet, the, 174
Redding, Otis, 154
Redman, Dewey, 56–58, 96, 241,
    243
Redman, Don, 274

Reed, Rex, 202
Reed, Waymon, 33
Reid, Rufus, 125
Reid, Vernon, 99–100, 248
Reinhardt, Django, 48–49, 139–
    45
Reinhardt, Joseph, 140
Revolutionary Ensemble, the, 208
Rich, Buddy, 13, 192
Richards, Johnny, 276
Richards, Red, 14–15
Richmond, Dannie, 105
Riddle, Nelson, 202–5, 228, 230–
    31, 233
Rivers, Sam, 134, 267, 276
Roach, Max, 34–38, 133, 269
Robinson, Jackie, 54
Robinson, Jim, 184
Roche, Betty, 254–55, 257
Roderick, Judy, 63–65
Rodgers, Richard, 30, 32, 229
Rodney, Red, 89, 134, 189–91
Rodrigo, Joaquin, 27
Rogers, Shorty, 114, 261, 275
Rollins, Sonny, 23, 35, 51, 110,
    133, 142, 164, 171–73, 177, 190,
    216, 221, 224, 236, 266, 268–70
Roney, Wallace, 135
Ronstadt, Linda, 201–4, 206–7
Rosenberg, Harold, 79
Rosolino, Frank, 41
Ross, Annie, 137
Roth, Philip, 203, 214
Rouse, Charlie, 220, 223, 225
Rowles, Jimmy, 33, 129, 131, 261
Royal, Marshal, 193
Rozie, Lee, 99–100
Rudd, Roswell, 41–44, 168–71,
    261–62
Ruegg, Mathias, 164
Ruiz, Hilton, 135–36
Rushing, Jimmy, 93, 162
Russell, George, 102, 237, 276–77
Russell, Luis, 40
Russell, Pee Wee, 51, 89, 130
Rutherford, Paul, 43

Saint-Saens, Camille, 150
Sauter, Eddie, 275
Savoy Sultans (Al Cooper's), 13–14
Savoy Sultans (Panama Francis's), 12–16, 181
Schlippenbach, Alexander von, 207–9
Schlitten, Don, 109, 125
Schoenberg, Arnold, 9, 163, 214
Schuller, Ed, 5
Schuller, Gunther, 158, 216, 272
Schwartz, Arthur, 45
Schwartz, Jonathan, 202
Scofield, John, 153–55
Scott, Cecil, 168
Scott, Henry, 247–48
Scott, Raymond, 89
Scriabin, Alexander, 16
Sex Pistols, the, 238
Shange, Ntozake, 174
Shapiro, Dave, 118
Sharon, Ralph, 66
Shavers, Charlie, 70
Shaw, Artie, 255, 275, 277
Shepp, Archie, 36, 41, 52, 102, 171, 173, 236
Shirelles, the, 202
Shorter, Wayne, 58, 84, 134, 160, 194, 265–66
Silva, Alan, 10, 210
Silver, Horace, 20, 132–36
Simeon, Omer, 91
Simmons, Norman, 189
Simon, Carly, 202
Simon, George, 114
Simpkins, Andy, 33
Sims, Zoot, 7, 33, 107, 110, 115, 156, 212–13
Sinatra, Frank, 28, 47, 66, 162, 201–5, 212, 225–35
Singleton, Zutty, 263
Sirone, 10–11
60 Million Buffalo, 64
Smith, Bessie, 40, 162
Smith, Brian, 24–25
Smith, Jimmy, 166–68

Smith, John, 14
Smith, Marvin, 265
Smith, Warren, 24–25
Smith, Willie, 254–55
Smithsonian Jazz Repertory Ensemble, the, 15
Sokal, Harry, 164
Sondheim, Stephen, 34
Soskin, Mark, 269–70
Sosnick, Harry, 112
Sour, Robert, 45, 47
Sousa, John P., 244
Spellman, A. B., 266
Sphere, 169, 222
Spoles, Victor, 189
Stabenow, Thomas, 165
Stark, Bobby, 70
Starr, Kay, 203
Stern, Chip, 239
Stern, Mike, 81, 153–54
Stewart, Bob, 87, 208, 210
Stewart, Rex, 70, 159
Stewart, Slam, 50, 179
Stitt, Sonny, 108–11, 169
Stokes, Irvin, 14, 182
Stone, David, 187
Stone, Jesse, 274
Strauss, Richard, 126
Stravinsky, Igor, 8, 114, 126, 215, 277
Strayhorn, Billy, 4, 25, 29–31, 62, 127, 129, 187–88, 275
Stubblefield, John, 77
Sullivan, Ira, 189–91
Sumac, Yma, 165
Sun Ra, 208, 276
Swallow, Steve, 57
Swanson, Howard, 60
Swope, Earl, 41

Tacuma, Jamaaladeen, 238, 240–41, 243, 248–49
Tate, Buddy, 52
Tate, Grady, 33–34, 168
Tate, Greg, 240

Tatum, Art, 4, 23, 49, 54–55, 60–61, 94, 125–26, 130, 140
Taylor, Billy, 134
Taylor, Cecil, 7–12, 60–61, 76–77, 79, 95–96, 99, 101, 133, 165, 200, 209–10, 237, 242, 246
Taylor, James, 122
Taylor, J. R., 205
Teagarden, Jack, 39–40, 91
Terry, Clark, 118, 165, 254, 257
Thielemans, Toots, 53
Thomas, Leon, 102, 163
Thomas, Michael Tilson, 205
Thornhill, Claude, 273, 275
Threadgill, Henry, 61, 176–77, 183, 185–88, 237, 267
Timmons, Bobby, 134
Tiny Tim, 202
Tio, Lorenzo, 263–64
Tizol, Juan, 31, 41
Tolstoy, Leo, 267
Tough, Dave, 114, 118
Towers, Jack, 256, 274
Tristano, Lennie, 5
Trumbauer, Frank, 16
Tucker, Mickey, 135–36
Turner, Big Joe, 65, 92–94
Turney, Norris, 14, 183
Turre, Steve, 43
Turrentine, Stanley, 166–67
Tyler, Charles, 97
Tyner, McCoy, 51, 109, 135

Ulmer, James Blood, 80, 95, 99, 172, 178, 237–41, 243–49, 267

Valentine, Dave, 265
Van Heusen, Jimmy, 227
Varèse, Edgard, 222
Vaughan, Sarah, 26–34, 52, 137–38, 162, 204–6, 212
Venuti, Joe, 91
Verdurmen, Rob, 199
Ver Planck, Billy, 261
Vienna Art Orchestra, the, 164–65, 277
Vivaldi, Antonio, 272

Wakeman, Alan, 104
Waller, Fats, 4–5, 16, 54–55, 72, 125, 137, 142, 275
Walrath, Jack, 190
Walton, Cedar, 134
Ward, Billly, 149
Ware, David, 76–77
Warren, Peter, 18
Washington, Dinah, 162, 204
Washington, Kenny, 194
Waters, Ethel, 137, 212
Waters, Muddy, 238
Watrous, Bill, 39, 41, 193
Watson, Leo, 162–63, 165
Watson, Robert, 135
Watts, Jeff, 160
Webb, Art, 265
Webb, Chick, 14, 40, 190, 237, 248, 272, 274–75
Webb, Clifton, 45
Webern, Anton, 163, 222
Webster, Ben, 30, 49, 70, 130, 171, 173, 180, 261, 275
Webster, Freddie, 26, 79
Weill, Kurt, 77, 102, 198
Wein, George, 156
Welk, Lawrence, 91
Welles, Orson, 71, 201
Wells, Dickie, 40, 157, 260
West, Paul, 20, 94
Westbrook, Kate, 102, 104
Westbrook, Mike, 102–5
Wheeler, Kenny, 210
Whitaker, Harry, 138
Whiteman, Paul, 162, 272
Wiedoft, Rudy, 200
Wiggins, J. J., 259
Wilber, Bob, 16, 90–91
Wilder, Alec, 131, 168
Wiley, Lee, 63
Wilkins, Ernie, 276
Williams, Buster, 96
Williams, Claude, 94
Williams, Cootie, 21, 251–52, 259
Williams, Franc, 14–15
Williams, Hank, 65, 276
Williams, James, 194

Williams, Martin, 16, 216, 272
Williams, Mary Lou, 214, 222, 255, 275
Williams, Richard (critic), 103
Williams, Richard (trumpet), 136, 182
Williams, Rudy, 13
Williams, Sandy, 40
Williams, Tony, 6, 81, 159, 236, 246
Williamson, Stu, 41
Wills, Bob, 65
Wilson, Dennis, 43
Wilson, Jackie, 27, 146–52
Wilson, Phillip, 174
Wilson, Quinn, 275
Wilson, Teddy, 46–48, 53–56, 125, 138
Winding, Kai, 41, 261
Wolf, Howlin', 96
Wonder, Stevie, 66, 123, 138, 149
Wood, Booty, 40

Woodman, Britt, 41, 254
Woodyard, Sam, 255, 257
Workman, Reggie, 178
World Saxophone Quartet, the, 18, 156, 172, 174–75, 237
Wyands, Richard, 179, 182–83

Yancey, Jimmy, 167, 217–18
Yancey, Yousef, 25
Yeats, William Butler, 75
Young, Lester, 19, 22, 49, 70, 73–75, 93, 107, 137, 173, 212–14, 217–18, 240
Young, Snooky, 192–93
Young, Trummy, 40
Young Lions, the, 157, 159
Young Tuxedo Brass Band, the, 183–86, 188

Zawinul, Joe, 133
Zedong, Mao, 35
Zion, Sid, 202, 204